The Complete
HOT AND SPICY
Cookbook

The Complete
HOT AND SPICY
Cookbook

edited by
Emma Callery

Grange
BOOKS

A QUINTET BOOK

Published by Grange Books
An imprint of Books & Toys Ltd
The Grange
Grange Yard
London SE1 3AG

Copyright © 1991 Quintet Publishing Limited.
All rights reserved. No part of this publication
may be reproduced, stored in a retrieval system
or transmitted in any form or by any means,
electronic, mechanical, photocopying, recording
or otherwise, without the permission of the
copyright holder.

ISBN 1 85627 129 3

This edition printed 1992

This book was designed and produced by
Quintet Publishing Limited
6 Blundell Street
London N7 9BH

Creative Director: Terry Jeavons
Designer: Annie Moss
Project Editor: Emma Callery

Typeset in Great Britain by
Central Southern Typesetters, Eastbourne
Manufactured in Hong Kong by
Regent Publishing Services Limited
Printed in Singapore by
Star Standard Industries Private Ltd

The material in this book appeared in previous
publications.

How to use this book:
Imperial, metric and American measurements are provided
for each recipe. The countries of origin are represented by the
following symbols:

From India

From Japan

From Thailand

From Mexico

From China

Contents

INTRODUCTION

Spices are more than just a food, they are an idea which has both changed the course of history and enriched the very language which we speak. To 'spice it up', 'the spice of life,' of just plain 'spicy' are words and phrases which suggest not merely specialness but the exotic; a little bit of fun; even the *risqué*.

Diversion, or the escape from boredom, has remained a constant human quest which began long before history itself. People lacked books, telephones, televisions and so on, but they did have to eat. No wonder those tiny, but powerful packages of exotic pleasure came to be so cherished.

Growing everywhere – just outside the kitchen door, so to speak, were and are another group of plants used primarily to add flavour to other foods – the herbs. Of course, they have their own story, but it was always spices which triggered the passions of people and fired their imaginations.

So what are spices? Unfortunately, there is no absolutely clear, simple and universal definition. Surely some readers will find it rather strange that an introduction admits that the book's very subject matter is impossible to define. The problem is that nature does not operate for the purpose of neatness in botanical classification. Or, to put it another way, spices are a human concept rather than an immutable law of the universe.

There are, of course, a number of general statements which can be made about both spices and herbs. The first is that their use in food is primarily aromatic rather than nutritional. The spice or herb is used to flavour another food which forms the major part of the meal or dish. Exceptions exist even for this fundamental statement. There are a number of dishes for which garlic is cooked as a vegetable rather than treated only as a spice. Herbs, generally, are the green leafy bits and perhaps parts of the stems of aromatic plants, but what of spices? It is true that most often they are dried, while herbs are used in forms both fresh and dried, but the odd exception can be found even here. Spices come from virtually every conceiv-able part of plants: pepper and allspice (or pimento) are dried berries; cinnamon and its sister spice, cassia, are tree bark; ginger and turmeric are rhizomes; nutmeg is the kernel of the seed of an apricot-like fruit, while mace is the seed coating, or aril of the same fruit; chillies (chilis), vanilla and cardamom are all fruits themselves, and cloves are unripened flower buds. Incidentally, if the clove buds are not picked but left, they become lovely pink and fragrant blossoms, but are no longer cloves. And garlic . . . Some say garlic is not a spice, and others call it a herb. The plant does have spear-like green leaves, but that is not the part used as a flavouring.

In order to end the confusion, some writers, who must have been in dire need of something to think about, proclaimed that true spices had to grow in the tropics. They also invented

Opposite: *Garlic on sale in a market*

Below left: *Pickers removing the buds from the flower stalks of a tropical evergreen tree belonging to the myrtle family. The cloves are the dried unopened flower buds*

Right: *Ginger roots being sorted for purchase.*

Below right: *The cinnamon quills are prepared from the valuable inner bark, after the outer bark has been stripped off.*

a third category over and above herbs and spices called 'aromatic seeds.' This works perfectly well for, say, pepper, which everyone agrees is a spice and always grows near the equator. It does mean, though, that garlic, which grows in temperate regions, cannot be considered a spice, but it can hardly be called an aromatic seed when it is not even a seed! Before returning to the drawing board, perhaps we should agree that exact definitions really are not necessary and get on with the fun.

The earliest trading caravans transported salt, but even before the dawn of human history they were also carrying spices. The early civilizations of the Mediterranean and the Near East craved the spices of India and lands eastward. Records exist of Egyptian spice expeditions to the east coast of Africa between three and four thousand years ago. Particularly treasured were the two aromatic barks, cinnamon and cassia. The Egyptians used them not only to flavour foods but in cosmetics and an assortment of ceremonial functions including the important burial rites. Consider this excerpt from Exodus:

> *Moreover the Lord spake until Moses, saying, Take thou also unto thee principal spices, of pure myrrh five hundred shekels, and of sweet cinnamon half so much, even two hundred and fifty shekels, and of sweet calamus two hundred and fifty shekels. And of cassia five hundred shekels, after the shekel of the sanctuary, and of olive oil an him: And thou shalt make it an oil of holy ointment after the art of the apothecary: it shall be an holy annointing oil. And thou shalt anoint the tabernacle of the congregation therewith, and the Art if the Testimony.*

Today calmus grows throughout Europe and America and is known as sweet flag or sedge. Myrrh, of course, figures significantly in later biblical episodes, especially as a mild potion of love in the Song of Solomon and as one of the gifts brought by the wise men for the baby Jesus. The point is that they both still grow in the Middle East and have done so since ancient times. By contrast, cinnamon and cassia do not, nor ever have grown in the region, yet were commanded for the most sacred of duties, the ointment for the holy Ark itself. From where then did they come?

The ancient Greek historian Herodotus asked this very question and came up with the area around the Red Sea, which he called the 'cinnamon growing lands.' He wrote of great birds using the spice to build their nests and of Arabs coming near with large sides of meat. The birds would take the meat up to the nests which would break under the strain of its weight, allowing the Arabs to collect the cinnamon. According to the historian, cassia was collected by an equally bizarre plan in which snakes figured prominently.

It was left to the Roman historian Pliny the Younger to come close to the real story. Pliny's investigation of the matter arose because as a Roman treasury official he became alarmed at a crisis in the balance of payments. The luxury-loving Romans, in order to secure supplies of eastern spices, were sending vast amounts of gold out of the Empire in the direction of India. Pliny described a series of fantastic voyages across thousands of kilometres of open ocean, starting east of India and ending on the east coast of Africa. The cinnamon carriers, on tiny open rafts, used only the stars for navigation and often took as long as five years to complete a round trip. For their troubles, they took home bits of glass, bracelets and baubles.

Remarked Pliny, referring to both the Romans and the remarkable spice sailors, '... hence it is, that this traffic depends chiefly upon capricious female fidelity to fashion.' It appears that the numerous Arab middlemen got most of the gold.

Had Pliny been a linguist he would have known that our word and the Roman word 'cinnamon' were derived from the almost identical Hebrew word used in the Bible which itself was derived from ancient Malay, meaning 'sweet wood.' To suggest some idea of the antiquity of this long-distance spice trade, consider the fact that the Roman, Pliny, lived and wrote closer in time to today than to the time of the Exodus! So Biblical cinnamon probably originated in the region of modern Malaysia. Cassia likely first came from the Khasi Hills of Assam, a region lying between the northern parts of Bangladesh and China. It could have been carried on packs or by animals across the tortuous width of Asia itself by a trail which later would be called 'The Silk Route.'

So the spice trade is very ancient indeed. When Europeans were running barefoot through the woods dressed in animal skins, a thriving commerce between East and West flourished throughout the Indian ocean and Asia. Ultimately, that was destined to change.

The point about spices is that they travel and keep. They are their own best containers.

The herbs were springing in the vale:
Green ginger plants and liquorice pale,
And cloves their sweetness offer,
With nutmegs too, to put in ale,
No matter whether fresh or stale,
Or else to keep in coffer.

These words were written by an Englishman who lived between 1340 and 1400, Geoffrey Chaucer. His ginger could have come from India or East Africa, and the liquorice from southern Europe, but it is the cloves and nutmeg which have a story to tell. Remember in Chaucer's time European ships could scarcely venture into open ocean and only rarely out of sight of land. The idea of sailing around Africa would have been considered as madness. Nobody even knew if Africa had an end: indeed, most people then had probably never even heard of Africa or the Indian Ocean.

Yet, at the time, all the cloves in the world came from a tiny group of islands lying on the equator between Borneo and New Guinea, the Moluccas, or Spice Islands. Even more astonishingly, all the world's nutmegs grew on an even tinier set of nearby islands known as Banda. Known, that is, to the Indonesian and Arab traders who, for thousands of years, had come to the islands. Certainly, neither Chaucer, nor anyone else in England had the slightest idea of the area's existence.

Left: *Green berries are laid out in the sun to dry.*

Right: *After the green berries have been dried for about 1½ weeks they turn into the familiar black pepper corns.*

Below: *The nutmeg fruit showing the nut covered with mace.*

Today, it is almost impossible to imagine the epic journey across half the world's surface those spices had to make to end up in Chaucer's ale. No wonder he wrote: '. . . or else to keep in coffer.'

In Chaucer's time the magnificent and powerful city-state of Venice ruled the Mediterranean. Much of her wealth came from agreements made with Arab traders to control the spice trade. All the fabulous spices of the Orient flowing into Europe passed through Venice, as did vast quantities of gold and silver flowing eastward. The Venetians grew rich, but the rest of Europe began to suffer the same balance of payment crises which had so worried the Romans. Far to the west, in the tiny but newly independent kingdom of Portugal one man decided to challenge the supremacy of Venice. Ultimately, his decision changed the whole course of human events.

Prince Henry of Portugal's plan was simple: find the end of Africa, sail around it all the way to India, and buy the spices directly from the producers, cutting out the Venetians and the Arabs. In hindsight it seems mad. Henry might just as well have chosen the moon or Mars to sail to. But he was driven not only by his lust for spices, but his hatred of the Moslem Arabs and the hope of finding a fabled Christian empire in the East. He gathered the world's greatest scholars and navigators about him and set out upon his grand plan. Henry died before it was accomplished, but the Portuguese did develop new ships which could sail against the wind and new methods of navigation which let them venture out into the open ocean.

By the 1480s, the Portuguese had rounded Africa and were ready for the final push upon India itself. This so worried Portugal's neighbour and rival, Spain, that the Spanish decided to finance an Italian navigator who claimed that he could reach India ahead of the Portuguese by sailing, not around Africa, but westward into the Atlantic. Christopher Columbus' astounding voyage was to alter everything, but more about that later.

In 1497 the Portuguese reached their goal, India. Their leader, Vasco da Gama announced, so the story goes, 'I have come for Christians and spices.' It is worth noting that India would remain under European subjugation for the following 450 years! Columbus, of course, to his lasting disappointment never found India. He did find islands, continents and empires which his fellow Europeans were quick to claim as their own. For the next half a millennium, the dominant world geo-political fact would be European colonialism, and it all started with the search for the source of spices.

The discovery of the new world forever changed the eating habits of the old. It is difficult to imagine a pre-America Europe void of tomatoes, potatoes, chocolate, vanilla, maize (corn), peanuts and turkey. Columbus caused everlasting confusion by calling all the peoples he encountered Indians. Similarly, he continued to muddy the linguistic waters by bestowing upon two very different plants in two different parts of the world the name of yet a third, pepper.

The first 'pepper' he discovered boasted berries somewhat larger than the Indian variety, the 'Asian' Indian variety. Also, it possessed a glorious aroma at the same time reminiscent of cloves, cinnamon and nutmeg. This was dubbed 'la pimenta de Jamaica', or Jamaican Pepper. Today it is called pimento by Jamaicans, but is known in its ground form as allspice. Allspice

Left: A field of croci being harvested.

Right: Green pimento berries which when dried are called allspice.

Far right: A selection of different types of rice, pulses and beans.

Bottom right: Turmeric is sold in powdered form which quickly loses its aromatic qualities.

or, if you prefer, pimento, is a marvellous spice used in a vast array of commercial foods. It is surprising that more people do not employ it in the kitchen.

It was, however, the other spice found by Colombus which set the culinary world on its ear. Capsicums in their many colours and varieties had been cultivated by the peoples of Mexico, Central and South America for no less than 9,000 years! Along came the lost sailor Colombus and called them 'pimientos' or 'peppers.' Today, we still call those large mild red and green capsicums, along with the much smaller and hotter yellow and red varieties, peppers. In no way are they related to the sneeze-inducing powder which resides in the shakers beside the salt. To avoid confusion, we shall refer to the hot capsicums by a name derived from their native American cultivators – chillies (chilis).

Aside from flavour, spices always have been called upon for pungency or heat. Until the European arrival of the chilli at the beginning of the 16th century, the spices used for pungency were pepper, mustard, horseradish and, perhaps, ginger. Each of these spices carries along with its heat an entire flavour complement. With chillies (chilis) the additional flavour is minimal and piquancy can be obtained without upsetting other flavour balances. As they are easily cultivated, it is little wonder that the little hot fruits flourished wherever the Spanish and later Portuguese sailors went. Surely it was a great day in the history of food when the chilli (chili) arrived in India. Today that country is the world's largest grower and it simply is inconceivable to consider Indian food without the heat of the chilli (chili). So central is the chilli (chili) to Indian cookery that many there still refuse to believe that the plant is not native to the land but was brought by the Europeans. It is ironic that the quest for the spices of India finally led to the transformation of the food of India itself.

The two 'Christian' nations, Spain and Portugal, started to interfere with each other's conquests to such an extent that the Pope drew an imaginary line down the centre of the Atlantic ocean to separate their spheres of interest. Portugal could have all the heathen lands east of the line while Spain could take those to the west. It is not clear, however, from the early charts whether the Moluccas and Banda, the homes of cloves and nutmegs, fell into the Portuguese or the Spanish sphere of influence.

The Spanish felt that their claim would be strengthened if the islands could be reached by sailing westward and following Columbus's original plan. An expedition of five ships and 230 men was mounted, led ironically, by a Portuguese, Ferdinand Magellan. They journeyed westward into the Atlantic, down the coast of South America and finally into the Pacific ocean. The expedition did reach the Moluccas, but Magellan himself was already numbered among the many casualties. Three years after it set out, only one ship, with 18 emaciated sailors aboard, finally returned to Spain. Undoubtedly, these 18 were the very first human beings to sail around the world – for cloves and nutmegs!

The following century saw the decline of Spain and Portugal and the rise of new and ever more ruthless European empires: England, Holland and France. Great companies were formed to marshal the necessary capital to mount eastward expeditions. The Dutch, in particular, formulated and executed plans to corner the world market in various spices. They destroyed all the clove and nutmeg trees on earth except for those growing on closely guarded islands. Ultimately, cloves and nutmegs escaped to be cultivated elsewhere, breaking the Dutch stranglehold.

By the middle of the 18th century, the desperate desire for spices was slowing down. In fact, the spices of choice were

changing. In the early years, cinnamon and cloves were most valued because the primary method of cooking in Europe was the single pot on the hearth, in which various foods of widely differing flavours were cooked together. There was no distinction between sweet, sour and savoury dishes. Both cinnamon and cloves are binding spices; they bring together the opposite flavour of sweet and sour. For example, apple strudel with sour apples and sweet sugar would be unthinkable without cinnamon or cloves or both.

The introduction of the cooking stove meant that everything no longer had to be cooked together. A new type of main dish arose, savoury, and with it a different spice took prominence – pepper. The new nation, the United States, entered the pepper trade with fast ships out of the New England port of Salem. Profits from the trade were used to build much of the state of Massachusetts' industrial base.

Finally, the arrival of eastern spices in abundance meant the decline of the local European spices, mustard and saffron. Mustard was destined for a number of renaissances, especially in the French town of Dijon and the English company of J.&J. Colman. But, alas, widespread saffron use never returned. Today, saffron is cultivated principally in Spain where it is used in the local *paellas*.

Throughout the ages people have cherished spices not only for their flavour and piquancy, but their perceived benefit to health. It is only in relatively recent times that food and medicine have become separate and distinct. Each of the spices contain a number of often complex and powerful chemicals. Modern medical science makes no claims for the curative value of any of the spices, although we can take note that for thousands upon thousands of years people in every continent have extolled their virtues in this respect.

This book, however, will be primarily about food; about cooking with and using spices in the kitchen. Today spices are easier than ever to obtain. Any reasonable supermarket will have a wide variety, but mostly already ground. Spices in general should be kept in dry, dark and airtight conditions, especially ground spices which should be used quickly. This then is a simple plea that whenever possible you should buy whole spices and grind them yourself.

As grinders and whole peppercorns become more and more popular, whole pepper becomes easier to use. Here's a hint: try mixing a few whole allspice berries in with your peppercorns, and use as you would ordinary pepper.

Do try fresh whole nutmeg. The 18th century saw nutmeg proclaimed as a wonder drug and people used to carry their own nutmegs and grinders around with them. We do not advocate anything so extreme, but there is no substitute for freshly ground nutmeg and it is as easy to grind as shaking a bottle. You should also become familiar with the lovely spice mace, in its aril form. In fact, experiment with all the spices and, above all, have fun.

SPECIAL INGREDIENTS, EQUIPMENT AND TECHNIQUES

India

To many people outside India, Indian food means just curry. Indeed, many of the dishes now popular in the West are delicious and fiery curries such as the Goan favourite, vindaloo. Food is, however, a celebrated item all over India and you do not need to delve too deeply into the subject to discover that there is a stunning array of dishes, some steamed, some fried, some grilled (broiled); some subtle and delicate, some full-bodied and rich to reflect the great diversity of the country.

There is no one Indian and no one Indian cuisine. It is a vast country of more than one and a half million square miles of changing topography and more than 700 million people of various faiths.

There are about 25 spices on the shelf in the Indian pantry. Many of them will have come from the back garden along with fresh herbs and bulbs – onions, garlic and shallots. With this huge treasury of flavours the Indian cook can create an infinite number of different dishes. Spices can be used individually or combined, roasted or ground with water into a paste to produce flavours anywhere in the spectrum from sweet to sour, fiery to bland and fragrant to pungent.

The traditional way to serve Indian food is on a *thali* or large tray, often of beautifully wrought metal. Each different dish will be in a small metal or earthenware bowl perched around the edge of the tray, or laid out on a low communal brass table. The diners sit on the floor or on very low stools. The carpet is spread with coloured cloth to protect it and the guests are given giant coloured napkins. The dishes can be wrapped in cotton or silk, which is loosely folded back over the food after it has been served. Often banana leaves will serve as disposable plates.

Indians eat with their hands. The right hand only is used; the left is thought unclean. In some parts of India the whole hand is used, in others just the fingertips. Generally, food is scooped up with a piece of flat bread in the north and mopped up with rice in the south. This means that cleanliness is very important, so hands are washed before and after eating and water for washing is provided even on barrows selling snacks in the streets.

SPECIAL INGREDIENTS

SPICES

Spices are the main ingredient for Indian cookery. Whole spices have a different taste from ground spices, and when the spices are dry roasted, they taste entirely different again. Simple dishes may have just one or two spices, whereas more elaborate dishes might involve ten or twelve. By adding different spices, the entire taste of the dish can be changed.

In India, spices are normally bought whole and then ground for daily use on a grinding stone with a little water. If spices are required to be ground dry, a mortar and pestle is used. In the modern kitchen, the spices can easily be ground in an electric coffee grinder, so long as you make sure that you do not overheat it.

Cumin seed

Coriander seed

Left: *Fragrant mountains of vibrant colour characterize the spice merchant's store.*

Spices can be bought ready ground but these have to be stored in airtight jars as they lose their flavour very quickly.

As Indian cookery has become popular, more and more spices are easily available. Supermarkets sell many of the spices you will need, but for a few special ones you will have to make a trip to an Indian grocery store.

In Indian cooking, onions, coconut, poppy seeds and almonds are some of the thickening agents. Normally the spices are cooked a little before the meat, fish or vegetables are added so that you get all the flavour.

Asafetida: A strong-smelling gum resin. It is sold in pieces or in ground form. It is popular in India as a digestive and is used in small amounts only. A pinch is added to hot oil and allowed to sizzle for a few seconds before the other ingredients are added.

Black cumin seeds: These are smaller than the ordinary cumin seeds and dark in colour.

Black salt: This is a rock salt with a distinctive flavour. It is used in small quantities in chutneys, pickles and snacks.

Cardamom: When the recipe calls for cardamoms, take the whole, small cardamom pods and, just before using, press the cardamom on a hard surface with your thumb and forefinger to break the skin, so that the flavour mixes with the other ingredients while cooking.

Ground cardamom is available in Indian grocery stores or supermarkets, but cardamoms can be ground easily in an electric coffee grinder.

Chilli (chili), dried red: Available in whole or ground form. The whole chillies (chilis), when added to hot oil and fried for a few seconds, turn darker and give a lovely flavour to the dish.

Cinnamon: This is the dried inner bark of the cinnamon tree. It is mainly used whole in rice, meat and fish dishes for its aroma and flavour.

Cloves: This is the flower bud of the clove tree and when dried it is used as a spice. Cloves also contain essential oils. They are used whole in rice and meat dishes for their aroma and flavour.

Coriander, fresh: This is also known as Chinese parsley or cilantro. It is used in small amounts to garnish or added towards the end of the cooking time for its aroma; it is also used for making chutney.

Coriander seeds: The seeds are small and round in shape and beige in colour. Ground coriander is used a great deal in cooking vegetables and meats.

Cumin: Like caraway seeds, but with a lightly pungent flavour. Whole and ground forms are used greatly in Indian cooking.

Curry leaves: Used mainly in South Indian cooking.

Fenugreek

Mustard seed

Onion seed

Poppy seed

Ground turmeric

Ground asafetida

Small cardamoms

Bay leaves

Stick cinnamon

Fennel: Light green, oval shaped seeds with a liquorice flavour – used a great deal in Kashmiri cooking.

Fenugreek: Used in small amounts only, either whole or ground after dry roasting.

Ginger: The rhizome of a plant with a pungent flavour; it can be stored in the refrigerator for about one month. To use, peel the skin and use either grated or cut into strips.

Kalonji (Onion seeds): Small, black seeds that are an important spice for pickling.

Mango powder: This is made by peeling and slicing the unripe mango and drying it in the sun until it shrivels up. It is then powdered.

Mustard: White and dark purple mustard seeds are available. In Indian cooking the darker variety is used. They are tiny and round in shape. When added to hot oil they start to splutter. At this stage, either the oil is poured over a cooked dish or vegetables are added to the oil.

Panch phoron: A combination of five spices mixed in equal proportions: cumin, kalonji (onion seeds), fennel, fenugreek and mustard. Used for lentil or vegetable preparations and normally used whole.

Pistachio nuts: The kernel is green with a reddish brown skin, and the flavour is delicate. They are used as a garnish on desserts either chopped or slivered.

Poppy seed: Tiny, white, round seeds with a nutty taste, used in both sweet and salt dishes. Sometimes used as a thickening agent.

Saffron: These threads are orangey red and are the dried stems of a flower of the crocus family. A small amount of good quality saffron is enough to colour and flavour a dish. It is usually soaked in warm milk for 15–20 minutes before using.

Sesame: Tiny, beige seeds with a nutty flavour. The sesame seed oil is used for cooking.

Tamarind: Tamarind trees grow in tropical climates. The pods are 5–7 in/12.5–17.5 cm in length and become dark brown when ripe. The pulp is dried in the sun and sold in packets at Indian grocery stores. A little tamarind pulp is soaked in hot water for 30 minutes and then squeezed to drain out all the juice. It has a sour taste.

Turmeric: Mainly found in ground form at Indian grocery stores or supermarkets. It is the root of a plant of the ginger family. Pungent in taste and yellow in colour.

OILS

Many different kinds of oil are used for cooking in India. Some of the vegetable and fish dishes from Eastern India are normally cooked in mustard oil, but you can use vegetable oil.

Masoor dal

Moong dal

Right: Panch phoron is a combination of five spices: **clockwise from top:** cumin, fennel, mustard, fenugreek and kalongi (onion seeds).

Chole

Channa dal

Rajma

Urid dal

Lobia

Matar

Coconut oil: Has a delicate flavour and solidifies at low temperatures.

Groundnut oil: This is the oil from peanuts. It is used for cooking in Southern India and has a nutty flavour.

Mustard oil: Yellow, with a strong smell. Fish cooked in mustard oil has a distinctive flavour.

Sesame seed oil: Has a strong, distinct flavour and is dark.

DALS

There are many varieties available in India and a great many of these can be found in North America at Indian grocery stores. They are available whole or split.

Black-eyed beans: (*Lobia*) White, kidney-shaped beans with a black 'eye'.

Channa dal: These are similar to split peas, but slightly smaller.

Chole: (*Chickpeas or garbanzos*) Beige, round, dried peas Should be soaked overnight to reduce the cooking time. Chickpea flour is called gram, and is widely used in cooking.

Masoor dal: (*Split red lentils*) Salmon-coloured, small, flat, round lentils which cook easily.

Matar: (*Split peas*) Round, yellow lentils, uniform in size.

Moong dal: Small, yellow, split lentils. Bean sprouts are made by sprouting these beans.

Rajma: (*Red kidney beans*) Large, dark red kidney-shaped beans. Should be soaked overnight to reduce cooking time.

Toovar dal: Also called arhar dal, this is the main dal used in southern India.

Urid dal: (*Black gram*) The bean is reddish black, is very small in size and takes a long time to cook. The split urid dal is pale cream. It is usually soaked and ground to a paste.

EQUIPMENT

A degchi: A pan without handles, made of polished brass, stainless steel or other metals. The lid of the degchi is slightly dipped so that sometimes live coal can be placed on it to cook food slowly or to keep food warm. Ordinary saucepans with lids can be used in the same way and the oven can be used to cook food slowly or to keep it warm.

A karai: This is found in every Indian kitchen. It is a deep concave metallic dish with two handles – one on each side. It looks like a Chinese wok but it is a little more rounded. It is used for deep frying.

A tava: Made from cast iron, it is slightly concave, and is about 10 in/25 cm in diameter. It is ideal for making chappatis or parathas because it distributes the heat evenly. A griddle or heavy skillet will serve the same purpose.

Metallic stirrers: These are used in India because the pans are not nonstick. Use wooden spoons when using nonstick pans. Wooden spoons are easier to use as they do not get hot, although if left in hot oil they tend to burn.

A thick stone slab: This is used with a round stone roller like a rolling pin for grinding. Whole spices are ground with a little water; if dry ground spice is required, a mortar and pestle is used. Lentils are also ground on the slab.

Tongs: These are used to remove a karai from the fire, or to remove the hot lid from the degchi. To remove the degchi from the fire it is normally held at either side with a cloth.

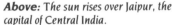

Above: The sun rises over Jaipur, the capital of Central India.

Top right: The tropical landscape of Southern India.

Right: Assam, in eastern India, lies at the foothills of the Himalayas, and is renowned for its tea.

Left: Traditional kitchen equipment includes the karai, shown on the left with tongs to lift it from the heat and a wooden stirrer. The heavy frying pan and saucepan on the right are suitable modern substitutes for the tava and the degchi. Also shown are a rolling pin, wooden spatula and sieve.

A tandoor: This is a clay oven used in northern India. Tandoori chicken, whole or in pieces, different kinds of breads and kebabs are baked in this oven. It is about 3–4 ft/90 cm–1.2 m deep and about 2 ft/60 cm wide on top with a hole of 12 inches/30 cm diameter through which the food is put. It is fuelled by wood and coal and intensive heat builds up inside.

Tandoori chicken can be cooked easily in the modern oven, and then put under a very hot grill (broiler) for a few minutes to dry out. It can also taste excellent barbecued.

TECHNIQUES

Adding spices to hot oil: Oil is heated until it is very hot, and whole spices, crushed garlic or green chillies (chilis) are added until the spices swell up or splutter or change colour. This is then added to a cooked dish, or vegetables, or other spices are added and cooking continues.

Dry roasting: Place whole spices in a small, heavy-based frying pan and heat gently, stirring the spices constantly so that they do not burn. Soon the spices will turn a few shades darker and a lovely aroma will emerge.

Frying onions: Place the oil in a frying pan over a medium high heat. When hot, add the onions, and, stirring occasionally,

fry until the onions start to change colour. Lower the heat and continue to fry until they are reddish brown.

Adding yogurt while cooking: When a recipe calls for yogurt, always whisk the yogurt until smooth, and add slowly, otherwise it curdles.

Peeling tomatoes: Place the tomatoes in boiling water for 30 seconds. Drain and cool under running cold water. Peel, chop and use as required.

Cleaning chillies (chilis): Pull out the stalks of the chillies (chilis) and, holding them under cold running water, slit them open with a sharp knife and remove the seeds. The seeds are the hottest part of the chillies (chilis) and most Indians do not remove them. Be very careful, when handling chillies (chilis), not to put your hands near your eyes as the oil will make your eyes burn.

China

There *is* an abiding love of food among all Chinese: it verges on worship. The ways that ingredients are chosen, prepared, cooked and balanced are a constant way of 'saying grace', of offering thanks to the gods. And the speed with which this form of 'worship' – the taste for Chinese food – has spread throughout the Western world over the last 30 years is remarkable. Yet despite the popularity of Chinese food, Chinese cooking is still regarded by most Westerners as being difficult and requiring special talents – mainly because the techniques used are so different from those of Western cuisines. But this does not mean that they are more complex.

In Western-style cooking, individual foodstuffs are conditioned by heat until they are ready to eat: meat is roasted or grilled (broiled); vegetables are boiled or fried. Chinese cooking, on the other hand, is dominated by compound dishes. Ingredients are mixed and cooked in different ways. It is the method – rather than the ingredients themselves – that determines the nature of the final dish. Thus, there is much more flavour- and texture-blending involved in Chinese cooking.

Most of the techniques used in Chinese cooking are the same as those used in the West, and those that are different form a few set patterns of using heat and marrying ingredients. The only completely different skill that needs to be mastered is stir-frying. Other techniques employed are quick, open steaming, steaming in a closed container and slow simmering. Red-cooking is simply slow-stewing in soy sauce. Each of these techniques is familiar to Western cooks.

The ingredients required will present no problem either. Most Chinese dishes can be prepared with no more than a handful of specifically Chinese ingredients, which are easily obtained from foodstores everywhere.

Many people may try to delude themselves that they 'eat to live', but the Chinese are honest enough to admit that they 'live to eat', and that a good appetite is a blessing.

SPECIAL INGREDIENTS

Bamboo shoots: There are several kinds of bamboo shoots available in the West – all in cans only, which is a pity since they lose much of their crispy texture and flavour. Try to obtain winter bamboo shoots; they are dug up from the cracked earth before the shoots grow to any great length or size, therefore they are extra tender and tasty. Spring bamboo shoots are much larger; they sometimes may reach several feet in length and 3–4 in/7.5–10 cm in diameter. Once the can is opened, the shoots may be kept in a covered jar of water in the refrigerator for several days. Braised bamboo shoots in cans should be eaten cold without any further cooking.

Bean-curd: Made from soaked yellow soy beans ground with water. A coagulant is added after some of the water is strained through muslin cloth, causing the ground beans to curdle and

Above: *A busy corner of Peking market.*

Opposite: *A monument to the Chinese people: the Great Wall of China.*

Chinese dried mushrooms

Dried shrimp

Five-spice powder

Ground and whole Sichuan
peppercorns

Wood ears

Green seaweed

Chinese cabbage: There are innumerable varieties of cabbage grown in China, of which only two or three types are available in the West. The one most commonly seen is known as celery cabbage or Chinese leaves, it has a pale green colour and tightly wrapped, elongated head. Two thirds of the vegetable is stem which has a crunchy texture; another variety has a shorter and fatter head with curlier, pale yellow leaves. Then there is the dark green-leaved variety, also with white stems, and the bright green-leaved variety with pale green stems, sometimes with a sprig of yellow flower in the centre which is very much prized by the Chinese. These last two varieties are sold only in Chinese stores.

Chinese dried mushrooms: There are two main types of Chinese mushrooms; those that grow on trees, known as Fragrant or Winter Mushrooms; and those cultivated on a bed of straw, known as Straw Mushrooms. Fragrant or Winter Mushrooms are sold dried; they are used in many dishes as a complementary vegetable for their flavour and aroma. Soak in warm water for 20–30 minutes, squeeze dry and discard the hard stalks before use. Straw Mushrooms are available in cans, but are completely different in texture and flavour. The Western varieties of common or field mushrooms can be used as substitutes.

Dried shrimp: These are small to very small, and are sold cleaned, shelled and whole. They add a salty, savoury seasoning to dishes.

Five-spice powder: A mixture of anise seed, fennel, cloves, cinnamon and pepper. It is very strongly piquant, so use a very small amount each time. It will keep for years if stored in a tightly covered container.

Fresh coriander: Sometimes known as Chinese parsley, this plant is available in oriental stores, or in Italian grocers where it is called *cilantro*.

Ginger root: Sold by weight. Should be peeled and sliced or finely chopped before use. Will keep for weeks in a dry, cool place. Dried and powdered ginger is not a satisfactory substitute for fresh ginger.

Gluten: A high-gluten flour and water dough is soaked and kneaded in water to wash out the starch; the remaining gluten is porous like a sponge. It is cut into pieces to be used like dumplings to carry flavour and provide bulk in sauces.

Green hot chilli (chili): Will keep fresh for a week or two in the vegetable compartment of the refrigerator in a plastic bag.

Green seaweed: This moss-like seaweed is dark green in colour. It is sold dried, in wads or in matted chips. When deep-fried in oil, it is crisp and has a toasted fragrance. Dried green cabbage leaves can be used as a substitute.

Hoisin sauce: Also known as barbecue sauce. Made from soy beans, sugar, flour, vinegar, salt, garlic, chilli (chili) and sesame.

become firm bean curd. Usually sold in squares about 2½ × 2½ in/6 × 6 cm, ¾ in/2 cm thick, they will keep a few days if submerged in water in a container and placed in the coldest part of the refrigerator. Dried bean curd skin is usually sold either in thick sticks or thin sheets. It should be soaked in cold water overnight or in warm water for at least an hour before use.

Bean sauce: Sometimes called 'Crushed bean sauce', this thick sauce is made from black or yellow beans, flour and salt. It is sold in tins and, once opened, must be transferred into a screw-top jar and then it will keep in a refrigerator for months. (NB Black bean sauce is very salty, while yellow bean sauce is sweeter with sugar added.)

Bean sprouts: Two kinds are available: yellow soy bean sprouts, only to be found in Chinese provision stores, and green mung bean sprouts, which can be bought from almost every large city supermarket. (Never use canned bean sprouts, they do not have the crunchy texture which is the main characteristic of bean sprouts.) They can be kept in the refrigerator for two or three days if bought fresh.

Cellophane or transparent noodles: Made from mung beans. They are sold in dried form, tied into bundles weighing from 2 oz/50 g to 1 lb/0.5 kg. Soak in warm water for five minutes before use.

Chilli (chili) paste: (Chilli (chili) purée). Is made of chilli (chili), soy bean, salt, sugar and flour. Sold in jars and will keep almost indefinitely.

Chilli (chili) sauce: Hot, red sauce made from chillies (chilis), vinegar, plums, salt and sesame.

Kao Liang liqueur: A spirit made from sorghum and millet. Brandy or vodka can be substituted.

Monosodium glutamate (MSG sometimes): This chemical compound, known as 'taste essence' is often used to heighten the flavour of food. It is rather frowned upon by true gourmets as it can wipe out the subtle distinction of a dish when used to excess.

Oyster sauce: A thick sauce made from oysters and soy sauce. Sold in bottles, will keep in the refrigerator indefinitely.

Red bean curd sauce: A thick sauce made from fermented bean curd and salt. Sold in cans or jars, will keep indefinitely.

Rice wine: Also known as Shaoxing wine, made from glutinous rice. Saké or pale (medium or dry) sherry can be substituted.

Salted black beans: Whole bean sauce, very salty.

Sesame seed oil: Sold in bottles. Widely used in China as a garnish rather than top cooking. The refined yellow sesame oil sold in Middle Eastern stores has less flavour and therefore is not a very satisfactory substitute.

The most commonly used oils in China are vegetable oils such as soy bean, peanut or rape seed oils. The Chinese never use butter or meat dripping, although lard and chicken fat are used in some regional cooking, notably in the Eastern School.

Sichuan preserved vegetable: This is a speciality of Sichuan province. It is the root of a special variety of the mustard green pickled in salt and hot chilli (chili). Sold in cans. Once opened it can be stored in a tightly sealed jar in the refrigerator for months.

Sichuan peppercorns: Reddish-brown peppercorns, much stronger than either black or white peppercorns of the West. Usually sold in plastic bags. Will keep indefinitely in a tightly sealed container.

Soy sauce: Sold in bottles or cans, this liquid ranges from light to dark brown in colour. The darker coloured sauces are strongest, and more often used in cooking, whereas the lighter is used at the table.

Golden needles (dried Tiger Lily buds): The buds of a special type of lily. Sold in dried form, should be soaked in warm water for 10–20 minutes and the hard stems removed. They are often used in combination with Wood ears.

Tomato sauce: Quite different from Western tomato ketchup. Italian tomato purée (paste) may be substituted when fresh tomatoes are not available.

Water chestnuts: Strictly speaking, water chestnuts do not belong to the chestnut family, they are the roots of a vegetable. Also known as horse's hooves in China on account of their appearance before the skin is peeled off. They are available fresh or in cans. Canned water chestnuts retain only part of the texture, and flavour of fresh ones. Will keep for about a month in a refrigerator in a covered jar.

Water chestnut powder: A flour made from water chestnuts. Cornflour is a good substitute.

Wood ears: Also known as Cloud ears they are dried tree fungus. Sold in dried form, should be soaked in warm water for 20 minutes; discard any hard stems and rinse in fresh water before use. They have a crunchy texture and a mild but subtle flavour. According to the Chinese, Wood ears contain protein, calcium, Phosphorous, iron and carbohydrates.

Below: Double wooden-handled wok with wok brush; single-handled wok on wok stand with long-handled metal sieve and smaller perforated ladle; long wooden chopsticks for cooking on, and chopstick stand and soft brush for cleaning woks.

EQUIPMENT

The wok: The best woks are traditional ones made of iron or carbon steel, with one long or two wooden side handles. The first is excellent for stir-frying since the cook can hold the wok, yet is far away from the very hot oil, using a long-handled spoon, chopsticks or wok scoop to toss the ingredients. The two-handled wok is better for deep-frying or for steaming food because it is steadier to move when full of liquid. When buying a wok it is important that it should have deep sides, is fairly large, about 14 in/35 cm in diameter, and that the metal is not too thin or stir-fried food will burn easily. Make sure your wok has a good fitting domed lid to use when steaming.

It is very important to season a wok before first cooking in it. Scrub it well to remove any protective coating, rinse, then dry it well. Place the wok over low heat, wipe it lightly with vegetable oil and let it heat for about 10 minutes. When cool, wipe the wok with absorbent kitchen paper to remove the dark film. Repeat the process until the paper wipes clean. Clean a seasoned wok in plain water without soap; never scrub it. Let the wok dry thoroughly over low heat before storing it. If the metal ever rusts, clean it with a scouring cream or fine sandpaper, rinse, dry and season it again. A wok brush is a stiff bundle of thin bamboo splints that is good for cleaning a wok.

Wok stand: A wok stand is necessary for wok cooking when deep-frying and steaming, as it provides a steady base for the pan. The stand is also used with a two-handled wok for stir-frying. If cooking over gas, be sure to use a solid wok stand that has ventilation holes. It gives the wok stability and prevents the flame from going out.

Bamboo steamer: Bamboo steamers are placed on a metal or bamboo trivet over water. When the food is in place, the wok can be covered with its lid or with the steamer's own tight-fitting bamboo lid, which is necessary when more than one type of food, each in its own steamer, is stacked one on top of the other. When new, wash then put the empty steamer over water and let it steam for five minutes.

Metal steamer: Metal steamers can be placed directly on the heat, fit snugly and have a tight-fitting lid. To prevent food sticking, place it on muslin (cheesecloth) or in a heatproof dish.

Cooking pots: Chinese earthenware cooking pots, also known as sand pots, come in a variety of shapes and sizes, all with unglazed exteriors and lids. They can be used over low heat, as in making soup, but not in the oven. They will crack if hot,

Right: A vast selection of sand pots, in a Chinese kitchenware shop.

Below left: Chinese earthenware cooking pot with basket ladle; and Mongolian hot pot with long-handled wire baskets for cooking.

Below right: Base and lid of a metal steamer; and Chinese bamboo steamer with lid and ornate wooden cooking chopsticks.

Resting on a chopping board, **far right:** smaller chopper (cleaver); and heavier, large chopper.

if put on a cold surface or if an empty pot is heated. Any heavy casserole makes a satisfactory substitute.

Mongolian hot pot: Mangolian hot pots, or fire-pots, heat stock or soup at the table from glowing charcoal under and in the middle of the pot. Small, long-handled wire baskets or bamboo sieves or chopsticks are used to add and remove ingredients from liquid.

Sieves and ladles: Long-handled sieves and perforated ladles are useful for lifting food from hot oil, when steaming or straining noodles. A wok scoop is a long-handled metal disk perfect for stirring and serving up stir-fried food. A long-handled wooden spoon or metal spatula can also be used.

Choppers: Chinese choppers, or cleavers, come in two sizes: heavy ones for chopping through bones and tough ingredients and smaller, thinner and lighter ones for cutting vegetables and slicing meat. Chopping boards should be fairly thick and made of either hard wood or white acrylic. A wooden board needs regular oiling. An acrylic board is easier to clean.

Chopsticks: Chopsticks for cooking are wooden and long so that they don't conduct heat and distance the cook from hot fat and steam. For eating, chopsticks can be wooden, plastic or for special occasions, ivory. Chopstick stands are useful for resting chopsticks on and make a decorative addition to a Chinese meal.

TECHNIQUES

Temperatures: The temperature of the cooking oil will also have to be varied according to the ingredients used and the dishes to be produced.

Hot pan with cold oil: Heat the pan until very hot, then add the cold oil. Put in the ingredients before the oil gets really hot and remove the ingredients after deep frying for a short time. This method requires the temperature of the oil to be 175–210°F/80–100°C. When you add the ingredients, there should be no smoke from the oil and no hissing sound. This method is used to prepare good cuts of meat as it helps to retain their natural flavour and preserves the tenderness of the meat.

Hot pan with hot oil: Heat the pan until very hot, then add the oil and heat it to a temperature of 350–425°F/180–220°C. The oil should start to smoke, and it will hiss if you stir it. This method is used to prepare seafood and food that requires a crunchy covering (often battered foods).

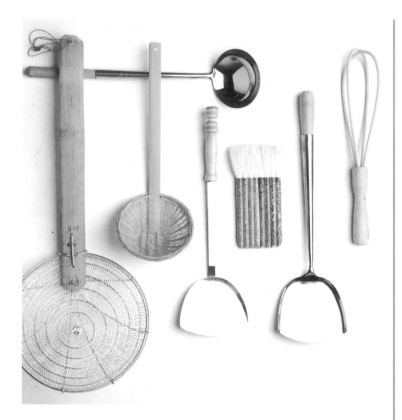

Left: *Metal ladle;* **across from left to right:** *bamboo sieve basket ladle; wok scoop; glazing brush; larger wok scoop; whisk.*

Right: *A Chinese housewife prepares a meal.*

Medium heat with hot oil: Heat the pan until very hot, then heat the oil until it reaches a temperature of 225–330°F/110–170°C. A small amount of smoke will begin to come off the surface of the oil. This method is used for frying large pieces of meat, whole fish, chicken or duck.

Stir-frying: The ability to stir-fry is an important part of any Cantonese chef's skill. It is essential to heat the pan over maximum gas or electricity until it is extremely hot. Then add the necessary quantity of oil. When that is hot, add crushed or chopped garlic, ginger and spring onion (scallion). As the mixture begins to cook, add the other ingredients, stir-fry and turn them to cook everything quickly and evenly. Sprinkle wine and sesame seed oil at the end to produce a fragrant smell.

Shallow frying: For shallow frying, heat the pan until it is extremely hot and then add oil. Lower the ingredient into the pan and, when it is slightly brown, reduce the heat to a minimum. Use this method to fry fish. It will stop the skin sticking to the pan and ensure an attractive appearance when it is served.

Deep frying: This is a popular technique in Chinese cooking. Strictly speaking, blanching the ingredients in oil can be regarded as deep frying. To deep fry you need, in most cases, adequate heat and hot oil to make the ingredients crunchy and tender. Be careful, however, with ingredients that are coated in batter: keep the temperature somewhat lower, otherwise you will overcook the outside of the food while the inside is still raw. In these cases, it might be better to use the 'soak-frying' method. Heat the oil, add the ingredients and turn off the heat. Let them soak for a while in the hot oil and

then take them out. Reheat the oil until it reaches a temperature of 350–425°F/180–220°C and then deep fry the ingredients for a second time, until done. This method is also known as double deep frying.

Steaming: There are two kinds of steaming. Short steaming, requiring high heat, and long steaming, requiring low heat. Some other Chinese cooks may call long steaming 'double boiling' because the foods are contained in a closed receptacle. In some recipes, those calling for the steaming of a duck, chicken or a large piece of meat for example, you should use long steaming, using low, medium heat, until the ingredients are tender.

Boiling: This is a very simple method of cooking. Simply add water to cook the ingredients, exactly as you would cook soup, rice or porridge. If you want to make a bowl of clear meat soup, you must blanch the meat with boiling water first, then

Slicing meat across the grain.

Meat is shredded into thin strips.

Shredding bamboo shoots.

frequently prepared by using a knife or sharp cleaver. Many recipes are prepared by the 'cut-and-cook' method, which requires that equal attention is paid to both the cutting and the cooking. Whether you are preparing ingredients by cutting them into chunky pieces, or by slicing, thick shredding, fine shredding, dicing into cubes or mincing, you must always ensure that everything is of equal size. If you do not, then the quality of the cooking will be affected because of the uneven heating that will result.

You need a good sharp cleaver and a heavy chopping-board. Any good quality Chinese chopper will be more than adequate, and a traditional chopping board made of solid wood 5–6 in/12–15 cm thick, is much better than the skimpy modern ones. Many Westerners are afraid of using a razor-sharp Chinese kitchen chopper. The secret for beginners is to avoid cutting horizontally. Instead, use your whole hand on the top of the blade, rather than chopping from the handle, and slice carefully into the ingredients at an angle. This is risk-free and easy, thanks to the sharpness of the blade.

Marinating: After cutting, the next stage in the preparation of food before actual cooking is marinating, sometimes called 'coating' or 'blending' in Chinese. The basic method is to marinate meat, fish or chicken in salt, egg-white and starch – usually water-chestnut flour, but cornflour (cornstarch) is a good substitute. Sometimes sugar, soy sauce and wine are added. The purpose of this 'coating' is to preserve the vitamins and protein content in meat after it is finely cut up, while retaining its tenderness and delicacy.

Seasonings: There are far too many seasonings to list here, but the most basic category of all are those made from soya beans. All kinds of soy sauce are made from beans, so are bean paste, preserved bean curd and preserved fermented black beans. You will begin to get the authentic Chinese flavour by combining any of the above with garlic, ginger and spring onion. Traditionally, Cantonese chefs enjoy using oyster sauce to flavour their cooking.

The following seasonings are sufficient: sweet soy sauce, soy sauce, oyster sauce, black bean paste, yellow bean paste, sesame seed oil, rice wine, pepper, sugar, rice vinegar and cornflour (cornstarch). Most ordinary Chinese dishes can be prepared using any of the above in combination with garlic, ginger and spring onions (scallions), and with dried orange peel.

Slicing: This is probably the most common form of cutting in Chinese cooking. The ingredients are cut into very thin slices, not much bigger than an oblong stamp, and as thin as cardboard. When slicing meat, always cut across the grain – this makes it more tender when cooked.

Shredding: The ingredients are first cut into thin slices, then shredded into thin strips as small as matches but twice as long.

Diagonal cutting: Traditionally, carrots, celery, courgettes (zucchini) and asparagus are normally cut into diamond-shaped pieces.

rinse it under cold water. Heat a bowlful of water in a pan and, when the water is boiling, put the ingredients into it. You should use the maximum heat at the start, reducing to medium heat and finally ending with low heat. This kind of soup is delicious once you have mastered the timing and the amount of water to add.

Braising: Cook ingredients over moderate heat with sufficient liquid to cover them. Reduce the liquid to 15 per cent of the original and add seasonings to make a sauce.

Stewing: Add more water or stock and use low heat to cook the ingredients until they are soft and tender. Only once the liquid has nearly all evaporated – or reduced to 10–20 per cent – should you add seasonings, ingredients and flavouring in order to make the sauce.

Knife and cleaver: The ingredients in Chinese cooking are

Japan

On first seeing a Japanese meal, one hardly dares to disturb the perfection of the tiny morsels of food arranged to form exquisite designs on the plates and bowls which form the background. The Japanese themselves tend to be more interested in the visual qualities of the meal before them than in its taste. A meal in the best restaurant in Tokyo may well taste heavenly, but what will most excite the admiration of the Japanese diner will be the way in which the chef has transformed simple vegetables, fish and meat into an edible masterpiece.

This concern with the visual quality of the meal is not the preserve of restaurants. A simple home-cooked meal will consist – not of a large plateful of food as in the West – but of tiny portions of various foods, selected as much for their variety of form, shape and colour, as for their taste. They are always neatly arranged and carefully garnished with tiny sprigs of green or a delicate scatter of poppy seeds.

There are several levels to the design of a Japanese meal. Each individual item of food is carefully prepared to enhance its visual qualities. Lowly vegetables may be used as decorative garnish, be it a carrot, cherry blossom or a turnip chrysanthemum. The prepared foods are then artistically arranged on small plates, sometimes forming a miniature landscape. The plates and serving dishes are laid out on the lacquered trays according to prescribed rules. The setting is one of harmony and stillness.

In the West we are relatively functional in our approach to food. We eat when we are hungry, to sustain our bodies. We plan a meal in terms of taste and nutritional content, vitamins, minerals and carbohydrates. In Japan, food has perhaps a wider significance than in the West. It is not just to fill the stomach and keep the body working: it has an aesthetic, ritual and social role to play too.

As with so many aspects of Japanese life, cooking techniques are neatly categorized. A Japanese meal is planned around a balance of techniques rather than nutritional considerations. A formal meal, such as one eaten in a restaurant or at a banquet, consists of a succession of dishes: first a clear soup, then a raw fish dish, followed by a simmered dish, a grilled dish, a deep-fried dish, a steamed dish and a dressed salad. A simpler home cooked meal is made up of a selection of dishes cooked using different techniques. In either case, the meal ends with the real food, rice, together with some crunchy pickles and probably a bowl of thick soup made from *miso*, a salty fermented soy bean paste.

SPECIAL INGREDIENTS

Dashi: Made from dried bonito flakes and kelp (*kombu*), is the basic stock of the Japanese kitchen. It is *dashi* which is responsible for giving the characteristic Japanese flavour to many dishes, and the ability to make well-flavoured *dashi* is the essential secret of the good cook.

Above: Kyoto, the cultural capital of Japan, is famous for its zen-inspired temple cuisine.
Far left: Japan's land mass is split into four main islands and nearly 4,000 islets. On the fourth island Hokkaido, Lake Mashu is said to be the clearest lake in the world.
Left: The fish market shows some of the many types of fish supplied by the lakes, rivers and the sea.

Below: The setting for this meal is a Japanese room with its muted colours and sparse furnishings, creating an atmosphere of harmony and stillness.

Ginger root: Fresh ginger root is much used in Japanese cookery as a seasoning and garnish; it is widely available, particularly in shops specializing in oriental or African foods.

Fish cake (Kamaboko): This is made from puréed white fish, pressed into solid cakes and sold ready cooked; it is usually white or tinted pink. It can be simply sliced and eaten raw, and is a popular ingredient in one-pot dishes, soups and rice and noodle dishes.

Horseradish (Wasabi): This is sold in Japanese food stores ready-made in tubes, and in powder form, to be mixed up as required with a little water to a smooth paste. Horseradish is the usual accompaniment for raw fish dishes.

Kinome: The fresh-tasting young leaves of the prickly ash, is the most widely used garnish in Japan.

Kuzu: This is produced from the root of the *kuzu* vine, and is a traditional Japanese thickener.

Mirin: A sweet, golden cooking wine with a very low alcohol content, is an essential item in the Japanese kitchen, giving a distinctive mild sweetness to simmering liquids, glazes and dipping sauces.

Miso: This is a rich and savoury paste produced by the fermenting action of a yeast-like mould on cooked soya beans, which are often mixed with rice or other grains. It takes at least six months and as much as three years to mature. M*iso* is a peculiarly Japanese food; indeed, as *miso* soup, it is probably eaten by every Japanese every day. It is much used in Japanese cooking as a basic flavouring, as a dressing for simmered and grilled foods and even for pickling.

Noodles: They are one of the most popular Japanese foods and come in many varieties and sizes.

Oils: The Japanese use pure vegetable oil, never animal fats, for cooking; any vegetable oil except olive oil is suitable.

Pickles (Tsukemono): No Japanese meal is complete without a dish of thinly sliced pickles of various types, colours and shapes. Pickles are made from many different vegetables; the most popular include *daikon* radish, aubergine (eggplant), Chinese cabbage and *shiso* buds.

Rice cake (Mochi): Rice cakes are made by pounding glutinous rice, traditionally in big tubs, to produce a chewy white cake, which is shaped into balls or squares. They are perhaps an acquired taste; it may be best to begin one's acquaintance with only a quarter of a rice cake.

Sesame seeds: These are a characteristic Japanese flavouring and garnish. They should be lightly roasted in a dry pan to bring out the nutty flavour before use.

Seven-spice pepper: (Shichimi): This is a grainy mixture of chilli (chili) pepper, black pepper, dried orange peel, sesame seeds, poppy seeds, slivers of *nori* seaweed, and hemp seeds; the exact blend of spices varies.

Soy sauce: A fermentation of soya beans, wheat and salt, is one of the primary seasonings of Japanese cooking. The thinner, lighter Japanese soy sauce, should be used in preference to the Chinese.

Soya bean curd: This is one of the most common ingredients in Japanese cooking, used in a wide variety of dishes. It has a delicate, slightly nutty, flavour and is an easily digestible source of vegetable protein.

Vinegar: Japanese rice vinegar has a light, delicate flavour. It is available in delicatessens as well as Japanese and Chinese food stores.

Yuzu: This is a tiny citrus fruit with a distinctively flavoured rind, much prized as a garnish and flavouring.

FOOD FROM THE LAND

Aubergine (eggplant): These are much used, in a variety of different types of dishes. They come in many shapes and sizes, all of which are smaller than those available in the West.

Bamboo shoots: The shoots of the young bamboo, which grow at an amazing rate, are a symbol of spring in Japan. A very common ingredient throughout the East, they are prized for their crunchiness and delicate taste.

Burdock: This long slender root vegetable with a crunchy texture and earthy taste is much used in Japanese cooking.

Chestnuts: Both large and small chestnuts are a popular food

*Below: A fine-meshed strainer is used for draining noodles. **Right:** A small round frying pan is sometimes used for making omelettes.*

Right: *Both metal steamers and bamboo steamers are used in Japan. Stacking bamboo steamers are readily available in Chinese stores and are most efficient. Bamboo makes a better insulator than metal, ensuring that more heat is retained.*

Steamers may be simply improvized. Use a large covered saucepan containing some support to keep the cooking vessels above the level of the water. A cloth stretched under the lid will absorb excess moisture.

in Japan, roasted and eaten as a snack or included in a variety of sweet and savoury dishes.

Napa or celery cabbage (Hakusai): This has a somewhat milder flavour than Western cabbage and is much used in Japanese cooking.

Chrysanthemum leaves: This delicious leaf vegetable is much used in one-pot dishes, particularly in *sukiyaki*.

Daikon: Huge white *daikon* roots – a kind of giant white radish – are a common sight in Japanese fields and markets.

Gingko nuts: These have a delicate flavour and texture and are a regular ingredient in steamed dishes.

Leeks: The Japanese leek is smaller, sweeter and finer than the Western leek. It is widely used as an ingredient in soups, simmered dishes and grilled dishes and, finely sliced, is a common garnish and condiment. Use long, slender leeks or large spring onions (scallions).

Lotus root: This crunchy root vegetable is served as *tempura* and in vinegared and simmered dishes.

Mushrooms: Many different varieties of fresh mushrooms, both wild and cultivated, are used in Japan – in soups, simmered dishes and one-pot dishes.

Yams: Many different varieties of yam and sweet potato are used in Japanese cooking in simmered and one-pot dishes and in *tempura*.

EQUIPMENT

Japanese meals may be successfully prepared using utensils available in any well-equipped Western kitchen, with just a little improvization. In fact, most Japanese kitchens are cramped and somewhat less complete and convenient than the average Western kitchen. However, with their characteristic love of precision and the right tool for each task, the Japanese have developed a range of kitchen utensils which, although not essential, are very useful in preparing Japanese dishes. They also make an aesthetically pleasing addition to the kitchen.

It is not essential to use Japanese knives, but you should have several good sharp knives which perform the same functions. Japanese knives are made of carbon steel, and are always honed on a whetstone.

Right: *This vegetable knife **(top)** performs all manner of delicate vegetable cutting operations – from chopping and slicing to fine paring – with efficiency and speed. It has no Western equivalent, and is a worthwhile investment. The long thin-bladed knife **(centre)** is used for cutting fish fillets. A Western meat slicer may be used instead. A basic kitchen knife **(bottom)** is used for both general fish and meat cutting and also for more delicate work. It is available in many sizes.*

TECHNIQUES

In Japanese cuisine, with its minimal approach to actual cooking, cutting techniques assume a greater importance than in the West. Foods are transformed more in cutting than in the cooking. The Japanese home-cook will often buy ready cut foods, deeming cutting to be one art best left to the experts. Many of the basic techniques are quite straightforward and within the reach of any home cook.

Preparing fish: Small fish look most attractive served whole, and need simply to be gutted. Larger fish are filleted according to their shape.

Salting fish: Fish is salted in order to firm the flesh and reduce colour. Thick fillets need more and longer salting than thin. Immerse fillets of white fish in a salt solution of 2 tbsp/30 ml salt in 5 cups of water, for 20–30 minutes. For heavier salting, dredge the fish in salt and set aside for 60–90 minutes.

Dried foods: In general, dried foods are first rinsed in cold water, then soaked in lukewarm water. After this they are shredded and simmered with fish, meat or vegetables.

Vegetable cutting: Decoratively cut vegetables add a great deal to the visual appeal of a dish. The main requirement for vegetable cutting is a good knife, a Japanese vegetable knife is ideal but any good, sharp knife will do.

Preparing fish to be served in fillets: The shape of a fish determines how it should be gutted and filleted. Round-bodied fish such as trout and mackerel are cut along the spine to produce two boneless fillets. Wide flat fish, such as sole, give four thin fillets.

Gutting:
1 Wash the fish in lightly salted water and scrape away the scales. Rinse and pat dry.

2 Place the fish with the head facing to the left. Make a diagonal cut at the base of the head. Make a second diagonal cut to remove the head.

3 Slit along the entire belly of the fish and carefully remove the stomach and intestines. Scrape the knife along the inside of the body to break blood pockets. Rinse thoroughly with cold water.

Two-piece filleting:
1 Rest the left hand gently on top of the fish and draw the knife lightly from the head to the tail. Retrace the cut several times, each time cutting closer to the spine; do not use a sawing motion.

2 Turn the fish and cut smoothly from the tail to the head.

3 Cut through to separate the fillets. The fish separates into two halves, one boneless and one containing the backbone.

VEGETABLE CUTTING:

ROUNDS Cylindrical vegetables like daikon radish and carrot are simply sliced through to make rounds.

CLAPPER CUT Thick rectangles are reminiscent of the wooden blocks clapped together at moments of excitement in Kabuki plays. Cut the vegetable into 2-in/5-cm lengths. Then cut into slices ⅛–⅜ in/3–5 mm thick. Turn and cut again to make small.

HALF-MOON CUT Cut rounds in half to make half moon slices; or halve the vegetable length-wise and slice.

DICE CUT Cut thick rectangles. Then cut across to make cubes of even size. These dice are about ⅜-in/5-mm square.

GINGKO LEAVES Cut rounds into quarters to make gingko leaves. This cut is used for large or tapering vegetables such as bamboo shoots and carrots.

PINE NEEDLES This particularly beautiful garnish makes use of the contrast of light and dark green in the cucumber.

FANCY CUTTING

DECORATIVE CARROT TWIST
Lemon peel as well as carrot is often formed into a decorative twist. Make two thin slits in a slice of carrot and twist.

Divide the vegetable into 3-in/7.5-cm lengths and halve it lengthwise. Score the top part of the cucumber closely with ¼-in/6-mm deep cuts.

Peel back a ¾-in/18-mm strip of skin and push to the side with your thumb. Repeat the cut, pushing the skin to alternate sides to form the pine needles.

Mexico

The best Mexican food is rarely found in restaurants, even in Mexico. It is a unique blend of Central American, of Spanish, and of the Arab cooking which in its turn influenced Spain. It can be brutally simple, or extremely complex: indeed, the same dish may well be prepared in ways which reflect the various influences in very varying degrees, so you may have an Aztec version, a poor Spanish soldiers' version, a rich hidalgo's version, and a Moorish version.

For the most part, though, Mexican cookery uses a relatively limited number of techniques, and a relatively limited number of ingredients, and it is not difficult to learn. It may be time-consuming, but anyone who likes to cook will have an excellent chance of complete success the first time they try to cook a dish. Also, Mexican food is mostly cheap, delicious and filling; it is as suitable for a student dinner-party as for a gathering of older and more well-to-do gastronomes.

Admittedly, there are some things which are easily available in Mexico itself, or in the south-western United States, that are much harder to come by in other parts of the world. Corn tortillas are one of the best examples. In Mexico, at the time of writing, they were about 1,000 pesos a kilo: say 25¢ a pound in US currency. In California, in the shops the Mexicans patronize, fresh corn tortillas cost approximately ten times the price of the Mexican version.

You can, however, compromise and improvise. In Mexico, *tortillas de harina* (flour tortillas) are much more expensive than corn tortillas – but flour tortillas are just as authentic, and are actually cheaper to make in many places. Or, if you live near an Indian shop, you can buy chapattis: these are so similar to some types of Mexican tortillas that you would never know the difference. In fact, if you live near an Indian shop, you will find that many of the spices and ingredients (especially the various kinds of chilli [chili] peppers) are suitable for use in Mexican cookery.

'No *hay reglas fijas*' – there are no fixed rules. This applies to many aspects of Mexican life, as anyone who has tried to drive through central Tijuana will attest, but it is arguably most true in Mexican cooking.

There are two main reasons for this. One is the inventiveness of the Mexican people, born partly of necessity and partly of sheer natural exuberance: you work with what you've got, and you modify any recipe to make it closer to what you want. The other is the sheer size and diversity of Mexico. The border with the United States is over 1,800 miles long, and the country is more than 1,000 miles from north to south. Add to this the fact that there are tropical and sub-tropical coastal areas (the 'Tierra Calda'), the temperate plateaux (the 'Tierra Templada') and the cold high mountains (the 'Tierra Fria'); allow for the mountain ranges which for centuries separated one valley from the next; and you will see that the scope for regional and local variations in recipes is enormous.

If, therefore, the recipes in this book differ greatly from the recipes in another book, it is by no means unlikely that *both*

Above and opposite: *Scenes in Inchitan.*

Right: *Chili peppers.*

are authentic. If you want to modify any recipe, for example by making it hotter or cooler or doubling the meat or halving the coriander, the chances are that it will still be authentic in the sense that someone, somewhere in Mexico, cooks it like that. As long as you stick to believable Mexican ingredients, whatever you cook will taste Mexican.

In fact, Mexican cooking (like most other types of cooking) is more a state of mind than a matter of following recipes slavishly. In so far as there are any rules, there are two things worth remembering. The first is that Mexicans often cook meat for far longer than North Americans or northern Europeans do: often, meat is boiled for hours, until it can be shredded with two forks, before it is added to the vegetables or *mole* (sauce). The second thing to remember is that you can ring the changes by using different meats (beef, pork, chicken, lamb or even goat) in one sauce, or by using different sauces with the same meat.

One very important point is that Mexican food is not all mouth-blisteringly hot. By choosing the types and quantities of chillies (chilis) that you use, you can vary the style of the food from mild to *muy picante*. It is, however, worth remembering that you can rapidly build up a tolerance for food that is *muy picante*, and that if you invite unsuspecting friends over to try a favourite recipe that you have made a number of times, you may make it in a way that makes their eyes water!

SPECIAL INGREDIENTS

There are several ingredients which give Mexican cooking its characteristic flavours and which it is almost impossible to do without. If there isn't a Mexican shop handy, some of these things should be available at any good supermarket, while others may require a bit of hunting. As already mentioned, Indian shops are a good place to look; so are Chinese and other oriental shops.

Avocados: There are far more varieties of avocado in Mexico than in most parts of the world, and they usually come to the market in better condition: ripe, and superbly flavoured. The ones with the thick, knobbly skins (Hass) are generally the best varieties outside Mexico. A ripe avocado yields to gentle finger pressure without being squashy or blackened. Underripe avocados, provided they were not picked too early, will improve if they are left in a bowl in the kitchen, preferably with a couple of bananas for company.

Chayote: Pear-shaped gourd or squash.

Cheeses and milk products: There are dozens, perhaps hundreds, of kinds of Mexican cheese. Some are made from cows' milk, some from goats' milk. If you can't get authentic Mexican cheeses, you can use Jack (or failing that, Cheddar) for most purposes where the cheese has to be melted, and sour cream as a substitute for the Mexican cream or 'crema agria' that is so often used as a garnish in Mexico.

Chillies (chilis): According to whom you believe, there are between 50 and 250 varieties of chilli (chili) peppers used in

Above: Mexican cheeses

Below: Dried chillies (chilis)

Opposite: A basketful of chillies (chilis) and peppers.

Opposite below: Fresh chillies (chilis).

Mexican cooking. For our purposes, there are four groups. Inside each group, substitutions are normally possible.

Fresh hot chillies (chilis): Serrano and jalapeno chillies (chilis) are the best-known here; they are very hot indeed. Generally, they are interchangeable. Use two or three of the smaller serranos in place of a single larger jalapeno. When cutting these, wash your hands and the knife blade carefully afterwards: rubbing your eyes with a chilli-contaminated finger is an agonizing experience, though you are unlikely to do yourself any lasting harm.

Fresh large chillies (chilis): These are much milder: the big anaheim and poblano chillies (chilis) are only slightly hotter than bell peppers (green peppers). The seeds and veins (in which the heat chiefly resides) are removed before use: see Chilli (chili) Preparation (page 37).

Dried chillies (chilis): All of these are hot, though the small red ones are much hotter than the big brownish, dark red or black Californias, New Mexicos, anchos, pasillas, negros, etc. Many are available powdered. Seeds and veins are usually removed from the larger chillies (chilis) (see page 37), but not the smaller ones.

Other prepared chillies (chilis): Various forms of pickled chillies (chilis) are available. Many recipes call for pickled jalapenos, though fresh peppers can be substituted, while pickled chillies (chilis) in sauce (en escabeche) add a unique flavour of their own. Chipotle chillies (chilis) are smoked, and usually sold en escabeche.

Coriander: Fresh coriander or 'Chinese parsley' (*cilantro* in Spanish) is used in many salsas and in several other kinds of cooking, and as a garnish. Ask for *dhaniya* in Hindi, or grow your own: coriander seeds will sprout, and fresh-picked coriander (with green coriander seeds) adds an extra dimension to salsa cruda.

Corn-husks: Not strictly an ingredient, these are used to wrap tamales while cooking; they are discarded before eating. They are normally available only in Mexican stores.

Herbs and spices: Apart from chillies (chilis), the main herbs and spices used in Mexican food are oregano and black pepper. Fresh oregano (and sage and thyme, for that matter) are much more aromatic than the dried herbs. Don't use old spices that have been sitting on your shelf for years: throw them out and buy more, if they have lost their aromatic scent.

Hominy: This is maize treated with lye; it tastes surprisingly different from untreated maize. It comes in various forms, including the old Southern 'hominy grits', and canned.

Jicama: A root vegetable with an unusual flavour something between a raw potato or turnip, an apple, and a sweet radish.

Masa: This is the ready-mixed corn dough from which tortillas and tamales are made. If you can't get masa, you may be able to get the flour or dry mix called masa harina, which is *not* the same as cornflour and then make your own. Otherwise, you are going to have to buy your tortillas and tamales ready made.

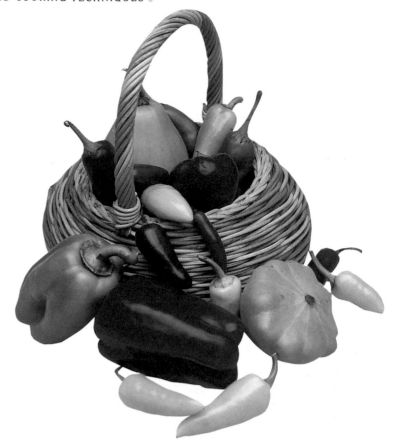

Piloncillo: Coarse, partially refined sugar. Also available in Indian stores as *gur* or *jaggery.*

Pipian: Raw, unsalted pumpkin seeds. These are used (like other nuts) for thickening and flavouring sauces and stews. You may find these in some Mexican shops: otherwise, you will need to slaughter and dress your own pumpkin.

Plantanos: Banana-like fruit used instead of bananas in cooking. It never becomes quite as sweet as a banana, but it breaks up less in stews. Use very slightly unripe bananas if you can't find these. Called 'plantains' in West Indian stores.

Ready-made foods: There are recipes for both corn and flour tortillas on pages 276–7, but most people find it easier to buy ready-made as do most Mexicans. Unless you have a mould or former, it is also easier to buy taco shells, but there is no point in buying tostadas when it is so easy to fry tortillas and make them at home.

Many kinds of salsa can be bought ready-made, but these are much better if you make them yourself: it is not difficult. Serve with freshly fried tostaditas to see how chips and salsa *should* taste.

Refried beans are readily available canned, and are perfectly adequate. The first time you try freshly made frijoles refritos, though, you realize how much better they can be.

Innumerable other prepared Mexican foods are available from a wide variety of manufacturers, and many of them are astonishingly good. Canned and frozen burritos, tamales, enchiladas, etc. are mostly edible, but they don't bear much resemblance to the real things, especially when these are made properly.

Tamarind: Seed pod of the tamarind plant. Used to make an astringent drink, and in some dressings. Available in some Mexican, Indian and oriental shops.

Tomatillos: These look rather like green tomatoes with a brown, papery husk. They are essential for some dishes, and green tomatoes are *not* a substitute.

Top: *Some fresh ingredients characteristic of Mexican food.*

Above: *A roasted and blistered chilli (chili) pepper.*

A *scene* in Inchitan.

EQUIPMENT

You do not need a fancy *batterie de cuisine* for Mexican cookery: indeed, the traditional earthenware *cazuelas* (casseroles) and *ollas* (pots) are a lot less convenient than modern utensils.

The most useful single cooking-pot is a large, heavy 'Dutch oven' or flameproof casserole: this replaces the clay *olla* which for centuries was the main cooking-pot of all Central American cultures. You also need a heavy skillet or large frying-pan (cast iron is ideal). Another smaller skillet and a saucepan or twoo will equip you to cook almost anything you like.

A selection of bowls of varying sizes, a couple of sharp knives, and a cutting board are necessary for food preparation.

Traditionally, a pestle and mortar were used to pound and purée food, and a large, strong pestle and mortar will make life very much easier today; add a second, smaller one for spices if you like.

Among electrical appliances, a blender is virtually essential: this makes it far easier to purée sauces to the degree of liquidity that is required. A food processor may be useful, but it cannot produce a fine enough purée for many applications. For grinding spices, a small electric coffee-mill is ideal – but don't use it for coffee afterward without a very thorough cleaning, or you will get some very strange flavours with your breakfast.

TECHNIQUES

There are a few basic techniques which are applicable in many recipes, and which are easiest to cover here.

Chilli (chili) preparation: The larger dried chillies (chilis) (ancho, California, New Mexico, etc) are first de-seeded and de-veined: the veins along the inside of the flesh contain much of the heat. Then, tear them into reasonably flat pieces, and toast them briefly on a hot, dry frying-pan or griddle. Hold them down for a few seconds, until they change colour and crackle. Then flip them over and hold the other side down for a few seconds. Do not allow them to burn, or they will become bitter.

Next, put the shredded, toasted chillies (chilis) in a bowl, and just cover them with boiling water. Put a saucer on top to hold them under water, and leave to soak for at least half an hour. The soaking liquid is used in some recipes, but not in others.

The larger fresh chillies (chilis) (Anaheim, Poblano) are often toasted over an open flame until the skin is blistered all over; if you don't have an open flame, try 'dry-frying', below, or use a grill (broiler). When they are thoroughly blistered, put them in a plastic bag for 20 minutes to steam. They will then be quite easy to peel.

'Dry-frying': Because ovens and overhead grills (broilers) do not play a large part in traditional Mexican cooking, many things are cooked on a hot, seasoned griddle or frying-pan, without any oil or liquid. Tomatoes are often cooked like this before being added to sauces; garlic is softened this way; nuts and seeds are roasted or toasted; and as already mentioned, chillies (chilis) are toasted. Grilling (broiling) is an acceptable substitute in many cases.

Thailand

In its layout and contents, a traditional Thai kitchen reflects both the living conditions of this tropical country and the basic cooking styles. It is built around the stove, which can vary from a built-in range of tiled cement to a simple earthenware charcoal pot. All cooking is done over open heat sources, never enclosed, so an oven is unnecessary. As there is a large amount of frying involved, over high heat, ventilation is an important concern, and in many old-style houses the kitchen is actually a separate building, with slatted rather than solid walls.

Of course, traditional kitchen design, like the traditional Thai ways of life, are changing extremely rapidly; Thailand for many years now has been undergoing an economic boom. As the older style of wooden houses are replaced with concrete structures and European designs (apartment blocks, particularly in Bangkok), the kitchens come more and more to resemble Western ones. Nevertheless, some of the original principles persist. Steaming, boiling and frying are the main cooking techniques, so that it is the hob of a cooker that is used, not the oven.

One of the essentially Chinese traditions that has been adopted by the Thais is a considerable amount of rapid cooking over a high heat – stir-fried dishes in a kata (wok) are prominent in the cuisine. This means it is a considerable advantage to have a strong source of open heat. Charcoal cooking is, naturally, out of the question in a Western house, but overall gas is more useful than electricity. Thailand itself does not have piped gas supply, but gas tanks are a common sight in modern kitchens.

The year-round hot climate has also had an effect on cooking and the kitchen. Until recently, neither refrigerators nor air-conditioning have been widely available, and Thai cooking has evolved to cope with conditions in which food does not keep for long. Traditionally, most food is bought daily at the market, and there are few dishes constructed from leftovers (rice dishes are an exception: khao phad, or fried rice, is the basic Thai leftover recipe). In addition, there is a large range of preserved foodstuffs: pickled, sun-dried, salted and fermented. A selection of some of the most well-known includes pickled garlic (*krathiam dong*), dried chillies (chilis) and dried fish (*phrik haeng* and *plaa haeng*), salted eggs (*khai khem*) and fish sauce (*nam plaa*). These, and perhaps some pre-cooked rice, are traditionally stored in a larder cupboard protected from flies by mesh screens. Nowadays, however, the refrigerator is taking over.

SPECIAL INGREDIENTS

Rice (*khao*): The staple of Thai cooking, and while no Thai cook would give a second thought to preparing the day's rice, if you are not familiar with rice steaming techniques, it is important to perfect them. Thai rice is long-grain, and should be fluffy and well-separated when properly cooked. The easiest

Opposite: The use of the wok is fundamental to Thai cuisine.

Above: A traditional Thai kitchen with slatted walls to ensure the necessary ventilation.

Right: A typical Thai market stall with its produce.

way by far is to use an electric rice cooker – a good investment if you eat rice regularly and a main item in modern Thai kitchens. Otherwise, use a saucepan in the following manner: wash the rice well with several changes of water until the water that your pour off is clear. For 8 oz/225 g/generous 1 cup of rice add 1 pint/600 ml/2½ cups of water; bring both together to the boil over a high heat. Turn the heat down to low, cover the pan and allow to cook for about 20 minutes. Fluff up the rice before serving. In Thai, cooked steamed rice is called *khao suay* or *khao plao*.

Coconuts and coconut milk (*maprao and nam katii*): As in virtually every other country where the coconut tree forms a natural part of the landscape, it plays an important part in the traditional economy. The whole tree, from fruit to palm fronds, is made use of. In Thai cooking, its contribution is mainly for the milk, a thickening and flavouring for various curries, as well as in other dishes. It is important to distinguish between two kinds of coconut milk: 'thick' and 'thin'. Both are made from the shredded meat of mature coconuts, and have nothing to do with the refreshing water content of the young green fruit. The dry coconut is cracked open and the white meat scraped out; the meat is then shredded, placed in boiling water, and squeezed to express the milky liquid. This first pressing produces 'thick' coconut milk; repeated squeezings with fresh water produce the 'thin' milk. The problem in the

West is obtaining ripe coconuts; the closest substitute is desiccated coconut, but then you may find better results by using (cow's) milk instead of water, or perhaps a mixture of milk and water.

To make coconut milk in this way, use 1 pint/600 ml/2½ cups of shredded dried coconut and 1½ pints/900 ml/3¾ cups of liquid (water, water-and-milk or milk) to make 1 pint/600 ml/ 2½ cups of 'thick' coconut milk. Bring the water to the boil in a saucepan or, if you are using milk, scald it. Add the shredded coconut, stir, remove from the heat and allow to cool. Strain through a sieve until the residue is dry. Add more water or cow's milk if you want to make a second pressing for 'thin' coconut milk. Treat as cow's milk as far as keeping is concerned; you can refrigerate it for several days.

This is the authentic method of preparation, but an acceptable substitute is canned coconut milk.

Chillies (chilis) (*phrik*): Chillies (chilis) are so characteristic of modern Thai cooking that it seems strange to many people that they are an import from the New World. They arrived with Portuguese traders, probably in the 16th century, and the enthusiasm with which they have been incorporated into Thai cuisine shows that they obviously fulfilled a latent need for strong, fiery flavour. Black pepper, originally from the Indonesian Spice Islands, probably had a similar role earlier, and is known as *phrik Thai*, or 'Thai pepper'. The Thais use a variety of chillies (chilis), although not as extensive as those available in Latin America, with different degrees of fieriness. The smallest and hottest are *phrik kii noo*, which translates with characteristic Thai lack of euphemism as 'mouse dropping chillies (chilis)' (apart from the colour, green, orange and red, there is some similarity of shape!). The colour is green when immature, changing to yellow and red as they ripen. Other chillies (chilis) are *phrik chiifaa*, which are finger-sized; *phrik num*, which are a northern variety, slightly larger; and *phrik yauk*, which are large and pale-green. They can be stored for up to about a week in a sealed, dry container in a refrigerator; after that they begin to grow mould and blacken.

Chillies (chilis) are also sun-dried, in which form they can be stored indefinitely, and appear wrinkled and crisp, with a colour between deep red and brown-black. The hottest part of a chilli (chili) is the seeds, and if you wish, you can remove these by holding the stem in one hand and slicing down the length of the chilli (chili) with the tip of a sharp knife, scraping out the seeds and interior ribs with the knife tip.

Dried chillies (chilis) can be de-seeded simply by breaking off the stem, holding the open end of the chilli (chili) pointing down and rolling it between your fingers; the seeds just fall out. Note, however, that Thais normally leave the seeds in; the fieriness is, after all, the main point of using chillies (chilis). Needless to say, be careful of the oil when handling chillies (chilis): never rub your eyes, for example, before washing your hands thoroughly. Chillies (chilis) are fairly easy to grow yourself; they need sunlight, water and well-drained soil.

Garlic (*krathiam*): This is used extensively in Thai cooking, pounded in a mortar, sometimes added whole, with some dishes sliced and deep-fried to make golden flakes. Thai garlic cloves are rather different from those in Europe and America: not only considerably smaller, but with a skin thin enough to be used in cooking.

Coriander (*phakchii*): Also called *cilantro* and Chinese parsley, coriander is as easy to grow as parsley, which it resembles. It adds a distinctive flavour which is very characteristic of Thai food (and also Cambodian). The fresh leaves are commonly used as a garnish, but for cooking the roots are also used. In the West, the stems are usually sold trimmed, sometimes with just the top part of the root.

Lemon Grass (*takrai*): Also known as *citronnelle*, this gives a lemony flavour to dishes, but more aromatic than lemon fruit. The lower several inches are used, from the whitish 'bulb'. In soups and curries, the fibrous stalks are usually partly crushed by pounding with the back of a knife; another use is in some salads, in which case the stalks are cut into thin rings (it may be necessary to peel off the outer, more fibrous leaves).

Fish sauce (*nam plaa*): An essential ingredient in Thai cooking and as a condiment. Salty and fermented, it is highly distinctive, a clear brown liquid sold in bottles. Use either the Thai version, *nam plaa*, or the Vietnamese, *nuoc mam*; they are very similar. In cooking, use straight from the bottle; also, serve as a condiment in a small Chinese sauce dish with meals, adding the fish sauce, two or three chopped small chillies (chilis) (*phrik kii noo*) and a squeeze of lime.

Shrimp paste (*kapi*): Traditionally, shrimp paste was a by-product of *nam plaa*, made from the residue of shrimps and salt left to dry in the sun. Now, however, its manufacture is a Thai industry in its own right. The best quality has a fine texture and is not very salty. The colour is either pinkish or a dark brown (but inferior quality *kapi* has dye colouring added to make it darker). It is available in shops in the West in vacuum-sealed jars.

Sticky rice (*khao niaow*): This is a different strain of rice from the familiar one, and forms an important part of the diet in the northeast of Thailand and parts of the north. The grains are short, and opaque white (rather than translucent in the case of regular rice). Use it to accompany the regional dishes from

Opposite: *A rice field, common to the country's landscape in which rice is a staple ingredient in the Thai diet.*

Above: *A selection of dried seafood, which, like fish sauce, is used as a condiment in much Thai cooking.*

Left: *Floating noodle stall.*

these areas. Sticky rice must be steamed, never boiled, and the secret of success is to soak it in cold water for a considerable time before cooking – up to several hours. This both cleans the grains and softens them, so that they do not clump together in glutinous masses. In Issaan, the heartland of sticky rice, most cooks use a steaming basket woven from bamboo known as a *huad*. Filled with rice, this is fitted on to a wide-mouthed, deep pan containing water. The ensemble is placed on the stove, and the steam from the boiling water cooks the rice (the time this takes depends on how much soaking the rice has received). Turn the rice once during the steaming, as the lower part cooks more quickly. Well-cooked sticky rice should be firm and dry and the grains adhere to each other. It should not be hard, which is sign of it having been cooked too long before being served, nor gooey, which happens if you overcook it. A *couscoussière*, available in French kitchen supply shops, makes an ideal alternative, otherwise line a lage sieve or collander with muslin (cheese cloth), and place over a large pan with boiling water.

Tamarind (*makhaam*): This fruit gives a sourish flavour to certain dishes, such as *kaeng sam*. It grows as long, fleshy pods that hang from the tamarind tree, and in Thailand is eaten as a fruit and candied. In cooking, it is normally used as tamarind water (the pulp itself is usually too tough to leave in the dish). If you have the actual fruit, open the pod case and remove the pulp and seeds, which are difficult to separate. Soak the pulp in about twice the quantity of hot water, stirring, and leave it until it has dissolved (this may take 10 minutes); then strain through a sieve. Alternatively, buy tamarind concentrate, which needs no straining. Do not, however, buy tamarind juice which has sugar added to it.

EQUIPMENT AND TECHNIQUES

The basic cooking utensils are the *katta* (wok), saucepan and steamer. Woks are usually of the Chinese variety – large, wide and round-bottomed with two metal handles on opposite sides of the rim. This fits on the circular opening of a traditional stove, but if you have only an electric range, the alternatives are to buy a flat-bottomed wok or to buy a circular metal rim that sits on a hot-plate and holds the wok securely. Because maximum heat transmission is important, the former is generally more useful. In stir-frying, the important technique is to add just a little oil but to bring this to a very high heat very quickly (to minimise burning and smoke). The food to be stir-fried is added all at once and moved around constantly with a spatula, at the same time the wok should be rocked. The high heat seals in the juices and flavour of the individual pieces so that they stay crisp and tasty. Slow stir-frying produces limp, partially steamed vegetables. A tip for dealing with hard, solid vegetables is not only to cut them into small pieces but after a minute or two of stir-frying to turn off the heat (or turn it right down) and cover the wok with a large saucepan lid. This has the effect of adding a little steaming.

For boiled dishes, a deep saucepan is necessary. For adding and removing ingredients, Thais use attractively made bamboo-

handled brass wire mesh baskets and scoops, but a large perforated spoon or sieve will do as well. A saucepan is also needed for cooking plain rice, but nowadays in Thailand any family that can afford one will have an electric rice-steamer. The results are more reliable for an inexperienced cook, and save time.

Steaming is the third main technique, used for many fish dishes. The standard utensil for this in Thailand is an aluminium Chinese steamer set, consisting of a saucepan for the water, on top of which fits one or more perforated trays, and a lid for the top. These are available, and not expensive, in Chinese supermarkets, but a makeshift alternative is a colander suspended over a deep saucepan, again with a lid large enough to seal in the steam. Do not overfill the saucepan base with water, but make sure that it does not dry out during the steaming process. One traditional Thai steaming method is to wrap food in parcels of leaves: this imparts some of the leaf's flavour to the food, and looks very attractive when served. Banana leaves are the standard, but pandanus leaves (*bai toei*) make a good wrapping for chicken pieces.

One of the most important features of Thai cooking is the emphasis on preparation. Very many of the recipes here are actually cooked quite quickly, and with a minimum of complication, but much more of the total time necessary to make the dishes is taken up with preparing the ingredients. Often this is mainly a matter of peeling and chopping and arranging into piles: with wok-cooked dishes you will usually need to add ingredients in rapid succession, so they must be close to the cooker and easy to scoop up. If you are entertaining guests to a Thai dinner, you may find that some of the dishes have to be cooked at the very last moment, so arrange your pre-dinner drinks accordingly! This is an additional reason for varying the types of cooked dish in a menu: steamed dishes can be left to cook by themselves, but fried dishes need constant last-minute attention.

Equipment for preparation includes a chopping board (better still, two), cleaver or large kitchen knife, medium and

Left: An itinerant food vendor.

Right: Although refrigeration is becoming more common, traditionally food that cannot be kept is bought daily at the market.

Below: Intricate preparation in Thai cuisine often takes the form of elaborately carved vegetables.

Bottom: A mortar and pestle.

the cross-section of the inside of the mortar is shallower and more or less circular. Pounding with these involves a grinding action as well.

The carving of fruit and vegetables occupies a special place in Royal or Palace style cooking. This decorative preparation of raw ingredients is a study in itself, but at a simpler level it provides an attractive touch to a Thai meal if you carve rather than just chop vegetables. The essential equipment is not complicated: a sharp paring knife with a finely pointed blade and a bowl of water, preferably iced, to prevent discoloration of the carved pieces. It is definitely time-consuming, although how much depends on the degree of elaboration you go for. Also buy a packet of plasters.

One of the simplest cuts for smallish round vegetables such as tomatoes and *makeua puang* is to halve them by means of consecutive diagonal cuts. Chillies (chilis) can be given a flower-like appearance by making two deep cuts through the length of the chilli (chili), at right angles to each other, from the tip to near the base. Hold the stem on the chopping board so that the chilli (chili) lies flat and cut straight down and through from the tip end. Scrape out the seeds and drop into the bowl of water; the ends will curve outwards naturally. You can give a similar treatment to a spring onion (scallion); first cut it down to the point where the stem begins to turn from white to green. Hold this end with one hand, and then make the same kind of deep lengthwise cuts from the bulb end. As with the chillies (chilis), these white ends will curve outwards; store temporarily in the bowl of cold water.

Cucumbers are an easy vegetable to carve with designs, for not only are they firm, but the contrast between the dark skin and the pale flesh makes surface designs very effective – rather like making a cameo. Cut the design just through the skin. A common Thai treatment for cucumbers is to make them into leaf shapes. Thai cucumbers are smaller and so lend themselves to this, but with the larger European and American cucumbers, you will need to cut them down to the basic leaf shape first.

small kitchen knives, mortar and pestle. Professional Thai cooks use a Chinese cleaver for virtually all cutting jobs with considerable delicacy, but if you are used to Western-style knives, use one of those. It must, however, be kept perfectly sharp. There are two kinds of mortar and pestle used in Thailand. One, for lighter work, is a relatively deep rough ceramic mortar and wooden pestle; the pounding action is up and down. The second kind is for heavy duty pounding; both the mortar and pestle is made from heavy stone, like granite, and

SOUPS AND STARTERS

From India
SAVOURY POTATO SNACK 46
CHEESE CUTLET 47
DEEP FRIED PASTRY 48
VEGETABLE FRITTERS 49
SAMOSAS 50
LENTIL CAKES IN YOGURT 51
FRIED POTATO CAKES 52
VEGETABLE CUTLET 53
ONION BHAJIS 54

From China
HOT AND SOUR SOUP 55
SHARK'S FIN SOUP 56
SPINACH AND BEAN CURD SOUP 57
DRIED BEAN CURD SKIN AND VERMICELLI SOUP 58

From Japan
MISO SOUP WITH TOFU AND LEEKS 59
THICK VEGETABLE SOUP WITH TOFU 60
THICK NEW YEAR'S SOUP WITH CHICKEN AND RICE CAKES 63
EGG DROP SOUP WITH MANGE-TOUT (SNOW) PEAS 63
CLEAR SOUP WITH PRAWNS (SHRIMP) AND SPINACH 64

From Mexico
TAMALES 65
TORTILLA SOUP 66
TLALPEN-STYLE SOUP 66
MACHOMO 69
PICO DE GALLO 69
EMPANADAS 70
QUESADILLAS 70

From Thailand
ISSAAN-STYLE SOUP 71
SOUP WITH STUFFED SQUID 72
SOUR CURRY SOUP 73
SATAY CHICKEN OR PORK 74
SATAY SAUCE 74
SPICY VEGETABLE AND SHRIMP SOUP 75
BOILED RICE SOUP WITH CHICKEN 75

Left: *Fresh produce in a Thai vegetable market.*

Savoury Potato Snack

12 oz/325 g/¾ lb potatoes, boiled
and peeled
1 small onion, finely chopped
1–2 green chillis (chilis), finely
chopped
½ tsp/2.5 g/½ tsp salt

½ tsp/2.5 g/½ tsp chilli (chili)
powder
5–6 tbsp/75–90/6–7 tbsp ml
tamarind juice
1 tbsp/15 g/1 tbsp coriander
leaves, chopped

1 Cut the potatoes into ¼-in/0.5-cm slices and cool thoroughly.
2 Gently mix in all the other ingredients. Serve cold.

Below: *Savoury potato snack.*

Above: Cheese cutlets.

Cheese Cutlets

1 tbsp/15 g/1 tbsp ghee
8 fl oz/225 ml/1 cup milk
6 oz/175 g/1 cup panir, drained
4 oz/100g/⅔ cup semolina
1 medium onion, finely chopped
2 green chillis (chilis), finely
chopped

1 tbsp/15g/1 tbsp coriander
leaves, chopped
½ tsp/2.5 g/½ tsp salt
2 tbsp/30 g/2 tbsp flour
4 fl oz/100 ml/½ cup milk
breadcrumbs
oil for deep frying

1 Heat the ghee in a karai over medium heat, add the milk, panir, semolina, onions, chilli (chili), coriander leaves and salt and mix thoroughly. Stirring constantly, cook until the mixture leaves the sides and a ball forms, about 3–4 minutes.
2 Spread the mixture ¾ in/1.5 cm on a greased baking tin. Cut into 1-in/2.5-cm squares and chill for about 2 hours.
3 Make a smooth batter with the flour and milk. Dip each square in the batter and then roll it in breadcrumbs.
4 Heat the oil in a karai over high heat and fry the cutlets for 2–3 minutes till crisp and golden. Serve with chutney.

Deep Fried Pastry

4 oz/100g/1 cup flour
½ tsp/2.5 g/½ tsp salt
pinch of kalonji
pinch of ground roasted cumin

1 ½ tbsp/22.5 ml/1 ½ tbsp oil
approx. 2 fl oz/50 ml/1 ¼ cup hot
water
oil for deep frying

1 Sieve the flour and salt together. Mix in the kalonji and cumin. Rub in the oil.
2 Add enough water to make a stiff dough. Knead for 10 minutes until soft and smooth.
3 Divide the dough into 12 balls. Roll each ball into thin rounds 4 in/10 cm across. Make 5 or 6 small cuts in the rounds.
4 Heat oil in a karai over medium heat. Fry until crisp and golden. Drain on paper towels. Serve with chutney.

Deep fried pastry and vegetable fritters.

Vegetable Fritters

Batter:
4 tbsp/60 g/5 tbsp (chick pea) flour
2 tsp/10 ml/2 tsp oil
1 tsp/5 g/1 tsp baking powder
½ tsp/2.5 g/½ tsp salt
3 oz/75 ml/⅜ cup water
Any of the following vegetables can be used:
aubergines (eggplant), cut into very thin rounds
onions, cut into ⅛ in/0.25 cm rings
potatoes, cut into very thin rounds
cauliflower, cut into ¾-in/1.5-cm florets
chilli (chili), left whole
pumpkin, cut into thin slices
green pepper, cut into thin strips
oil for deep frying

1 Mix all the batter ingredients together and beat until smooth.
2 Wash the slices of vegetables and pat dry.
3 Heat the oil in a karai till very hot.
4 Dip a slice of the vegetable in the batter and put into the hot oil. Place as many slices as you can in the oil. Fry till crisp and golden. Drain and serve with mint or coriander chutney.

Samosas.

Samosas

DOUGH:

1 Sieve together the flour and salt. Rub in the oil. Add enough water to form a stiff dough. Knead for 10 minutes until smooth.
2 Divide into 12 balls. Roll each ball into a round of about 6 in/ 15 cm across. Cut in half.
3 Pick up one half, flatten it slightly and form a cone, sealing the overlapping edge with a little water. Fill the cone with 1½ tsp/7.5 ml of the filling and seal the top with a little water.
4 In a similar way make all the samosas.
5 Heat oil in a karai over medium heat. Put in as many samosas as you can into the hot oil and fry until crisp and golden. Drain. Serve with a chutney.

Filling:
3 tbsp/45 ml/4 tbsp oil
¼ tsp/1.25 g/¼ tsp whole cumin seeds
1 lb/450 g/4 cups potatoes, diced into ½-in/1-cm cubes
1 green chilli (chili), finely chopped
pinch of turmeric
½ tsp/2.5 g/½ tsp salt
3 oz/75 g/scant ½ cup peas
1 tsp/5 g/1 tsp ground roasted cumin
Dough:
8 oz/225 g/2 cups plain (all-purpose) flour
1 tsp/5 g/1 tsp salt
3 tbsp/45 ml/4 tbsp oil
approx. 3½ fl oz/90 ml/scant ½ cup hot water
oil for deep frying

FILLING:

1 Heat the oil in a karai over medium high heat and add the cumin seeds. Let them sizzle for a few seconds.
2 Add the potatoes and green chilli (chili) and fry for 2–3 minutes. Add the turmeric and salt and, stirring occasionally, cook for 5 minutes.
3 Add the peas and the ground roasted cumin. Stir to mix. Cover, lower heat and cook a further 10 minutes until the potatoes are tender. Cool.

Lentil cakes in yogurt.

Lentil Cakes in Yogurt

8 oz/225 g/2 cups washed urid dal
15 fl oz/425 ml/scant 2 cups water
3 green chillis (chilis)
½ tsp/2.5 g/½ tsp salt
¼ tsp/1.25 g/¼ tsp asafetida
oil for deep frying
1½ pints/850 ml/3¾ cups plain
yogurt

¼ tsp/1.25 g/¼ tsp ground
roasted cumin
¼ tsp/1.25 g/¼ tsp garam
masala
½ tsp/2.5 g/½ tsp chilli (chili)
powder

1 Wash the dal and soak in the water overnight.
2 In a blender or food processor put in the dal, green chillis (chilis), salt and asafetida and some of the soaking liquid. Blend until you have a thick paste, adding more soaking liquid as necessary.
3 In a karai, heat the oil over medium high heat.
4 Add tablespoons of the mixture to the hot oil and fry for 3–4 minutes, until they are reddish brown, turning once. Drain them on paper towels.
5 When all the vadas are fried put them in a bowl of warm water for 1 minute. Squeeze out the water gently and put in a large dish.

6 Combine the yogurt, roasted cumin, garam masala and chilli (chili) powder and pour over the vadas.
7 Chill and serve with tamarind chutney.

Above: Fried potato cakes.

Fried Potato Cakes

1 lb/450 g/2 cups potatoes, boiled and mashed
1–2 green chillis (chilis), chopped
½ tsp/2.5 g/½ tsp salt
1 tbsp/15 g/1 tbsp coriander leaves, chopped
2 tbsp/30 g/2 tbsp onions, chopped
oil for frying

1 Mix the mashed potatoes with the chillis (chilis), salt, coriander leaves and onions.
2 Form into small balls and flatten.
3 Heat oil for shallow frying till hot and fry the potato cakes for a few minutes each side till golden. Serve with a chutney.

Vegetable Cutlet

4 oz/100 g/1 cup beetroot (beet),
diced
4 oz/100 g/1 cup carrots, diced
8 oz/225 g/2 cups potatoes, diced
4 oz/100 g/1 ½ cups cabbage,
shredded
½ tsp/2.5 g/½ tsp chilli (chili)
powder

½ tsp/2.5 g/½ tsp ground black
pepper
¾ tsp/4 g/¾ tsp salt
a big pinch sugar
1 tbsp/15 g/1 tbsp raisins
(optional)
2 oz/50 g/½ cup flour
4 oz/100 ml/½ cup milk

½ tsp/2.5 g/½ tsp ground roasted
cumin

breadcrumbs
oil for deep frying

1 Boil the beetroot (beet), carrots, potatoes and cabbage together until tender. Drain.

2 Mash the boiled vegetables with the chilli (chili), roasted cumin, black pepper, salt, sugar and raisins. Divide into 12 balls and flatten. Chill for 1 hour.

3 Make a batter with the flour and milk and dip a cutlet in it. Then roll it in breadcrumbs until well coated.

4 Heat the oil in a large frying pan and fry the cutlets for 2–3 minutes turning once, until crisp and golden. Serve with coriander chutney.

Below: Vegetable cutlet.

Onion bhajis.

Onion Bhajis

2 tbsp/30 ml/2 tbsp oil	pinch chilli (chili) powder
½ tsp/2.5 g/½ tsp ground	(optional)
mustard seed	½ tsp/2.5 g/½ tsp salt
1 tsp/5 g/1 tsp fenugreek seed	1 egg
1 tsp/5 g/1 tsp ground turmeric	4 oz/100 g/scant 1 cup gram
1 medium onion, finely chopped	(chick pea) flour
	oil for frying

1 Heat the oil and fry the spices for a minute. Add the onion, and stir untill well coated.

2 Turn down the heat, cover, and cook until the onion is tender but not mushy. Leave to cool.

3 Add salt, egg and gram (chick pea) flour and stir well.

4 Fry generous ½ tbsp/7.5 g/½ tbsp of the mixture in ½ in/1 cm hot oil, turning them almost immediately. As soon as they are puffy and brown remove them with a slotted spoon and drain on kitchen paper (paper towels). Serve warm.

5 Onion bhajis can be kept warm in a moderate oven for 20 minutes or so before serving, but they cannot be made in advance and reheated.

VARIATION Make the bhajis half-size and serve with cocktail sticks (toothpicks).

Hot and sour soup.

Hot and Sour Soup

3 dried Chinese mushrooms, soaked in warm water for 30 minutes
2 cakes of bean curd (tofu)
2 oz/50 g/½ cup Sichuan preserved vegetables
2 oz/50 g/½ cup pickled vegetables, such as cucumber, cabbage or French (green) beans
2 spring onions (scallions), finely chopped

2 slices ginger root, thinly shredded
1½ pt/900 ml/3¾ cups water
1 tsp/5 g/1 tsp salt
2 tbsp/30 ml/2 tbsp rice wine or sherry
1 tbsp/15 ml/1 tbsp soy sauce
freshly ground pepper to taste
1 tsp/5 ml/1 tsp sesame seed oil
1 tsp/5 g/1 tsp cornflour (cornstarch) with 2 tsp/10 ml/2 tsp water

1 Squeeze dry the mushrooms after soaking. Discard the hard stalks and cut mushrooms into thin shreds. Reserve the water for use later.

2 Thinly shred the bean curd, Sichuan preserved vegetables, pickled vegetables and ginger. Finely chop the spring onions (scallions).
3 In a wok or large pot, bring the water to the boil. Add all the ingredients and seasonings and simmer for 2 minutes.
4 Add the sesame seed oil and thicken the soup by stirring in the cornflour (cornstarch) and water mixture. Serve hot.
NOTE A little vinegar can be added to the soup if you find that the pickled vegetables do not give a sour enough taste.

Shark's Fin Soup

This recipe is included here purely for academic interest. Should any reader be adventurous enough to attempt it, be warned that to start with, one or two of the ingredients are unobtainable in the West. If that does not deter you from going ahead, it takes days to clean the shark's fin in the preliminary stage before you can even proceed to the preparation proper, which is in itself lengthy and fiddly.

1 ½ lb/0.75 kg/1 ½ lb shark's fin, which has been soaked for at least 3 days with several changes of water
4 oz/100 g/4 oz 'yolk' (roe) of the female or hen crab extracted from 2 lb/1 kg/2 lb cooked crab meat
6 tbsp/90 ml/7 tbsp rice wine (or sherry)
2½ tsp/12 g/2½ tsp salt
1½ tsp/7.5 ml/1½ tsp monosodium glutamate
2–3 slices ginger root

2–3 spring onions (scallions)
2½–3 pt/about 1.5 l/6¼–7½ cups stock (made from simmering a whole chicken and a whole duck in 5–6 pt/about 3 l/6–6½ pt water until the liquid is reduced by half, discarding both the chicken and duck and straining the stock for use)
4 oz/100 g/½ cup lard
2 tbsp/30 ml/2 tbsp cornflour (cornstarch)

1 After the shark's fin has been soaked, it is cleaned again before simmering for 4–5 hours or until the sandy skin and decayed bone hidden in the meat at the top of the fin can be removed, but do not boil it hard. Rinse in cold water and scrub off the sandy skin and decayed bone. After simmering gently for a further 8 hours or so the fin will gradually reveal itself as a transparent colour and curl into the shape of a crescent.

2 Place the absolutely clean fin in a bowl, add 2 tbsp/30 ml/2 tbsp rice wine or sherry, 1 tsp/5 g/1 tsp salt, ½ tsp/2 ml/½ tsp monosodium glutamate, ginger root, and onion. Use about a third of the stock to cover the fin.

3 Place the bowl in a steamer and steam over a high heat for about 1–1½ hours or until the fin is really soft.

4 Place about half of the remaining stock in a *wok* or pan, add ¼ tsp/1 ml/¼ tsp monosodium glutamate, ¼ tsp/1 g/¼ tsp salt, and 1 tbsp/15 ml/1 tbsp rice wine or sherry together with the fin, but discard the stock in which it has been steamed. Simmer gently for about 15 minutes or until the fin is quite tender.

5 Remove and discard the stock in which it has been cooking, and start all over again with fresh stock, wine, salt and monosodium glutamate. After a further simmering, remove the fin (yes, again discard the stock!) and place it neatly on a plate.

The fin is now ready for its last stage of cooking.

6 Warm about half of the lard in a wok, put in the crab 'yolk', add the remaining 2 tbsp/30 ml/2 tbsp rice wine or sherry, 1 tsp/5 g/1 tsp salt, ½ tsp/2.5 ml/½ tsp monosodium glutamate together with the last 3–4 tbsp/45–60 ml/4–5 tbsp of stock and cook gently for 10 minutes. the crab 'yolk' will then have broken up and the flavour of both the lard and rice wine will have merged into it.

7 Thicken it with cornflour (cornstarch) until smooth. Take it off the heat and add the remaining lard, stirring and pouring it all over the fin. It is now ready to be served.

Below: Spinach and bean curd soup.

Above: Shark's fin soup.

Spinach and
Bean Curd Soup

8 oz/225 g/½ lb fresh spinach
2 cakes bean curd (tofu)
2 tbsp/30 ml/2 tbsp oil
2 tsp/10 g/2 tsp salt

1 pt/600 ml/2½ cups water
2 tbsp/30 ml/2 tbsp soy sauce
1 tsp/5 ml/1 tsp sesame seed oil

1 Wash the spinach well, discarding the tough and discoloured leaves. Shake off the excess water and cut the leaves into small pieces.
2 Cut the bean curd into about 14 pieces.
3 In a wok or large pot, heat the oil until hot. Stir-fry the spinach until soft. Add the salt and water and bring to the boil.
4 Add the bean curd and soy sauce and cook for 1½–2 minutes. Add the sesame seed oil just before serving.

Dried Bean Curd Skin and Vermicelli Soup

½ oz/15 g/½ oz dried bean curd skin
1 oz/25 g/1 oz golden needles (dried, tiger-lily buds)
¼ oz/5 g/¼ oz black moss
2 oz/50 g/2 oz bean thread vermicelli
1½ pt/900 ml/3¾ cups water
1 tsp/5 g/1 tsp salt

2 tbsp/30 ml/2 tbsp light soy sauce
1 tbsp/15 ml/1 tbsp rice wine or dry sherry
1 tsp/5 g/1 tsp fresh root ginger, finely chopped
2 spring onions (scallions), finely chopped
2 tsp/10 ml/2 tsp sesame seed oil
fresh coriander to garnish

1 Soak the bean curd skin in hot water for 30–35 minutes and then cut it into small pieces.

2 Soak the lily buds and black moss in water separately for about 20–25 minutes. Rinse the lily buds until clean. Loosen the black moss until it resembles human hair. With a pair of scissors, cut the vermicelli into short lengths.

3 Bring the water to the boil in a wok or large pot, and add all the ingredients together with the seasonings. Stir until well blended.

4 Cook the soup for 1–1½ minutes. Add the sesame seed oil and serve hot, garnished with coriander.

Below: *Dried bean curd skin and vermicelli soup.*

Above: *Miso soup with tofu and leeks.*

Miso Soup with Tofu and Leeks

8 oz/225 g/1 cup tofu
1 young leek

30 fl oz/850 ml/3¾ cups dashi II
3 tbsp/45 ml/4 tbsp red miso

1 Wash the leek and slice very finely; divide between four soup bowls. Cut the tofu into small cubes and distribute between the four bowls.
2 Heat the dashi in a small saucepan. Put a little of the hot dashi in a bowl, add the miso and soften with a wire whisk. Strain the miso mixture into the hot dashi. Do not reboil.
3 Ladle the dashi over the tofu and leeks in each bowl and serve immediately.

Thick Vegetable Soup with Tofu

8 oz/225 g/1 cup tofu
2 medium carrots
3 medium potatoes
1 bamboo shoot, fresh or tinned
8 fresh or dried & reconstituted
shiitake mushrooms

1 cake konnyaku (arum root)
2 tbsp/30 ml/2 tbsp vegetable oil
30 fl oz/850 ml/3¾ cups dashi
4 tbsp/60 ml/5 tbsp red miso

1 First drain the tofu: set a weight such as a chopping board or dinner plate on the tofu and set aside for at least 30 minutes to drain.

2 Prepare the vegetables. Wash and peel the carrots and potatoes and cut into small chunks. Cut the bamboo shoot into pieces of the same size. Trim away the hard stems of the mushrooms and cut into quarters.

3 With a teaspoon, cut the konnyaku into chunks. Heat the vegetable oil in a frying pan, add the vegetables and sauté over high heat, until lightly browned and evenly coated with oil.

4 Turn the vegetables into a saucepan and ladle the dashi over them. Bring to the boil. Squeeze the drained tofu through your fingers and into the soup. Ladle a little of the hot soup into a bowl and add the miso. Soften with a wire whisk.

5 Strain the miso into the soup. Reheat the soup until nearly boiling, but do not boil. Ladle the soup into warmed soup bowls and serve immediately.

Thick vegetable soup with tofu.

Thick New Year's Soup with Chicken and Rice Cakes

4 rice cakes	2 young leeks
8 oz/225 g/1 cup boned chicken, leg and breast, with skin	30 fl oz/850 ml/3¾ cups dashi
	3 tbsp/45 ml/4 tbsp white miso

1 Grill (broil) the rice cakes under a hot grill (broiler) or over a hot flame, turning so that the cakes do not burn. When the surface is crisp and brown, remove from the heat and pierce with a fork a few times.

2 Trim the chicken and slice into thin strips. Blanch in a little lightly salted water for 2 minutes, and drain. Slice the leeks diagonally into fine slices.

3 In a large saucepan, bring the dashi to a boil; add the chicken pieces and simmer until tender.

4 Ladle a little of the hot soup into a bowl, add the miso and soften with a wire whisk. Strain the miso into the soup. Reheat the soup but do not boil.

5 Warm four soup bowls and put a rice cake into each. Ladle the soup into the bowls, distributing the chicken pieces evenly. Top with thin slices of leek and serve immediately.

Egg drop soup with mange-tout (snow) peas

4 oz/125 g/1 cup mange-tout (snow) peas	sauce
	salt
30 fl oz/850 ml/3¾ cups dashi	2 eggs
½ tsp/25 ml/½ tsp light soy	

1 Wash the mange-tout (snow) peas, pat dry, and slice diagonally into very thin slices. Parboil in lightly-salted water for 1 minute, remove and plunge into cold water to stop further cooking. Drain and pat dry.

2 Bring the dashi just to a boil; turn the heat to low and season to taste with soy sauce and salt. Beat the eggs lightly in a small bowl.

3 Add the peas to the simmering dashi, and pour over the egg in a thin stream. Remove from heat immediately and ladle into warmed soup bowls.

Above: *Egg drop soup with mange-tout (snow) peas.*

Opposite: *Thick New Year's soup with chicken and rice cakes.*

Clear soup with prawns (shrimp) and spinach.

Clear Soup with Prawns (Shrimp) and Spinach

4 medium raw prawns (shrimp)
salt
1 oz/25 g/¼ cup kuzu, potato flour or cornflour (cornstarch)

2 oz/50 g/2½ cups spinach
30 fl oz/850 ml/3¾ cups dashi
a few slivers yuzu or lemon rind

1 Shell and de-vein the prawns (shrimp), leaving the tail attached. Wash and pat dry.
   Slit the backs of the prawns (shrimp) open and press out flat.
2 For each prawn (shrimp), cut a lengthwise slit in the middle and push the tail through this slit to make a prawn (shrimp) 'flower'.
3 Salt the prawns (shrimp) lightly, and dredge in kuzu or cornflour (cornstarch). Drop the prawns (shrimp) into lightly-salted boiling water and parboil for 2 minutes. Drain on absorbent paper.

4 Wash the spinach and parboil in lightly salted boiling water for 2 minutes, until just tender. Plunge immediately into cold water to retain the brilliant green colour.
5 Lay the leaves of spinach evenly on a bamboo rolling mat and roll firmly to squeeze out moisture. Unroll the spinach and cut into four 2-in/5-cm pieces.
6 Warm four soup bowls and arrange a roll of spinach in each. Arrange a prawn (shrimp) beside each roll of spinach.
7 Bring the dashi to the boil, season with a little salt to taste and ladle over the ingredients in each bowl, taking care not to disturb the arrangement.
8 Float a few slivers of yuzu on each bowl and serve.

Tamales

Tamales.

1 Use a basic masa (see tortillas on page 266), or for extra luxury make it with chicken, pork or beef stock. Mix 1 lb/500 g/ 1 lb of this masa with about half as much lard.
2 Cream the lard; it must be light and fluffy. Beat the dough and the lard together until you have a light, soft, slightly mushy dough. A spoonful of the dough should float in water.
3 If you are using dried corn-husks, soak them in hot water to soften them; this takes about half an hour to an hour.
4 Put 1 tbsp/15 g/1 tbsp of dough in the centre of each husk; spread it out until it is about ½-in/1.25-cm thick. Use your fingers or (much easier) a tortilla press.
5 Put 1 tbsp/15 g/1 tbsp filling in the centre of the dough; roll up the dough-plus-husk to enclose the filling, and fold the top and bottom of each husk over.
6 Wrap another husk around the first, and tie the ends.
7 Put the tamales in a steamer with the bottom end of the corn-husk down. Steam for about an hour, or until the dough starts to come away from the husks.

FILLING:

4–6 *cloves garlic*	1 *lb/450 g/1 lb well-cooked beef,*
3 *California chillies (chilis)*	*pork or chicken*
	1 *ancho chilli (chili)*

1 Prepare the chillies (chilis) as described on page 37. While they are soaking, shred the meat with two forks.
2 Liquidize the chillies (chilis) in a blender with the garlic and a little of the soaking broth. Fry the purée for 5 minutes, stirring and scraping constantly, then add the shredded meat.

VARIATIONS In the masa include adding 4 fl oz/100 g/½ cup of cream to the stock used to make it, and adding ¼ tsp/1.25 g/ ¼ tsp each of cumin and oregano plus one puréed, soaked dried chilli(chili) to the basic dough recipe. Variations in the filling include using tomatoes, onions, and different herbs.

Left: Tortilla soup.

Right: Caldo tlalpeno.

Tortilla Soup

1 large or 2 small tomatoes
12 corn tortillas
lard or olive oil for frying
1 medium onion, chopped

2 cloves garlic
1 ½ pt/1 l/4 cups chicken stock
salt and pepper

1 Halve and grill (broil) the tomato or 'dry-fry' it.
2 The tortillas should be slightly dry; stale ones are ideal. Cut them into strips about ½ × 2in (1.5 × 5 cm). Deep-fry them until they are crisp and brown. Set them aside; pour off all but 1 tbsp/15 ml/1 tbsp of the lard or oil.
3 Fry the onion and garlic until golden-brown. In a blender, purée them with the tomato. Return the mixture to the frying pan with 1 tbsp/15 ml/1 tbsp of lard or oil. Fry until thick, stirring constantly.
4 Add the stock. Simmer for half an hour. Season to taste. Pour over the crisp tortillas in individual bowls.

VARIATIONS Add diced leftover chicken or meat, or cheese, and offer the following separately as garnishes: sour cream, chopped raw onion, chopped hard-boiled (hardcooked) eggs, lime wedges, dried pasilla chillies (chilis). To prepare the chillies (chilis), remove the seeds and veins; tear into pieces and deep-fry for a few seconds, until crumbly. You can do them at the same time as the tortillas.

Tlalpen-style Soup

4 oz/100 g/½ cup chicken (white meat)
1 ½ pt/1 l/4 cups chicken stock
1 or 2 dried red chillies (chili arbole)
1–5 cloves garlic

3 tbsp/45 ml/3 tbsp water
salt to taste
1 avocado
coriander to garnish (about half a handful)

1 Slice the chicken into julienne strips. If the chicken is not cooked, bring the chicken stock to a boil; simmer the meat until it is cooked (less than 5 minutes). Otherwise, bring the stock and chicken to a simmering boil. Doubling the amount of chicken will not do any harm.
2 De-seed the chillies (chilis); tear into pieces; grind in a pestle and mortar with the garlic and water. Strain into the stock. Stir, simmer for a couple of minutes, and add salt to taste.
3 Peel the avocado and slice into strips. Separate the slices carefully before dropping them into the soup, or they will stick together. They will sink for a few moments, then float to the surface. When they do, the soup is ready. Chop some coriander and float it on the surface for a garnish.

Machomo

1 lb/450 g/1 lb beef	1 bay leaf
2 cloves garlic	2 small onions
6 peppercorns	1 tbsp/15 g/1 tbsp lard
1 clove	

1 Chop the beef into approx. 2-in/5-cm cubes. Put in a saucepan with just enough water to cover. Add all the other ingredients except one of the small onions and the lard. Bring to the boil and simmer until the beef is soft enough to be shredded with two forks.

2 Strain off the stock and save it for use in another recipe; discard the onion, garlic, etc.

3 Shred the beef as finely as possible. Chop the onion finely. Melt the lard in a frying pan or skillet and fry the onion until it is light golden. Add the shredded beef, and continue to fry, stirring constantly. Slowly, the beef will begin to dry out. When it is crisp, or at least very dry, the machomo is ready: this takes about ten minutes.

Pico de Gallo

| 1 medium-to-large jicama | juice of 1 large lemon or 2 limes |
| 2 medium-to-large oranges | bottled hot sauce |

1 Peel and slice (or chip or dice) the jicama. Peel and slice (or dice) the oranges. Mix, in a bowl, with the lemon or lime juice. Sprinkle with hot sauce – it brings out the flavours of the other ingredients.

2 Some people add cantaloupes, apples and fresh chopped coriander. Others add lots of salt. Some use tangerines instead of oranges.

Left: Machomo. **Above:** *Pico de Gallo.*

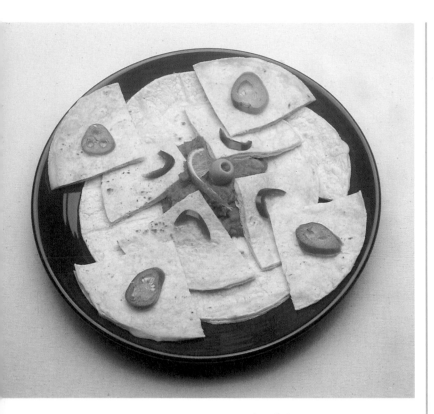

Quesadillas

Quesadillas are a very simple, very economical, and surprisingly filling and delicious snack. They consist of nothing more than tortillas with a melted cheese filling. The best cheese is Oaxaca, but mozzarella is fine, and Cheddar (or Jack) will do.

1 Fry a tortilla in an almost dry pan (or on a griddle) until it is soft; flip it over.
2 Put a lump or a handful of grated cheese in the middle; fold it in half; and continue to cook it, turning it over occasionally, until the cheese melts.

VARIATIONS Quesadillas Sincronizadas, or 'synchronized quesadillas' are made as shown, with two quesadillas stuck together with melted cheese; they are quartered for serving. If you are making quesadillas with uncooked tortillas, you can pinch together the edges of a basic turnover quesadilla and fry the whole thing in deep fat.

Above right: Empanadas.

Above left: Quesadillas sincronizadas.

Empanadas

Empanadas are little turnovers that may contain sweet or savoury ingredients. As so often, you can use both your imagination and your leftovers to the full; this is a basic savoury empanada.

1 lb/500 g/1 lb shortcrust pastry (pie pastry)	1 tbsp/15 g/1 tbsp sultanas (golden raisins)
8 oz/250 g/1 cup minced (ground) beef	1 dried red chilli (arbol chili or similar)
1 medium onion	½ tsp/2.5 g/½ tsp cumin seed
1 small pepper, red or green	2 tbsp/30 ml/2 tbsp olive oil
2 medium tomatoes	pepper and salt

1 Skin, seed and chop the tomatoes. Remove the seeds and veins from the pepper; chop. Chop the onion finely. Fry these ingredients together in the oil, and fry until soft. Add the beef; fry until the meat is brown and crumbly.
2 Crumble the dried pepper. Use the cumin seeds whole, or for still better flavour, crush them using a pestle and mortar. Add the dried pepper, cumin and sultanas (golden raisins) to the mixture in the pan. Season to taste, and cook for another ten minutes or so. Set aside to cool.
3 Roll the dough into 5-in/12-cm rounds; you should get about eight. Divide the filling equally between them, placing it on one half of the round and folding over to seal. Overfilling will make cooking difficult!
4 Cook in a pre-heated oven at 375°F/190°C (mark 5) until the pastry is golden brown – about 35 minutes. Serve hot. Some people prefer to deep-fry their empanadas.

Issaan-Style Soup

Issaan-style soup.

4 oz/100 g/¼ lb beef or calves heart
4 oz/100 g/¼ lb beef or calves liver
4 oz/100 g/¼ lb beef of calves lung
4 oz/100 g/¼ lb beef or calves kidney
4 oz/100 g/¼ lb beef or calves small intestines
Any offal (variety meats) may be used or excluded, depending on your preference
5 cups water

3 pieces lemon grass, cut into 1-in/2.5-cm pieces and crushed
5 pieces kaffir lime leaf, shredded
1 oz/25 g/1 oz galanga, sliced
2 tbsp/30 g/2 tbsp Lao parsley, sliced into 1-in/2.5-cm pieces
½ tsp/2.5 g/½ tsp salt
1½ tsp/7.5 g/1½ tsp fish sauce
1 tbsp/15 ml/1 tbsp lemon juice
1 tsp/5 g/1 tsp crushed dry chilli (chili)
2 tbsp/30 g/2 tbsp spring onion (scallions), cut into ½-in/1.25-cm pieces

1 Boil the offal (variety meats) in water till tender. Rinse and slice fairly small.
2 Take the offal (variety meats) and place in a pot with the water.
3 Bring to the boil and add all ingredients except spring onions (scallions).
4 Bring to the boil again and add spring onions (scallions).
5 Remove from heat and serve in soup cups with steamed rice or sticky rice.

Soup with stuffed squid.

Soup with Stuffed Squid

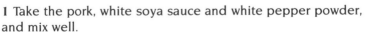

1 lb/450 g/2 cups minced (ground) pork
½ tsp/2.5 g/½ tsp white soya sauce
¼ tsp/1.25 g/¼ tsp white pepper powder
32 fl oz/900 ml/4 cups chicken stock
½ tbsp/7.5 g/½ tbsp salt-preserved cabbage

7 pieces white peppercorns, crushed
5 cloves garlic, crushed
11 oz/300 g/11 oz squid, body not tentacles, cleaned
1 tsp/5 ml/1 tsp fish sauce
¼ tsp/1.25 g/¼ tsp sugar
1 tbsp/15 g/1 tbsp coriander, cut into ½-in/1.25-cm pieces
¼ cup spring onions (scallions) sliced to ½-in/1.25-cm pieces

1 Take the pork, white soya sauce and white pepper powder, and mix well.
2 Heat the chicken stock, add the preserved cabbage, crushed white pepper and garlic and bring to a boil.
3 Meanwhile stuff the squid with the pork mixture and place in the boiling stock (if there is extra pork make into small meatballs and add to soup also).
4 Add the fish sauce and sugar and cook until stuffed squid is done. Finally, add the coriander and spring onions (scallions) and remove from heat. Serve with rice.

Sour curry soup.

Sour Curry Soup

1 lb/450 g/1 lb whole fresh water
fish, cleaned well
40 fl oz/1.25 l/5 cups water
2 oz/50 g/½ cup cucumber,
quartered and sliced
2 oz/50 g/½ cup French (green)
beans, cut into 2-in/5-cm pieces
2 oz/50 g/½ cup morning glory,
cut into 2-in/5-cm pieces

2 oz/50 g/½ cup Chinese
cabbage, cut into 2-in/5-cm pieces
3 tbsp/45 ml/4 tbsp tamarind
juice
2 tsp/10 ml/2 tsp lemon juice
2 tbsp/30 ml/2 tbsp fish sauce
1 tsp/5 g/1 tsp sugar

CHILLI (CHILI) PASTE
8 pieces dry red chilli (chili)
2 oz/50 g/½ cup shallots

1 tbsp/15 g/1 tbsp salt
½ tsp/2.5 g/½ tsp shrimp paste

1 To make the chilli (chili) paste pound all the ingredients together well.

2 To make the soup, take fish and cut into small pieces. Boil 5 oz/150 g/5 oz in water till cooked.

3 Discard water, cool fish, remove all bones. Add the fish meat to the chilli (chili) paste and pound until fine.

4 Place this paste in a pot large enough to hold all ingredients. Add the water, boil, and add the rest of the fish. Bring to the boil again and then add the cucumber, beans and morning glory. Bring back to the boil once more.

5 Add the rest of the ingredients. Boil, remove from heat and serve with rice and dry salted beef or fish and pickled vegetables as condiments.

Satay chicken

Satay Chicken or Pork

1 chicken breast, sliced into long thin slices	1 tbsp/15 g/1 tbsp curry powder
2 pieces lemon grass, crushed lightly	1 tsp/5 g/1 tsp sugar
	½ tsp/2.5 g/½ tsp salt
5 pieces Kaffir lime leaf, roughly chopped	12 fl oz/300 ml/1½ cups coconut milk
	5 pieces coriander root, crushed

1 Mix together all the ingredients and leave to marinate for 3–4 hours.
2 Skewer chicken on to wood skewers or metal skewers.
3 Grill (broil), preferably over charcoal.
4 Serve with satay sauce, salad and pieces of toasted bread to dip in sauce. This dish is excellent with cocktails.

Satay Sauce

5 oz/150 g/5 oz chilli (chili) paste	1 tsp/5 g/1 tsp salt
32 fl oz/900 ml/4 cups coconut milk	1 cup unsalted peanuts, chopped very fine
2 tsp/10 ml/2 tsp tamarind juice	⅓ cup yellow beans, steamed and mashed
3 tbsp/45 g/4 tbsp palm sugar	

1 Mix together all the ingredients. Boil for 5 minutes. Remove from fire and cool.

Spicy vegetable and shrimp broth.

Spicy Vegetable and Shrimp Soup

10 pieces white pepper corn chilli (chili) paste
4 oz/100 g/1 cup shallots, sliced
3 pieces small green chillies (chilis)
½ tbsp/7.5 ml/½ tbsp shrimp paste
1 oz/25 g/¼ cup dried shrimp
8 cups chicken stock
4 oz/100 g/1 cup young butter nut squash, cut into wedges with seeds

5 oz/150 g/5 oz banana flower (optional)
7 oz/200 g/1¾ cups pumpkin, diced
4 oz/100 g/1 cup lemon basil
4 oz/100 g/1 cup French (green) beans
½ tbsp/7.5 ml/½ tbsp fish sauce
7 oz/200 g/1 cup shrimps, peeled and cleaned

1 Pound the chilli (chili) paste, shallots, green chillies (chilis), shrimp paste and dried shrimp into a fine paste.
2 Place chicken stock in a pot, add the chilli (chili) paste and bring to the boil.
3 Add the vegetables, boil, and add fish sauce.
4 Finally, add the shrimps and remove from fire. Serve with rice.

Boiled Rice Soup with Chicken

6 cups chicken stock
11 oz/300 g/1⅓ cups chicken breast, sliced
1 tbsp/15 ml/1 tbsp pickled cabbage (tong chi)
1 tsp/5 g/1 tsp salt
4 cups steamed rice
4 oz/100 g/1 cup celery, sliced small

4 tbsp/60 g/5 tbsp spring onions (scallions), sliced
3 oz/50 g/⅓ cup garlic, whole cloved not peeled
2 tbsp/30 ml/2 tbsp fish sauce
2 oz/50 g/½ cup sliced red chilli (chili) with vinegar (prik dong)

1 Boil the stock and add the chicken, cabbage, salt and rice. Boil till cooked.
2 Add the celery and spring onions (scallions) and remove from heat.
3 Place in a bowl and garnish with the garlic which has been previously fried in oil until soft. White pepper, the fish sauce and prik dong should be served separately.

MEAT DISHES

From India

MEAT CURRY WITH YOGURT 78
MEAT AND TOMATO CURRY 79
MEAT CURRY IN A THICK SAUCE 79
SWEET AND SOUR MEAT CURRY 80
FRIED SPICED MEAT KEEMA 80
MEAT CURRY WITH ROASTED SPICES 81
MEATBALL AND CAULIFLOWER CURRY 82
MEAT CURRY WITH NUTS AND COCONUT MILK 83
MEAT KEBABS 83
PORK VINDALOO 84
MEAT AND VEGETABLE CURRY 85
KASHMIRI LAMB CURRY 85

From China

STEAMED GROUND RICE-PORK WRAPPED IN LOTUS LEAVES 86
DEEP-FRIED CRISPY FINGERS OF PORK 86
DRY-FRIED BEEF, FLAVOURED WITH AGED ORANGE PEEL 87
MONGOLIAN BARBECUE OF LAMB 88
TUNG-PO MUTTON 89
STUFFED GREEN PEPPERS 89
STIR-FRIED BEEF WITH VEGETABLES 90
SWEET AND SOUR PORK 90
RED-COOKED LAMB 91
STEAMED SPARERIBS IN BLACK BEAN SAUCE 91
BRAISED TRIPE 92
PORT IN HOT AND SOUR SAUCE 92
ANTS CLIMBING TREES 93
SHREDDED PORK IN 'FISH SAUCE' 93
TWICE-COOKED PORK 94
HOT AND SOUR KIDNEY 94
CHICKEN, HAM AND MUSHROOM SOUP 95
DRUNKEN SPARERIBS 95
SALT AND PEPPER SPARERIBS 96
SWEET AND SOUR SPARERIBS 96
TWICE-ROAST PORK 96
'WHITE-CUT' PORK 98
SHREDDED KIDNEYS IN WINE SAUCE 98
CLEAR AND THICK STOCK 99
RAPIDLY-FRIED BEEF STEAK 99
CASSIA LAMB 100
STEWED BEEF 100
RINSED LAMB IN FIRE-POT 101

SHREDDED BEEF WITH CELERY 102
GROUND (MINCED) FRIED PORK 102
FIVE-FRAGRANT KIDNEY SLICES 103
STIR-FRIED SICHUAN BEEF 104

From Japan

SHABU SHABU 105
SIMMERED PORK NAGASAKI STYLE 105
BEEF SALAD IN HOT CHILLIS (CHILI) DRESSING 106
SWEET-GLAZED BEEF 106

From Mexico

FAJITAS 108
PORK WITH CABBAGE AND CORN 109
PICADILLO 110
CARNE DE RES CON NOPALITOS 111
SHREDDED BEEF STEW 112
CARNE MOLIDA CRUDA 112
CARNE CON CHILE COLORADO 113
STUFFED PEPPERS 114
ADOBO SAUCE 114
PUERCO ADOBADO 114
PORK IN CHILLI (CHILI) SAUCE 116
GREEN SAUCE 117
PORK AND CHICKEN IN GREEN SAUCE 117

From Thailand

WILD BOAR CURRY 118
GRILLED BEEF TONGUE 119
MUSLIM CURRY 120
RAW MEAT SALAD 121
BEEF OR CHICKEN CURRY WITH COCONUT MILK 122
NAM TOK NUM 123
COCONUT CURRY BEEF 123
RED PORK WITH RICE 124
PORK FRIED WITH GARLIC 125
KAENG HANG LEY 125

Left: A Thai street vendor.

Meat Curry with Yogurt

2¼ lb/1 kg/2¼ lb meat, trimmed
and cubed
4–6 tbsp/60–90 ml/5–7 tbsp oil
2 onions, roughly chopped
1 oz/25 g/1 oz fresh ginger,
chopped
2 cloves garlic, chopped
1 green chilli (chili), chopped
cardamom seeds from 2 pods
1-in/2.5-cm cinnamon stick
3 cloves

½ tsp/2.5 g/½ tsp fennel seeds
1 tbsp/15 g/1 tbsp ground
coriander
1 tsp/5 g/1 tsp ground cumin
leaves from 2 sprigs coriander
½ tsp/2.5 g/½ tsp turmeric
1 tsp/5 g/1 tsp chilli (chili) powder
5 oz/125 g/½ cup yogurt
4–6 curry leaves
salt

1 Heat half the oil in a pan, add half the onion, the ginger, garlic, green chilli (chili), cardamom seeds, cinnamon, cloves, fennel seeds, ground coriander, cumin, half the coriander leaves, the turmeric and chilli (chili) and fry gently, stirring, for 10 minutes.

2 Take the pan off the heat and stir in the yogurt. Mix well and set aside.

3 Chop the remaining onion finely and fry in the remaining oil until golden. Add the meat and fry for about 15 minutes, stirring occasionally.

4 Stir in the spiced yogurt and cook gently for 8–10 minutes, stirring.

5 Pour on about 1 pt/600 ml/2½ cups boiling water, turn down the heat and cook, covered, for about 1 hour or until the meat is tender. Cook uncovered if a thicker sauce is required and stir frequently.

6 Sprinkle on the curry leaves and remaining coriander leaves and add salt to taste.

Meat and Tomato Curry

2¼ lb/1 kg/2¼ lb meat, trimmed and cubed
2 oz/50 g/¼ cup butter or ghee
1 small onion, finely chopped
½ oz/15 g/½ oz fresh ginger, finely grated
3 cloves garlic, finely chopped
8 oz/225 g/1 cup tomatoes, peeled and chopped
½ tsp/2.5 g/½ tsp turmeric

2 tsp/10 g/2 tsp chilli (chili) powder
1 tbsp/15 g/1 tbsp ground coriander
½ tsp/2.5 g/½ tsp ground cumin
salt
1 tsp/5 g/1 tsp garam masala
8 oz/225 g/1⅓ cups potatoes, peeled and diced
leaves from 1 sprig of coriander

1 Heat the butter or ghee in a large saucepan, add the onion, ginger and garlic and fry until the onion is golden.
2 Add the tomato, turmeric, chilli (chili) powder, ground coriander, cumin, ½ tsp/2.5 g/½ tsp salt and garam masala. Stir and continue to fry until the fat runs clear of the spices, then add 1 pt/600 ml/2½ cups boiling water and mix well.
3 Add the meat and cook, covered, over a low heat for about 1 hour, until tender and the sauce is thick.
4 Add the potato and a little extra water, if necessary, and cook for a further 10–15 minutes until tender but not soft.
5 Sprinkle on the coriander leaves and extra salt to taste.

Opposite: Meat curry with yogurt.

Above: Meat and tomato curry.

Right: Meat curry in a thick sauce.

Meat curry in a thick sauce

2¼ lb/1 kg/2¼ lb meat, trimmed and cubed
1 small onion, finely chopped
2 tbsp/30 ml/2 tbsp oil
1 tbsp/15 g/1 tbsp flour
1 tbsp/15 ml/1 tbsp lemon juice
½ tsp/2.5 g/½ tsp ground pepper

salt
2 oz/50 g/¼ cup butter or ghee
8 oz/225 g/1 cup tomatoes, chopped
1 green chilli (chili), sliced
leaves from 1 sprig of coriander
½ tsp/2.5 g/½ tsp garam masala

1 Fry the onion in the oil until golden. Add the flour and continue to fry, stirring, until the flour is coloured and has formed a paste.
2 Add the meat, lemon juice, pepper and ½ tsp/2.5 g/½ tsp salt, stir and pour on about 1½ pt/850 ml/3¾ cups water. Bring to the boil and simmer, covered, for about 1 hour, stirring occasionally, until the meat is tender and the sauce is thick.
3 Heat the butter or ghee in a pan, add the tomato and green chilli (chili) and fry gently, stirring, for 3–4 minutes, then add to the meat.
4 Sprinkle on the coriander leaves and garam masala.

Sweet and Sour Meat Curry

2¼ lb/1 kg/2¼ lb meat, trimmed and cubed
2 tbsp/30 ml/2 tbsp oil
2 oz/50 g/¼ cup butter or ghee
2 onions, finely chopped
1 green chilli (chili), chopped
½ oz/15 g/½ oz fresh ginger, finely grated
2 cloves garlic, crushed
8 oz/225 g/1 cup tomatoes, peeled and chopped
leaves from 2 sprigs of coriander
½ tsp/2.5 g/½ tsp garam masala
½ tsp/2.5 g/½ tsp turmeric
1 tsp/5 g/1 tsp chilli (chili) powder
8 oz/225 g/1⅓ cups potatoes, peeled and chopped
½ tsp/2.5 g/½ tsp ground pepper
1 tbsp/15 g/1 tbsp sugar
5 oz/125 g/½ cup yogurt
2 tbsp/30 ml/2 tbsp lemon juice

1 Heat the oil and butter or ghee in a pan, add the onion, green chilli (chili), ginger and garlic and fry until the onion turns golden.
2 Add the tomato, half the coriander leaves, the garam masala, turmeric and chilli (chili) powder and cook, stirring and squashing the tomato under the back of a wooden spoon until it makes a paste and the fat has run clear of the spices.
3 Add the meat and 1 pt/600 ml/2½ cups boiling water and cook over a low heat for about 1 hour, until tender.
4 Add the potato and cook for a further 10–15 minutes until tender but not soft.
5 Mix the remaining coriander leaves, the pepper and sugar with the yogurt, add to the curry and cook for 2–3 minutes, stirring, to heat through.
6 Sprinkle on the lemon juice and add salt to taste.

Above left: *Sweet and sour meat curry.*

Fried Spiced Meat Keema

1 lb/500 g/1 lb lean minced (ground) meat
4 oz/100 g/½ cup butter or ghee
1 onion, finely chopped
2 cloves garlic, finely chopped
½ oz/15 g/½ oz fresh ginger, finely grated
leaves from 1 sprig of coriander
6 oz/175 g/¾ cup tomatoes, peeled and chopped
cardamom seeds from 2 pods, crushed
1-in/2.5-cm cinnamon stick
3 cloves
1 bay leaf
½ tsp/2.5 g/½ tsp ground coriander
½ tsp/2.5 g/½ tsp turmeric
½ tsp/2.5 g/½ tsp ground cumin
½ tsp/2.5 g/½ tsp chilli (chili) powder
salt
8 oz/225 g/1⅓ cups potatoes, peeled and diced

1 Heat the butter or ghee in a pan, add the onion and fry until golden.
2 Add the garlic, ginger, half the coriander leaves, the tomato, cardamom, cinnamon, cloves and bay leaf and fry for 3–4 minutes, stirring.
3 Add the coriander, turmeric, cumin, chilli (chili) powder and ½ tsp/2.5 g/½ tsp salt and stir to make a thick paste.
4 Add the meat and potato and fry for about 15 minutes, stirring occasionally, then pour on ½ pint/300 ml/1¼ cups boiling water, cover and cook on a low heat for a further 15 minutes, until the meat and potato are cooked and the sauce is thick.
5 Add salt to taste and sprinkle on the remaining coriander leaves.

Above right: *Fried spiced meat keema.*

Meat curry with roasted spices.

Meat Curry with Roasted Spices

1 lb/500 g/1 lb meat, trimmed and cubed

3 tbsp/45 ml/4 tbsp oil

2 tbsp/30 ml/2 tbsp coriander seeds

2 red chillies (chilis), cut into pieces

1-in/2.5-cm cinnamon stick

3 cloves

2 oz/50 g/⅔ cup grated coconut

½ tsp/2.5 g/½ tsp turmeric

salt

2 green chillies (chilis), sliced

½ oz/15 g/½ oz fresh ginger, grated

1 small onion, chopped

8 oz/225 g/1⅓ cups potatoes, peeled and diced

8 oz/225 g/1 cup tomatoes, peeled and chopped

6 curry leaves

1 Heat half the oil in a pan and fry the coriander seeds, red chilli (chili), cinnamon, cloves and coconut for about 5 minutes, then transfer to a grinder or a mortar and reduce to a smooth paste.

2 Put the meat in a bowl with the turmeric, ½ tsp/2.5 g/½ tsp salt, green chilli (chili), ginger and half the onion, add the spice paste and mix well. Leave to marinate for 15 minutes.

3 Heat the remaining oil in a large saucepan and fry the remaining onion until golden.

4 Add the marinated meat, the potato and tomato, pour on 1½ pt/850 ml/3¾ cups boiling water, cover and cook on a low heat for about 1 hour, until the meat is tender and the sauce is thick.

5 Add extra salt to taste and sprinkle on the curry leaves.

Left: Meatball and cauliflower curry.

Above: Meat curry with nuts and coconut milk.

Right: Meat kebabs.

Meatball and Cauliflower Curry

FOR THE MEAT AND CAULIFLOWER

1 lb/500 g/1 lb lean minced (ground) meat
1 egg, beaten
½ oz/15 g/½ oz fresh ginger, grated
2 cloves garlic, chopped
½ tsp/2.5 g/½ tsp garam masala
½ tsp/2.5 g/½ tsp ground cumin
leaves from 1 sprig of coriander
salt
1 small cauliflower, cut into florets, tough stalks discarded

FOR THE SAUCE

3 oz/75 g/6 tbsp butter or ghee
1 small onion, finely chopped
cardamom seeds from 2 pods, crushed
2 cloves
1-in/2.5-cm cinnamon stick
½ oz/15g/½ oz fresh ginger, grated
2 cloves garlic, crushed
½ tsp/2.5 g/½ tsp turmeric
1 tsp/5 g/1 tsp chilli (chili) powder
½ tsp/2.5 g/½ tsp ground cumin
½ tsp/2.5 g/½ tsp ground coriander
8 oz/225 g/1 cup tomatoes, peeled and chopped or 2 tsp/10 g/2 tsp tomato purée (paste)
5 oz/125 g/⅔ cup yogurt
salt
leaves from 1 sprig of coriander

1 Mix the egg with the minced (ground) meat.

2 Grind, pound or blend in a blender the ginger, garlic, garam masala, cumin, coriander leaves and ½ tsp/2.5 g/½ tsp salt.

3 Mix the spice paste with the meat, form it into small balls and set aside.

4 For the sauce, heat the butter or ghee in a pan, add the onion and fry until golden.

5 Add the cardamom seeds, cloves, cinnamon, ginger, garlic, turmeric, chilli (chili) powder, cumin and coriander and fry for 3 or 4 minutes, stirring.

6 Add the tomato or tomato purée (paste) and cook, stirring, until the fat runs clear of the spices.

7 Stir in the yogurt with a pinch of salt and 1–2 tbsp/15–30 ml/ 1–2 tbsp water and bring gently to the boil.

8 Carefully slide in the meat balls and cauliflower florets and cook for about 20 minutes on a low heat, stirring occasionally and taking care not to break the meat balls.

9 Sprinkle on the coriander leaves and add salt to taste.

Meat Curry with Nuts and Coconut Milk

2¼ lb/1 kg/2¼ lb meat, trimmed and cubed
flesh of 1 coconut, grated
2 oz/50 g/½ cup cashew nuts
2 cloves garlic, chopped
½ tsp/2.5 g/½ tsp chilli (chili) powder
½ oz/15 g/½ oz fresh ginger, grated
½ tsp/2.5 g/½ tsp ground coriander
½ tsp/2.5 g/½ tsp turmeric
leaves from 1 sprig of coriander
½ tsp/2.5 g/½ tsp garam masala
½ tsp/2.5 g/½ tsp ground pepper
4 oz/100 g/½ cup butter or ghee
1 small onion, chopped
¼ tsp/1.25 g/¼ tsp saffron
1 oz/25 g/3 tbsp sultanas (golden raisins)
2 oz/50 g/½ cup almonds
salt
4–6 curry leaves

1 Blend the coconut in a blender with 1 tbsp/15 ml/1 tbsp boiling water. Transfer to a sheet of muslin (cheese cloth) and squeeze out the milk into a bowl. Return the coconut to the blender and repeat the process.
2 Grind, pound or blend in a blender the cashew nuts, garlic, chilli (chili) powder, ginger, ground coriander, turmeric, coriander leaves, garam masala and pepper.
3 Heat the butter or ghee in a pan, add the onion and fry until golden, then add the blended spices and fry for a further 5 minutes.
4 Add the meat, stir and fry for 5 minutes, then pour on the coconut milk, add the saffron, sultanas (golden raisins), almonds and ½ tsp/2.5 g/½ tsp salt and cook, covered, over a low heat for about 1 hour, until the meat is tender and the sauce has thickened.
5 Sprinkle on the curry leaves.

Meat Kebabs

1 lb/500 g/1 lb lean minced (ground) meat
½ oz/15 g/½ oz fresh ginger, finely grated
1 green chilli (chili), chopped
salt
½ tsp/2.5 g/½ tsp garam masala
1 onion, finely chopped
½ tsp/2.5 g/½ tsp chilli (chili) powder
½ tsp/2.5 g/½ tsp ground pepper
½ tsp/2.5 g/½ tsp ground cumin
leaves from 1 sprig of coriander
1 egg, beaten
6 tbsp/90 ml/7 tbsp oil

1 Grind, pound or blend in a blender the ginger, green chilli (chili), ½ tsp/2.5 g/½ tsp salt and the garam masala with 1–2 tbsp/15–30 ml/7 tbsp water to make a paste.
2 In a bowl, mix the spice paste with the meat and onion, sprinkle on the chilli (chili) powder, pepper, cumin and coriander leaves, add the egg and 1–2 tsp/5–10 ml/1–2 tsp oil and combine well.
3 Roll the mixture into small sausages and thread on skewers.
4 Grill (broil) the kebabs for 20 minutes, basting with a little oil, and turning frequently until cooked through.
5 Remove the kebabs from the skewers and fry in the remaining oil for about 10 minutes, turning gently.

Pork Vindaloo

2¼–3 lb/1–1.4 kg/2¼–3 lb shoulder of pork, trimmed and cubed
6 cloves garlic
1 oz/25 g/1 oz fresh ginger
4 red chillies (chilis), seeded
1 tsp/5 g/1 tsp mustard seeds
½ tsp/2.5 g/½ tsp fenugreek seeds
½ tsp/2.5 g/½ tsp turmeric
½ tsp/2.5 g/½ tsp ground cumin

4 tbsp/60 ml/5 tbsp white wine vinegar
2–3 tbsp/30–45 ml/2–3 tbsp oil
2 onions, finely chopped
8 oz/225 g/1 cup tomatoes, peeled and chopped
salt
4–6 curry leaves
6 cloves
1-in/2.5-cm cinnamon stick
1 tsp/5 g/1 tsp sugar

1 Chop 4 cloves garlic with half the ginger, then grind, pound or blend in a blender with the chillies (chilis), mustard seeds, fenugreek seeds, turmeric and half the vinegar.

2 Heat the oil, add the onion and fry until golden.

3 Add the spice paste, stir and fry gently for 15 minutes.

4 Add the tomato and continue to cook, mashing it under the back of a wooden spoon to make a paste.

5 When the oil has run clear of the spices, add the pork and fry for 5 minutes, turning the pieces in the spice mixture.

6 Add ½ tsp/2.5 g/½ tsp salt and pour on 1 pt/600 ml/2½ cups boiling water. Simmer, covered, for 40 minutes, until the pork is tender.

7 Slice the remaining garlic and ginger and add with the curry leaves, cloves and cinnamon stick. Cook for a further 5 minutes.

8 Add the sugar and remaining vinegar. Add salt to taste.

Pork vindaloo.

Meat and Vegetable Curry

1 lb/500 g/1 lb meat, trimmed and cubed	1 green chilli (chili), chopped
3 oz/75 g/6 tbsp butter or ghee	4–6 curry leaves
1 small onion, finely chopped	6 oz/175 g/¾ cup tomatoes, peeled and chopped
½ oz/15 g/½ oz fresh ginger, grated	4 oz/100 g/1 cup okra, trimmed and cut into 2 or 3 pieces
2 cloves garlic, chopped	4 oz/100 g/1 cup carrots, peeled and diced
½ tsp/2.5 g/½ tsp turmeric	
½ tsp/2.5 g/½ tsp chilli (chili) powder	8 oz/225 g/1⅓ cups potatoes, peeled and cubed
½ tsp/2.5 g/½ tsp ground coriander	6 oz/175 g/1½ cups aubergine (eggplant), peeled and cubed
½ tsp/2.5 g/½ tsp garam masala	2 oz/50 g/⅓ cup fresh peas
½ tsp/2.5 g/½ tsp ground cumin	salt

1 Heat the butter or ghee in a pan, add the onion and fry until golden.

2 Add the ginger, garlic, turmeric, chilli (chili) powder, coriander, garam masala, cumin, green chilli (chili) and curry leaves, stir and fry for a further 5 minutes.

3 Add the meat and fry for 5 minutes, then add the tomato, okra, carrot, potato, aubergine (eggplant) and peas, pour on 1½ pt/850 ml/3¾ cups water, add ½ tsp/2.5 g/½ tsp salt and cook over a low heat for 1 hour, until the vegetables and meat are tender and the sauce is thick.

4 Add extra salt to taste.

Kashmiri Lamb Curry

1½ oz/40 g/3 tbsp ghee or butter	½ pt/300 ml/1¼ cups stock or water
1 in/2.5 cm fresh ginger, scraped and grated or finely chopped	3 oz/75 g/¾ cup blanched almonds
1 lb/450 g/1 lb lamb, trimmed and cubed	ice water
1 tsp/5 g/1 tsp garam masala	3 tbsp/45 ml/4 tbsp double (heavy) cream
2 tsp/10 g/2 tsp ground coriander	salt to taste
pinch chilli (chili) powder	

1 Heat the ghee or butter in a heavy pan. Add the ginger and lamb and stir over high heat until the meat begins to brown.

2 Add the garam masala, coriander and chilli (chili). Stir, then add the water. Bring to the boil and simmer until the lamb is just tender, about 25 minutes.

3 Pulverize two-thirds of the almonds in a mortar, blender or food processor, adding enough ice water to make a smooth paste. Stir in the cream.

4 Add the almond mixture to the lamb and salt to taste. Cook very gently for a further 4 minutes.

5 Serve hot, sprinkled with the remaining almonds, coarsely chopped.

Top: Meat and vegetable curry.

Above: Kashmiri lamb curry.

Left: *Steamed ground rice-pork wrapped in lotus leaves.*

Below: *Deep-fried crispy fingers of pork.*

Opposite: *Dry-fried beef with aged orange peel.*

Steamed Ground Rice-Pork wrapped in Lotus Leaves

3–4 lotus leaves
1½ lb/700 g/1½ lb belly of pork (fresh pork sides), thick end
2 tbsp/30 ml/2 tbsp light soy sauce
vegetable oil for deep-frying
2 slices fresh root ginger
2 spring onions (scallions)

1½ tbsp/22.5 ml/1½ tbsp oyster sauce
½ tsp/2.5 g/½ tsp salt
1½ tsp/7.5 g/1½ tsp sugar
2 cloves garlic
3 tbsp/45 g/4 tbsp ground rice
1½ tsp/7.5 ml/1½ tsp sesame seed oil

1 Immerse the lotus leaves in warm water for 3–4 minutes to soften. Bring a large pan of water to the boil, add the pork and simmer for 10 minutes. Remove and drain.

2 Rub the pork with the soy sauce. Heat the oil in a wok or deep-fryer. When hot, fry the pork for about 3 minutes. Drain.

3 Cut the pork into ½-in/1-cm slices. Finely chop the ginger and spring onions (scallions). Mix together the oyster sauce, salt, sugar, ginger, garlic and spring onions (scallions).

4 Add the ground rice and sesame seed oil. Mix in the pork slices and make sure they are evenly coated.

5 Pile the slices neatly into a stack, then wrap in the softened lotus leaves. Tie securely with string.

6 Place the parcel in a heatproof dish, put in a steamer and steam for 3 hours. When ready, drain away any excess water and serve straight from the lotus leaves. By now, the pork will be tender and the ground rice will have soaked up any fattiness.

Deep-Fried Crispy Fingers of Pork

1½ lb/700 g/1½ lb lean pork
1 tsp/5 g/1 tsp salt
¼ tsp/1.25 g/¼ tsp pepper
½ tsp/2.5 g/½ tsp ground ginger

1 tbsp/15 ml/1 tbsp rice wine or dry sherry
1 tsp/5 ml/1 tsp sesame seed oil
vegetable oil for deep-frying

BATTER

1 egg	1½ tbsp/22.5 g/1½ tbsp
5 tbsp/75 g/6 tbsp plain (all-purpose) flour	cornflour (cornstarch)

SAUCE

1½ tbsp/22.5 g/1½ tbsp vegetable oil	5 tbsp/75 ml/6 tbsp good stock
	2 tbsp/30 ml/2 tbsp vinegar
1½ tbsp/22.5 g/1½ tbsp spring onion (scallions), chopped	2 tbsp/30 ml/2 tbsp light soy sauce
2 tsp/10 g/2 tsp garlic, crushed	1 tsp/5 g/1 tsp salt
2 tsp/10 g/2 tsp fresh chillies (chilis), chopped	1 tsp/5 g/1 tsp sugar
1½ tbsp/22.5 g/1½ tbsp fresh root ginger, chopped	radish rose and halved lemon slices, to garnish

1 Cut the pork into finger-sized strips. Mix the salt, pepper, ginger, wine or sherry and sesame seed oil together. Add the pork and mix thoroughly. Leave to marinate for 10 minutes.

2 To make the batter, mix the egg, flour and cornflour (cornstarch) together.

3 To make the dip sauce, heat the oil in a wok or pan. When hot, add the onion, garlic, chilli (chili) and ginger and stir for a few seconds. Add the rest of the dip sauce ingredients. Bring to the boil, then pour into a small heatproof bowl.

4 Heat the oil in a wok or deep-fryer. When very hot, dip the pork fingers in the batter and put gently into the oil. Fry for about 3 minutes. Drain. Allow the oil to reheat, then fry the pork again for 30 seconds. Drain. Arrange the pork fingers on a heated plate and serve with the dip sauce.

Dry-Fried Beef with aged Orange Peel

1½ lb/700 g/1½ lb lean beef, such as topside (eye of round), tenderloin, etc	20 fl oz/½ l/2½ cups peanut oil
	½ tsp/2.5 g/½ tsp salt
1 dried, aged orange or tangerine peel	1½ tbsp/22.5 g/1½ tbsp sugar
	1½ tbsp/22.5 ml/1½ tbsp dark soy sauce
3 slices fresh root ginger	1 tbsp/15 ml/1 tbsp hoisin sauce
2 green chilli (chili) peppers	2 tbsp/30 ml/2 tbsp good stock (see recipe)
2 dried red chilli (chili) peppers	
2 spring onions (scallions)	
6 tbsp/90 g/7 tbsp cornflour (cornstarch)	2 tbsp/30 ml/2 tbsp rice wine or dry sherry
1 egg, lightly beaten	1½ tsp/7.5 ml/1½ tsp sesame seed oil

1 Shred the beef into 'double matchstick-sized' pieces. Wash and drain the pieces thoroughly.

2 Soak the dried orange or tangerine peel in warm water for 20 minutes and cut it into matchstick-sized shreds. Cut the ginger and the green and red chilli (chili) peppers into similar-sized pieces and the spring onion (scallion) into 2-in/5-cm sections.

3 Mix together the cornflour (cornstarch) and lightly-beaten egg and coat the shredded beef, making sure that each piece is evenly covered.

4 Heat the oil in a pan or wok and, when a crumb dropped into the oil sizzles, add the beef. Using a fork or wooden chopstick to separate the shreds, stir-fry the beef over a medium heat for 6–7 minutes. Remove the beef from the pan with a perforated spoon and set it aside to drain.

5 Meanwhile, allow the oil in the pan to increase in temperature until it is smoking. Return the beef and stir-fry for a further 2 minutes. Remove the beef with a perforated spoon and drain thoroughly.

6 In a separate pan or wok heat 3 tbsp/45 ml/4 tbsp of oil. When the oil is hot, add the shredded ginger, orange or tangerine peel and green and red chilli (chili) peppers and the spring onion (scallion) pieces. Stir-fry them together for 1 minute before adding the salt, sugar, soy sauce, hoisin sauce, stock and wine or sherry. Continue to stir and cook for another minute, by which time the liquid should have reduced by about half.

7 Return the beef to the pan and stir well to mix the ingredients together for 1 minute. Sprinkle the sesame seed oil over the mixture and serve.

Left: Mongolian barbecue of lamb.

Mongolian Barbecue of Lamb

3–4lb/1.5–1.75 kg/3–4 lb leg of
lamb
4 slices fresh root ginger
5 spring onions (scallions)
1 tbsp/15 g/1 tbsp pounded
Sichuan peppercorns
1 tbsp/15 g/1 tbsp salt
3 tbsp/45 ml/4 tbsp soy sauce

1½ tbsp/22.5 ml/1½ tbsp yellow
bean paste
1½ tbsp/22.5 ml/1½ tbsp hoisin
sauce
¼ tsp/1.25 g/¼ tsp five-spice
powder
2 tbsp/30 ml/2 tbsp rice wine or
dry sherry
vegetable oil for deep-frying

WRAPPING AND EATING
12 lettuce leaves
2 small bowls of Peking Duck
sauce

3 saucers of matchstick-sized
pieces of cucumber
3 saucers of shredded spring
onions (scallions)

1 Cut the lamb along the grain into 6 long strips. Shred the ginger and spring onions (scallions). Mix with the peppercorns and salt and use to rub into the lamb.

2 Mix the soy sauce, yellow bean paste, hoisin sauce, five-spice powder and wine or sherry and place in a bowl with the lamb. Marinate for 1–2 hours.

3 Pack the seasoned lamb strips in a heatproof bowl, cover the top with foil. Place in a steamer and steam for about 2 hours or place the bowl in a pan containing 2 in/5 cm of water and double boil for 2 hours.

4 Remove from the bowl and leave to cool until required. When required, heat the oil in a wok or deep-fryer. When hot, fry the lamb for 4 minutes.

5 Place the lamb on a chopping board and chop into bite-sized pieces while still hot. To serve, spoon some duck sauce on to a pancake or lettuce, then place on a few slices of lamb, followed by a little cucumber and spring onion (scallion). Form into a neat roll and turn up the end so that nothing falls out, and then eat it.

Left: Tung-po mutton.

Below: Stuffed green peppers.

Tung-Po Mutton

½ lb/225 g/½ lb stewing mutton
4 oz/100 g/¼ lb potato
4 oz/100 g/¼ lb carrot
2 tbsp/30 ml/2 tbsp soy sauce
1 tbsp/15 g/1 tbsp sugar
2 spring onions (scallions)
1 slice fresh root ginger

1 clove garlic, crushed
1 tsp/5 g/1 tsp five-spice powder
3 tbsp/45 ml/4 tbsp rice wine or dry sherry
½ tsp/2.5 g/½ tsp Sichuan pepper
oil for deep-frying

1 Cut the mutton into 1-in/2.5-cm cubes, and then score one side of each square halfway down. Next, peel the potato and carrot and also cut them so that they are the same size and shape as the mutton.
2 Heat up quite a lot of oil in a wok or deep-fryer. When it is smoking, deep-fry the mutton for 5–6 seconds or until it turns golden; scoop out and drain, then fry the potato and carrot, also until golden.
3 Place the mutton in a pot or casserole, cover the meat with cold water, add soy sauce, sugar, onions, root ginger, garlic, pepper, five-spice powder and rice wine or sherry, and bring it to the boil. Then reduce the heat and simmer for 2–3 hours. Finally adding the potato and carrot, cook the lot together for about 5 minutes and serve.

Stuffed Green Peppers

8 oz/225 g/½ lb pork
4 oz/100 g/¼ lb fish fillet
1 lb/0.5 kg/1 lb small round green peppers
1 tsp/5 g/1 tsp salt
1 tbsp/15 ml/1 tbsp rice wine or sherry
1 tbsp/15 ml/1 tbsp soy sauce

1 tbsp/15 g/1 tbsp cornflour (cornstarch)
2 tsp/10 g/2 tsp sugar
1 clove garlic, crushed
½ tbsp/10 ml/½ tbsp crushed black bean sauce
2 tbsp/30 ml/2 tbsp oil

1 Finely chop the pork and fish; mix with a little salt and cornflour (cornstarch).
2 Wash the green peppers; cut them in half and remove the seeds and stalks. Stuff them with the meat and fish mixture; sprinkle with a little cornflour (cornstarch).
3 Heat up 1 tbsp/15 ml/1 tbsp oil in a flat frying pan; put in the stuffed peppers, meat side down; fry gently for 4 minutes adding a little more oil from time to time.
4 When the meat side turns golden, add the crushed garlic, bean sauce, rice wine or sherry, sugar and a little stock or water. Simmer for 2–3 minutes, then add soy sauce and a little cornflour (cornstarch) mixed with cold water. Serve as soon as the gravy thickens.

Stir-Fried Beef with Vegetables

¾ lb/350 g/¾ lb beef steak	1 tbsp/15 ml/1 tbsp rice wine or
4 oz/100 g/1 cup broccoli	sherry
4 oz/100 g/⅔ cup bamboo shoots	2 tbsp/30 ml/2 tbsp oyster sauce
3–4 Chinese dried mushrooms,	1 tbsp/15 ml/1 tbsp soy sauce
soaked	1 tbsp/15 g/1 tbsp cornflour
2 slices ginger root, peeled	(cornstarch)
1 carrot	3 tbsp/45 ml/3 tbsp stock
1 tsp/5 g/1 tsp salt	oil for deep-frying

1 Cut the beef across the grain into thickish slices the size of matchboxes; mix with rice wine or sherry, soy sauce, cornflour (cornstarch) and a little oil; leave to marinate for 10 minutes.
2 Cut the bamboo shoots and carrot into slices the same size as the beef, cut the broccoli into small florets.
3 Deep-fry the beef in warm oil for 1½ minutes; remove and drain.
4 Pour off the excess oil leaving about 2 tbsp/30 ml/2 tbsp oil in the wok. Wait until it smokes, toss in the ginger root, broccoli, bamboo shoots, carrot and mushrooms; add salt, stir a few times then add the beef with oyster sauce and stock; cook together for 1 minute. Serve hot.

Top left: *Stir-fried beef with vegetables.*

Top centre: *Sweet and sour pork.*

Top right: *Red-cooked lamb.*

Opposite: *Steamed spareribs in black bean sauce.*

Sweet and Sour Pork

½ lb/225 g/½ lb pork, not too	1 egg
lean	½ tbsp/7.5 g/½ tbsp cornflour
4 oz/100 g/⅔ cup fresh bamboo	(cornstarch)
shoots	2 tbsp/30 g/2 tbsp flour
1 green pepper	1 clove garlic
1 tsp/5 g/1 tsp salt	1 spring onion (scallion), cut into
1½ tbsp/22.5 ml/1½ tbsp Kao	short lengths
Liang spirit	oil for deep-frying

SAUCE:

3 tbsp/45 ml/4 tbsp vinegar	1 tbsp/15 ml/1 tbsp soy sauce
2 tbsp/30 g/2 tbsp sugar	½ tbsp/7.5 g/½ tbsp cornflour
½ tsp/2.5 g/½ tsp salt	(cornstarch)
1 tbsp/15 ml/1 tbsp tomato purée	1 tsp/5 ml/1 tsp sesame seed oil
(paste)	

1 Cut the meat into about two dozen small pieces, cut the bamboo shoots and green pepper into pieces of the same size.
2 Mix the meat pieces with salt and Kao Liang spirit for 15 minutes; add the egg, well beaten with the cornflour (cornstarch) dissolved in it; blend well, then coat each piece of meat with flour.
3 Deep-fry the meat in slightly hot oil for 3 minutes, then turn off the heat but leave the meat in the oil for 2 minutes; scoop out and drain. Heat up the oil again and re-fry the meat with bamboo shoots for another 2 minutes or until they are golden. Remove and drain.
4 Pour off the excess oil, put in the garlic and green pepper followed by onion and the sweet and sour sauce mixture; stir to make it smooth, add the meat and bamboo shoots; blend well. Serve.

Red-Cooked Lamb

1 ½ lb/0.75 kg/1 ½ lb lamb fillet
in one piece
4–5 Chinese dried mushrooms,
soaked
1 ½ tbsp/22.5 g/1 ½ tbsp Chinese
dried dates, soaked
4 oz/100 g/1 cup water chestnuts,
peeled
½ tsp/2.5 g/½ tsp five-spice
powder
2 slices ginger root, peeled
2 spring onions (scallions), cut
into short lengths

1 tsp/5 g/1 tsp salt
½ tsp/2.5 g/½ tsp Sichuan
ground pepper
½ tsp/2.5 g/½ tsp sesame seed oil
2 tbsp/30 ml/2 tbsp soy sauce
2 tbsp/30 ml/2 tbsp rice wine or
sherry
1 tbsp/15 g/1 tbsp cornflour
(cornstarch)
3 pt/1.5 l/7½ cups stock
oil for deep-frying

1 Wash the meat thoroughly; make a cut two-thirds the way through the piece of meat at ½-in/1-cm intervals. Blanch in boiling water for about 3 minutes; drain and coat with soy sauce.

2 Place the meat in a strainer and lower it into oil to deep-fry over a moderate heat for about 1½ minutes or until it turns red; remove and drain.

3 Pour off the excess oil; put the meat back with rice wine or sherry, salt, dates, water chestnuts, ginger root, onions, soy sauce, five-spice powder and stock; bring to the boil, then transfer into a sand-pot or casserole.

4 Simmer gently for 1½ hours or until the stock is reduced by half; add the mushrooms and cook for another 10 minutes or so. Now remove the meat and cut it into ½-in/1-cm thick pieces.

5 Place the water chestnuts, dates and mushrooms on a serving dish with the lamb pieces on top.

6 Remove the onions and ginger root from the gravy and discard them; warm up about 1 cup of the gravy in a small saucepan. Add sesame seed oil and thicken it with a little cornflour (cornstarch); stir to make it smooth, then pour it over the lamb and serve.

Steamed Spare Ribs in Black Bean Sauce

¾ lb/350 g/¾ lb pork spareribs
1 clove garlic, crushed
1 slice ginger root, peeled

1 tsp/5 ml/1 tsp oil
1 small red chilli (chili)

SAUCE:

2 tbsp/30 ml/2 tbsp crushed black
bean sauce
1 tbsp/15 ml/1 tbsp soy sauce

1 tbsp/15 ml/1 tbsp rice wine or
sherry
1 tsp/5 ml/1 tsp cornflour
(cornstarch)

GARNISH:
2 spring onions (scallions) cut into
short lengths

1 Chop the spareribs into small pieces, finely chop the garlic, ginger root and red chilli (chili). Mix them all together with the sauce; marinate for 15 minutes.

2 Grease a heatproof plate with oil; place the spareribs on it. Steam vigorously for 25–30 minutes. Garnish with onions cut into short lengths. Serve.

Pork in Hot and Sour Sauce

½ lb/225 g/½ lb pork fillet (tenderloin)   1 egg

3–4 Chinese dried mushrooms, soaked   2 tbsp/30 g/2 tbsp cornflour (cornstarch)

1 tbsp/15 g/1 tbsp Chinese pickled cabbage   1 tsp/5 g/1 tsp salt

2 tbsp/30 g/2 tbsp bamboo shoots   2 tbsp/30 ml/2 tbsp chilli (chili) paste

2 oz/50 g/⅓ cup green hot chillies (chilis)   1 tbsp/15 ml/1 tbsp soy sauce

1 leek   1 tsp/5 ml/1 tsp sesame seed oil

oil for deep-frying

1 First cut the pork into thick slices, score the surface with a criss-cross pattern, then cut them into small squares; marinate with salt, egg and 1 tbsp/15 g/1 tbsp cornflour (cornstarch).
2 Finely chop the mushrooms, pickled cabbage, bamboo shoots, green chillies (chilis) and leek.
3 Warm up the oil, deep-fry the pork until each piece opens up like a flower, scoop out and drain.
4 Pour off the excess oil leaving about 2 tbsp/30 ml/2 tbsp in the wok; stir-fry all the chopped ingredients, add chilli (chili) paste and pork; blend well. Now add soy sauce and the remaining cornflour (cornstarch) mixed with a little cold water. When the sauce thickens, add the sesame seed oil and serve.

Braised Tripe

2 lb/1 kg/2 lb tripe (pig's stomach)   4 tbsp/60 ml/5 tbsp soy sauce

salt   1 tbsp/15 g/1 tbsp sugar

2 slices ginger root, peeled   1 tsp/5 g/1 tsp five-spice powder

2 spring onions (scallions)   2 tbsp/30 ml/2 tbsp oil

2 tbsp/30 ml/2 tbsp rice wine or sherry   1 tsp/5 ml/1 tsp sesame seed oil

1 Wash the tripe thoroughly, rub both sides with the salt several times and rinse well.
2 Blanch it in boiling water for 20 minutes. Drain and discard the water.
3 Heat oil, brown the tripe lightly, add ginger root, onions, rice wine or sherry, soy sauce, sugar and five-spice powder. Add 2 pints/1.2 l/5 cups water and bring it to the boil, reduce heat and simmer under cover gently for 2 hours.
4 Remove the tripe and cut into small slices; garnish with sesame seed oil and serve hot or cold.

Top left: Braised tripe.

Top right: Pork in hot and sour sauce.

Opposite, top left: Ants climbing trees.

Opposite, top right: Shredded pork in 'fish sauce'.

Ants Climbing Trees

½ lb/225 g/½ lb pork
2 tbsp/30 ml/2 tbsp soy sauce
1 tbsp/15 g/1 tbsp sugar
1 tsp/5 g/1 tsp cornflour
(cornstarch)
½ tsp/2.5 g/½ tsp chilli (chili)
paste
1 small red chilli (chili)

4 spring onions (scallions),
chopped
4 oz/100 g/¼ lb transparent
noodles
3 tbsp/45 ml/4 tbsp oil
About ¼ pt/100 ml/⅔ cup stock
or water

1 Mince (grind) the pork; mix it with the soy sauce, sugar, cornflour (cornstarch) and chilli (chili) paste. Soak the noodles in warm water for 10 minutes.

2 Heat up the oil; first fry the chilli (chili) and onions, then the pork. When the colour of the meat starts to change, drain the noodles and add them to the pan. Blend well, then add the stock or water; continue cooking. When all the liquid is absorbed, it is done.

Shredded Pork in 'Fish Sauce'

½ lb/225 g/½ lb pork filllet
(tenderloin)
8 oz/225 g/½ lb soaked wooden
ears
2–3 stalks celery
1 tsp/2.5 g/1 tsp salt
1½ tbsp/22.5 g/1½ tbsp
cornflour (cornstarch)
1 slice ginger root, peeled and
finely chopped

1 clove garlic, finely chopped
2 spring onions (scallions), finely
chopped
1½ tbsp/22.5 ml/1½ tbsp soy
sauce
1 tbsp/15 ml/1 tbsp chilli (chili)
paste
1 tsp/5 g/1 tsp sugar
2 tsp/10 ml/2 tsp vinegar
3 tbsp/45 ml/4 tbsp oil

1 Cut the pork into thin shreds the size of matches; mix with salt and ½ tsp/2.5 g/½ tsp cornflour (cornstarch). Shred the soaked wooden ears and celery.

2 Heat 1 tbsp/15 ml/1 tbsp oil and stir-fry the pork until the colour changes; remove and add the remaining oil to the wok.

3 Put in wooden ears and celery together with ginger root, garlic and onions; add pork, soy sauce, chilli (chili) paste, sugar and vinegar. Cook together for 1–2 minutes, then add the remaining cornflour (cornstarch) mixed in a little water; blend well; serve.

Twice-Cooked Pork

½ lb/225 g/½ lb pork
1 leek
1 small green pepper
1 small red pepper

1 tbsp/15 ml/1 tbsp chilli (chili) paste
1 tbsp/15 ml/1 tbsp soy sauce
3 tbsp/45 ml/4 tbsp oil
1 tsp/5 g/1 tsp salt

1 Choose a piece of pork that is not too lean. Boil in water for 20 minutes; remove and cool a little then cut it into thin slices the size of a matchbox.
2 Cut the leek, green and red peppers into chunks of roughly the same size.
3 Heat up the oil, stir-fry the leek, green and red peppers till soft. Add salt, chilli (chili) paste and soy sauce followed by the pork slices. Blend well and cook together for 1–2 minutes; serve hot.

Top left: Twice-cooked pork.

Top right: Hot and sour kidney.

Hot and Sour Kidney

½ lb/225 g/½ lb pig's kidney
1 tsp/5 g/1 tsp salt
1 tbsp/15 ml/1 tbsp rice wine or sherry
½ tbsp/7.5 g/½ tbsp cornflour (cornstarch)
1 tbsp/15 g/1 tbsp dried red chilli (chili)

1 slice ginger root, peeled
2 spring onions (scallions)
1 clove garlic
oil for deep-frying
1 tsp/5 g/1 tsp Sichuan pepper, ground

SAUCE MIXTURE:
1 tbsp/15 g/1 tbsp sugar
1½ tbsp/22.5 ml/1½ tbsp vinegar
1½ tbsp/22.5 ml/1½ tbsp soy sauce

2 tsp/10 ml/2 tsp cornflour (cornstarch)
water or stock

1 Split the kidneys in half lengthwise and discard the fat and white parts in the middle. Score the surface of the kidneys diagonally in a criss-cross pattern and cut them into oblong stamp-size pieces. Marinate in salt, rice wine or sherry and cornflour (cornstarch).
2 Cut the dried red chilli (chili) into small bits, discard the seeds; finely chop the ginger root, garlic and onions. Mix the sauce in a bowl or jug.
3 Heat up the oil and deep-fry the kidney pieces for about 1 minute; scoop them out and drain. Pour off the excess oil leaving about 1 tbsp/15 ml/1 tbsp in the wok; put in the red chilli (chili) and cook until it turns dark.
4 Add kidney pieces, onions, garlic, ginger and pepper. Stir a few times, then add the sauce mixture; blend well. As soon as the sauce starts to bubble, dish out and serve.

Chicken, Ham and Mushroom Soup

4 oz/100 g/¼ lb chicken breast meat
2 oz/50 g/¼ cup pork fat
1 oz/25 g/¼ cup water chestnuts, peeled
1 oz/25 g/⅙ cup bamboo shoots
4–5 Chinese dried mushrooms
2 oz/50 g/¼ cup cooked ham
1 egg white
1½ tsp/7.5 g/1½ tsp salt

2 tsp/10 g/2 tsp cornflour (cornstarch)
2 spring onions (scallions)
3 tbsp/45 ml/4 tbsp oil
1½ pt/900 ml/3¾ cups thick stock
2 tbsp/30 ml/2 tbsp rice wine or sherry
½ pt/300 ml/1¼ cups clear stock
1 slice ginger root, peeled and finely chopped

1 Soak the chicken breast in cold water for 20 minutes, then remove the white tendon from the meat and finely chop it into a pulp.

2 Next peel the water chestnuts and parboil for a few minutes, then chop them finely. Finely chop the pork fat as well.

3 Soak the dried mushrooms in warm water for 20 minutes, squeeze dry and discard the hard stalks, then cut them into small pieces. Cut the bamboo shoots into thin slices of the same size. Cut the ham into thin slices roughly the same size as the bamboo shoots.

4 Beat the egg white until frothy, mix in the chicken meat, ½ tsp/2.5 g/½ tsp salt, cornflour (cornstarch), pork fat and water chestnuts; blend well.

5 Heat 2 tbsp/30 ml/2 tbsp oil in a wok, toss in 1 onion cut into short lengths, after a few seconds discard the onion and reduce the heat to as low as possible.

6 Now wet your hands and make the chicken mixture into small round balls no bigger than cherries; fry them in the oil,

turning them round, and press them flat with a spatula.

7 Put the chicken into a bowl, add bamboo shoots, mushrooms and ham, together with ¼ pt/150 ml/⅔ cup thick stock, ½ tbsp/7.5 g/½ tbsp rice wine or sherry and ½ tsp/2.5 g/½ tsp salt. Steam over a high heat for 5 minutes, remove and discard the stock, place the entire contents in a large serving bowl.

8 Heat up the remaining oil, fry the other onion (cut into short lengths) for a few seconds and discard, add the remaining thick stock plus the clear stock, salt, finely chopped ginger root and the remaining rice wine or sherry; bring it to the boil then pour it over the chicken.

Drunken Spareribs

10 oz/275 g/10 oz pork spareribs
1 tbsp/15 g/1 tbsp cornflour (cornstarch)
2 tbsp/30 ml/2 tbsp rice wine or sherry
1 tbsp/15 g/1 tbsp curry powder
1 tsp/5 g/1 tsp sugar
1 tbsp/15 ml/1 tbsp soy sauce
1 spring onion (scallion), finely chopped

1 clove garlic, finely chopped
1 small green pepper, shredded
1 small red pepper, shredded
1 tbsp/15 ml/1 tbsp sesame seed oil
1 tbsp/15 ml/1 tbsp tomato purée (paste)
oil for deep-frying

1 Chop the spareribs into small pieces; mix in cornflour (cornstarch), wine or sherry and curry powder. Deep fry in hot oil for 3 minutes; scoop them out and drain.

2 Pour the excess oil out, put in the finely chopped onion and garlic, followed by shredded red and green peppers; add sugar, soy sauce, tomato purée (paste) and sesame seed oil. Stir to make a smooth sauce, then put in the spareribs; blend together well; serve.

Above: Drunken spareribs.

Left: Chicken, ham and mushroom soup.

Salt and Pepper Spareribs

10 oz/275 g/10 oz pork spareribs
1 egg
1 tsp/5 g/1 tsp salt
2 tsp/10 g/2 tsp cornflour
(cornstarch)
½ tbsp/7.5 ml/½ tbsp Kao Liang
spirit

½ tsp/2.5 g/½ tsp five-spice
powder
1 tsp/5 g/1 tsp Sichuan pepper,
freshly ground
oil for deep-frying

1 Chop the spareribs into small pieces; marinate with salt, pepper, Kao Liang spirit and five-spice powder for 15 minutes. Add egg and cornflour (cornstarch), mix well.
2 Heat the oil until hot; deep fry the spareribs for 3 minutes, then soak them in cold oil for 1 minute. Just before serving, crisp them in hot oil once more.

Sweet and Sour Spareribs

1 lb/0.5 kg/1 lb pork spareribs
2 tbsp/30 ml/2 tbsp soy sauce
1 tbsp/15 ml/1 tbsp rice wine or
sherry
½ tsp/2.5 ml/½ tsp monosodium
glutamate
2 tbsp/30 g/2 tbsp cornflour
(cornstarch)

2 tbsp/30 g/2 tbsp sugar
1½ tbsp/22.5 ml/1½ tbsp
vinegar
lard for deep-frying
salt and Sichuan pepper for
dipping

1 Chop the spareribs into small bits using a cleaver. Mix ½ tbsp/7.5 ml/½ tbsp soy sauce with the rice wine or sherry and monosodium glutamate. When they are all well blended to-gether, add 1 tbsp/15 ml/1 tbsp cornflour (cornstarch).

Far left: Salt and pepper spareribs.

Left: Sweet and sour spareribs.

Right: Twice-roasted pork.

Thoroughly coat each bit of the sparerib with this mixture.
2 In a bowl mix the remaining soy suace with sugar and vinegar. Warm up the lard in a wok or deep-fryer, put in about half of the spareribs, fry for 30 seconds, scoop them out.
3 Wait for a while to let the lard heat up again, then fry the rest of the spareribs for 30 seconds, scoop out. Now wait for the lard to get hot before returning all the spareribs to the wok to fry for another 50 seconds or so; scoop them out when they turn golden and place them on a serving dish.
4 Pour off the excess lard, leaving about 1 tbsp/15 ml/1 tbsp in the pan; add the sauce mixture. When it starts to bubble, add the remaining cornflour (cornstarch) mixed in a little cold water; stir to make a smooth sauce, then pour it over the spareribs.

Serve with salt and pepper mixed as a dip.

Twice-Roasted Pork

3–4 lb/1.5–2 kg/3–4 lb loin of
pork (in one piece)
4 egg whites
4 oz/100 g/1 cup plain (all-
purpose) flour

3–4 spring onions (scallions)
2 oz/50 g/¼ cup Hoi Sin sauce
4 oz/100 g/½ cup Chinese pickles

1 Pierce the pork with a spit, singe the skin over a high flame then plunge it into a large pot of hot water for 5 minutes. Take the pork out and scrape off any burnt skin. Place it in a large pot, cover with cold water and cook for about 1 hour. Remove.
2 Make a paste with the egg whites and flour, rub it all over the meat (not the skin), roast in a moderate oven 400°F/200°C (Gas Mark 6) skin side up for 20 minutes, then turn it over and roast for a further 15–20 minutes.
3 To serve, carve the crackling, the fat, the meat and spareribs separately and arrange each in a row.
4 Cut the onions into shreds, to be eaten with the pork together with the Hoi Sin sauce and the Chinese pickles. Wrap the pork and its accompaniments in 'Lotus-leaf' pancakes, or place them inside Greek pitta bread which is very similar to a type of bread eaten in northern China.

'White-cut' Pork

2 lb/1 kg/2 lb leg of pork (skinned
and boned)

DIP:

4 tbsp/60 ml/5 tbsp soy sauce
1 tbsp/15 ml/1 tbsp Kao Liang
spirit (or brandy)
2 spring onions (scallions), finely
chopped
2 slices ginger root, peeled and
finely chopped

1 tsp/5 ml/1 tsp sesame seed oil
1 tsp/5 ml/1 tsp chilli (chili) sauce
(optional)
3–3½ pt/about 1.75 l/7½–9
cups water

1 Place the pork (in one piece, tied together with string if
necessary) in a large pot; add cold water, bring it to a rapid
boil; skim off the scum. Cover and simmer gently for about 1
hour.
2 Remove from the pot and leave it to cool under cover with
the fat side up for 6–8 hours.
3 Just before serving, cut off any excess fat, leaving only a very
thin layer (about 1/10 in/2 mm) of fat on top, then cut the meat
into small thin slices across the grain. Put any uneven bits and
pieces in the centre of a plate; arrange the well-cut slices in
two neat rows, one on each side of the pile, then neatly arrange
a third row on top of the pile so that it resembles an arched
bridge.
4 You can either pour the sauce mixture all over the pork and
serve, or use the sauce as a dip.

Shredded Kidneys in Wine Sauce

1 lb/0.5 kg/1 lb pigs' kidneys
5–6 Chinese dried mushrooms
2 oz/50 g/⅓ cup bamboo shoots
2 oz/50 g/½ cup green cabbage
heart or broccoli
1½ tbsp/22.5 ml/1½ tbsp rice
wine or sherry

1 tsp/5 g/1 tsp salt
1 tbsp/15 ml/1 tbsp soy sauce
½ tsp/2.5 ml/½ tsp monosodium
glutamate
1 slice ginger root, peeled
1 spring onion (scallion)
Sichuan peppercorns

1 Peel off the thin white skin covering the kidneys, split them
in half lengthways and discard the white parts in the middle.
Shred each half into thin slices and soak them in cold water
for an hour or so.
2 Soak the mushrooms in warm water for 20 minutes, squeeze
dry and discard the hard stalks, then cut them into thin shreds.
Cut the bamboo shoots and greens into thin shreds and blanch
them in boiling water for a few minutes (if using canned
bamboo shoots this will be unnecessary as they have already
been cooked). When blanched, drain and mix the bamboo
shoots with 1 tsp/5 ml/1 tsp salt.
3 Parboil the kidneys in about 1¾ pt/1 l/4¼ cups boiling
water for a few minutes, scoop them out, rinse in cold water
and drain. Place them in a bowl, add the bamboo shoots,
mushrooms, greens, soy sauce, rice wine or sherry and monosodium glutamate; mix well and marinate for 20 minutes or so.
4 Arrange the contents on a serving plate and garnish with
finely chopped onion, ginger root and freshly ground pepper.
   This is an ideal starter for a formal meal or dinner party.

Top left: 'White-cut' pork.

Above: Shredded kidneys in wine
sauce.

Clear and Thick Stock

1 duck weighing about 4 lb/ 1.75 kg/4 lb
3 chickens weighing about 2 lb/ 1 kg/2 lb each
1 hand of pork (picnic shoulder) weighing about 3 lb/1.5 kg/3 lb
3 lb/1.5 kg/3 lb pork bones
2–3 spring onions (scallions)
2 slices ginger root, peeled
2 tbsp/30 g/2 tbsp salt
2 tbsp/30 ml/2 tbsp soy sauce

CLEAR STOCK

1 Remove the breast meat from all three chickens and the meat from the legs of two chickens; put the meat aside. Break the leg bones of the third chicken and the duck. Cut through to the meat of the pork as far as the bone, then break the bone with the back of the cleaver.

2 Put 10–12 pt/about 5 l/12–14 pt cold water in a large pot. Place the pork bones in the water, then put in the chickens (but not the breast and leg meat you removed earlier), followed by the duck and finally the pork hand (picnic shoulder). Bring the pot to a rapid boil, skim off the scum, simmer for about 1 hour, then ladle out about 4–5 pt/about 2 l/5–6 pt of the stock into a bowl, add the chicken leg meat finely chopped, together with the ginger root and onions, and leave it to cool.

3 Now add about 5–6 pt/about 2.5 l/6–7 pt fresh boiling water to the pot, simmer for 1½ hours, then scoop out the pork, chickens, duck and pork bones.

4 Skim once more, turn off the heat and let it cool for about 20 minutes, then put it back on a high heat again; add salt, stir and add the stock containing the chicken leg meat; continue stirring. When all the leg meat starts floating on the surface, reduce heat and scoop it out with a perforated spoon, then ladle out about 4–5 pt/about 2 l/5–6 pt stock into a bowl.

5 Let it cool a while before putting in the finely chopped chicken breast meat, blend well and pour it back to the stock pot.

6 Increase heat, add soy sauce, stir until all the meat is floating on the surface, scoop it out then pour the stock through a fine sieve, and you will have the famous clear stock.

THICK STOCK

1 Use the pork hand (picnic shoulder), pork bones, chickens and the duck carcass and bones with the meat removed left over from the previous recipe.

2 Place first the pork bones on the bottom of a large pot, then the chickens all the way around the bones with the pork hand (picnic shoulder) in the middle, and finally place the duck carcass and bones on top. Fill the pot up with 10–12 pt/about 5 l/12–14 pt water, bring it to a rapid boil then reduce heat to moderate and simmer for 2½ hours or until the stock is reduced by half, remove all the bones and meat, then strain the stock through a fine sieve.

Rapidly-Fried Beef Steak

½ lb/225 g/½ lb best beef steak
1½ tbsp/22.5 ml/1½ tbsp soy sauce
1 tbsp/15 g/1 tbsp cornflour (cornstarch)
2 cloves garlic, finely chopped
2 spring onions (scallions), white parts only, cut into ½ in/1 cm lengths
1 tsp/5 ml/1 tsp vinegar
2 tsp/10 ml/2 tsp rice wine or sherry
oil for deep-frying

1 Cut the beef into thin slices and marinate with 1 tbsp/15 ml/1 tbsp soy sauce and cornflour (cornstarch).

2 Heat up the oil until smoking, deep-fry the beef slices for about 30 seconds only, stir with chopsticks to separate them, then quickly scoop them out with a perforated spoon.

3 Now heat up about 1 tbsp/15 ml/1 tbsp oil in a wok and toss in the onions and garlic. When they start to turn golden, put in the beef slices, add vinegar, rice wine (or sherry) and the remaining soy sauce, stir-fry for about 30 seconds, then it is done.

4 A simple dish, but the quality of the beef steak, the degree of heat and the timing all must be right.

Left: Rapidly-fried beef steak.   *Above: Clear and thick stock.*

Cassia Lamb

4 oz/100 g/¼ lb fillet tenderloin lamb	2 tsp/10 ml/2 tsp rice wine (or sherry)
3 eggs	1 tsp/5 g/1 tsp salt
½ tsp/2.5 ml/½ tsp monosodium glutamate	1 slice ginger root, peeled
	2 tbsp/30 ml/2 tbsp chicken fat

1 Cut the lamb into thin shreds. Finely chop the ginger root. Beat up the eggs and mix them with the lamb shreds and ginger root.

2 Heat up the chicken fat in a wok or pan, put in the egg mixture, stir and scramble for about 10 seconds and add salt, monosodium glutamate and rice wine or sherry. Stir and scramble for another 10 seconds. Serve.

Stewed Beef

2 lb/1 kg/2 lb shin of beef (shank cross cuts)	1 tsp/5 g/1 tsp five-spice powder
2 tbsp/30 ml/2 tbsp sugar	3–4 spring onions (scallions)
6 tbsp/90 ml/7 tbsp soy sauce	2–3 slices ginger root
2 tbsp/30 ml/2 tbsp rice wine or sherry	2 tbsp/30 ml/2 tbsp oil

1 This dish makes excellent use of a cheap cut of meat. It is cooked slowly so that the meat becomes really tender. Cut the beef into 1-in/2.5-cm cubes. Cut the onions into 1-in/2.5-cm lengths.

Rinsed Lamb in Fire-Pot

3–3½ lb/1.5 kg/3–3½ lb boned
shoulder, loin or leg of lamb
1 lb/1.5 kg/1 lb Chinese cabbage
1 lb/0.5 kg/1 lb spinach
2 cakes of bean-curd (fresh or
frozen)

4 oz/100 g/¼ lb transparent
noodles
4–5 pt/about 2 l/5–6 pt water or
stock

SAUCE:

finely chopped spring onions
(scallions)
garlic and ginger

root; soy sauce; sherry; Hoi Sin
sauce; vinegar; sugar; chilli (chili)
sauce and sesame seed oil

1 Cut the lamb into fairly large but very, very thin slices – you will find that it is much easier to do this if the meat is half frozen.

2 Wash and cut the cabbage and spinach into biggish pieces; cut each cake of the bean-curd into 10 to 12 slices; soak the transparent noodles in warm water for a few minutes, then drain.

3 Now arrange the cabbage, spinach, bean-curd, transparent noodles and the meat in separate serving dishes and place them on the table with the fire-pot in the middle. Here a round table would be ideal, a square one is almost as good, but not a long table – you will have to arrange your seats in such a way that nobody is too far from the fire-pot.

4 While waiting for the water or stock to boil in the moat of the fire-pot, each person prepares his or her sauce by mixing a little of the various ingredients in individual sauce dishes according to his or her own taste.

5 When the water or stock is boiling vigorously, each person picks up a piece of lamb with chopsticks and dips it in the water to cook it, occasionally dunking it as if rinsing – hence the name of the dish.

6 Depending on the thickness and cut of the meat, it should not take more than 20–30 seconds to cook, otherwise it will be too tough. Now you dip the cooked meat in the sauce mixture and eat it. Delicious!

7 After a while, you can start adding the vegetables to the moat and eating them with the meat. As the cooking progresses, the pot is re-charged with charcoal; the remaining water or stock is put in the moat, and the contents get tastier and tastier.

8 When all the meat is eaten, put the rest of the vegetables into the moat, to make a delicious soup.

2 Heat up the oil and brown the beef before blanching it in a pot of boiling water for a few seconds. Pour the water away and cover with fresh cold water, add onions, ginger root, five-spice powder, sugar, soy sauce and rice wine or sherry, and place a tightly fitting lid over the pan. Bring it to the boil over a high heat, then reduce the heat and simmer gently for 3–4 hours, after which there should be very little juice left. Serve hot or cold.

Top left: Cassia lamb.

Left: Stewed beef.

Above: Rinsed lamb in fire-pot.

Shredded Beef with Celery

½ lb/225 g/½ lb beef steak	2 tbsp/30 ml/2 tbsp soy sauce
2 oz/50 g/½ cup celery	½ tsp/2.5 g/½ tsp salt
2 oz/50 g/½ cup leek or spring	1 tsp/5 g/1 tsp sugar
onion (scallion)	1 tbsp/15 ml/1 tbsp rice wine or
2 slices ginger root	sherry
1 tbsp/15 ml/1 tbsp chilli (chili)	1 tsp/5 ml/1 tsp vinegar
paste	3 tbsp/45 ml/4 tbsp oil

1 Shred the beef into thin strips about the size of matches. Shred the celery and leeks the same size (Chinese leeks are a cross between the Western leek and spring onion (scallion) with thin skin and green foliage). Peel the ginger root and cut it into thin shreds as well.

2 Heat up the wok or pan and put in the oil. When it starts to smoke, stir-fry the beef for a short while, add the chilli (chili) paste, blend well. Then add the celery, leek and ginger root, followed by the soy sauce, salt, sugar and wine. Stir for 1–2 minutes, then add vinegar and serve.

Minced (Ground) Fried Pork

1 lb/0.5 kg/1 lb pork fillet	½ tsp/2.5 g/½ tsp salt
(tenderloin)	½ tbsp/7.5 ml/½ tbsp soy sauce
4 oz/100 g/½ cup Sichuan	1 slice ginger root
preserved vegetable	1 spring onion (scallion)
1 tbsp/15 ml/1 tbsp crushed	1 tbsp/15 ml/1 tbsp rice wine or
yellow bean sauce	sherry
2 tsp/10 ml/2 tsp brown sugar	1 tsp/5 ml/1 tsp sesame seed oil

1 Trim off all sinew and gristle from the meat, but keep the fat; now chop the pork coarsely with a cleaver into rice grain-sized pieces. Chop the Sichuan preserved vegetable into small pieces.

Finely chop the ginger root (peeled) and onion.

Five-Fragrant Kidney Slices

½ lb/225 g/½ lb pigs' kidneys
1 tsp/5 ml/1 tsp red colouring
12 fl oz/350 ml/1½ cups chicken stock
1 tbsp/15 ml/1 tbsp soy sauce
1 tbsp/15 ml/1 tbsp rice wine or sherry
1 slice ginger root
1 tsp/5 g/1 tsp salt
1 tsp/5 g/1 tsp five-spice powder
1 spring onion (scallion)

1 Place the kidneys in cold water in a pan; bring to the boil; skim off any impurities floating on the surface; reduce heat and simmer for 30 minutes. Remove and drain.

2 Place the kidneys in fresh cold water (just enough to cover), add the red colouring (if Chinese red-powder is unobtainable, then use a little cochineal). Bring to the boil, then remove and rinse in cold water and drain.

3 Put the chicken stock in a pot or pan; add the soy sauce, wine or sherry, ginger root, onion, salt, five-spice powder and the kidneys. Boil for 5 minutes, then place the kidneys with the stock in a large bowl to cool. This will take 5–6 hours.

4 Take the kidneys out and cut them into as thin slices as you possibly can – it is possible to cut 80–90 slices from each kidney if your cleaver is really sharp!

5 Place the unevenly cut slices in the middle of a plate to make a pile, then neatly arrange the rest of the slices all the way around it in two or three layers like the petals of an opened flower, then through a sieve pour a little of the juice in which the kidneys have been cooking over the 'flower', but be careful not to disturb the beautiful 'petals'. Serve cold as an hors d'oeuvre. The name 'five-fragrant' is, of course, referring to the five-spice powder used.

2 Heat up a wok or frying-pan over a high heat and stir-fry the pork for 1 or 2 minutes; as soon as it starts to stick on the bottom, reduce the heat to low and scrape the pan well. After about 1 minute, increase the heat to high again until it starts to stick, then reduce heat.

3 Repeat this rather fiddly high-low heat procedure three or four times, when the pork will turn pale in colour. Then drain off the fat which the meat will have produced.

4 Over high heat add the bean sauce, sugar, salt and soy sauce, mixing well; by now the meat should have turned light brown. Now add the chopped Sichuan preserved vegetable, ginger root, onion and wine or sherry, blend well, and finally add the sesame seed oil and serve.

Left: *Shredded beef with celery.*

Above: *Minced (ground) fried pork.*   **Right:** *Five-fragrant kidney slices.*

Stir-Fried Sichuan Beef

12 oz/350 g/¾ lb (trimmed weight) lean steak
1½ tbsp/22.5 ml/1½ tbsp light vegetable oil
½ tbsp/7.5 ml/½ tbsp light soy sauce
1 tbsp/15 g/1 tbsp finely chopped spring onion (scallion)
1 tsp/5 g/1 tsp whole Sichuan pepper, lightly bruised
salt to taste
1 tsp/5 ml/1 tsp sesame oil

1 Chill the beef well. Slice into 4 × 1 in/10 × 1 cm strips, no more than ⅛ in/3 mm thick.
2 Combine two thirds of the vegetable oil with the soy sauce and spring onions (scallions), mix into the meat and leave to marinate, covered, for 2 hours.
3 Heat the remaining oil in a wok or heavy frying pan and toss the Sichuan pepper in it for 30 seconds. Add the meat and its marinade and stir-fry until just cooked, no more than 3 minutes.
4 Off the heat, stir in the sesame oil and serve immediately, perhaps with buttered egg noodles.

Above left: Stir-fried Sichuan beef.

Shabu Shabu

7 oz/200 g/scant 1 cup bean curd
7 oz/200 g/2 cups napa cabbage
4 oz/100 g/4 cups spinach, washed and trimmed
4 oz/100 g/⅔ cup bamboo shoots
12 flat mushrooms, wiped and trimmed
1 package shirataki noodles
4 leeks, washed and trimmed
1¼ lb/500 g/1¼ lb top sirloin of beef, in paper-thin slices

SESAME SAUCE
2 tbsp/30 g/2 tbsp white sesame seeds
salt
3 tbsp/45 ml/4 tbsp dashi
2 tbsp/30 ml/2 tbsp rice vinegar
2 tbsp/30 ml/2 tbsp light soy sauce
1 tbsp/15 ml/1 tbsp mirin

SOY SAUCE
red maple radish
daikon radish, grated
lemon wedges
spring onions (scallions) or leeks, shredded and rinsed
1 piece kombu seaweed

1 Cut the bean curd into 1¼-in/2-cm squares. Wash the cabbage and cut into large chunks; parboil in plenty of rapidly boiling salted water for 2–3 minutes, then drain well and pat dry. Wash the bamboo shoots and cut into strips.
2 Remove the stems of the mushrooms and cut a cross in the top of each. Parboil the shirataki for 1–2 minutes and drain. Cut the leeks diagonally into 1-in/3-cm lengths. Arrange the ingredients attractively on a large platter, grouping each type of ingredient together.
3 Lightly toast the sesame seeds with a little salt until golden-brown. Transfer to a suribachi and grind until oily. Gradually

Above: Simmered pork Nagasaki style.

Left: Eating shabu shabu.

blend in the remaining sesame sauce ingredients. Pour into small individual bowls for dipping. Fill 4 other small bowls with soy sauce and prepare and distribute the condiments in yet more bowls.

4 Wipe the kombu and make a few slashes in it to help release the flavour. Place in a large ovenproof casserole and fill three-quarters full of water. Bring to the boil and remove the kombu. It is now up to the diners to cook the meal. With chopsticks, pick up slices of beef and move them around in the simmering stock for ½ minute, until the meat becomes pink. Dip into sauces and eat.

5 Continue to cook the ingredients. Allow the vegetables to cook for a little longer than the meat. When ingredients have been consumed, ladle the broth into bowls, season with a little salt and serve as soup.

Simmered Pork Nagasaki Style

2¼ lb/1 kg/2¼ lb pork shoulder
1 pt/600 ml/2½ cups water
piece fresh root ginger, peeled and crushed
1 pt/600 ml/2½ cups dashi
4 tbsp/60 g/5 tbsp sugar

5–6 tbsp/75–90 ml/6–7 tbsp dark soy sauce
½ pt/300 ml/1¼ cups sake
1 tbsp/15 ml/1 tbsp mirin
mustard

1 Chop the pork into manageable pieces. Place them in a steamer and steam for 30 minutes. Remove the pork from the steamer and place in a large saucepan. Cover with the water and add the ginger.

2 Bring to the boil, skim the surface carefully and cover with a drop lid. Simmer over the lowest possible heat for at least 2 hours, topping up the water if necessary, until the pork is very tender.

3 Drain the pork, discarding the cooking water and ginger. Rinse well and refrigerate for at least 3 hours, preferably overnight.

4 An hour before you are ready to cook the pork, remove it from the refrigerator and allow it to come to room temperature. Cut the pork into small chunks.

5 In a dry frying pan, sauté the pork to brown it lightly. Transfer the browned pork to a saucepan.

6 Ladle the dashi over the pork. Add the sugar, soy sauce, sake and mirin. Bring to a rapid boil, reduce the heat, cover with a drop lid and simmer for 30–40 minutes, until the simmering stock is considerably reduced.

7 Arrange a few pieces of pork on each serving dish and ladle a little of the thickened simmering stock over them. Serve with a dab of mustard.

3 De-seed the pickled plums. Grind the plum flesh with the miso in a suribachi.
4 Combine the vinegar, ½ the chilli (chili) pepper and the sugar in a small saucepan and heat to dissolve the sugar. Remove from heat and cool. Blend the cooled vinegar mixture with the 2 pickled plums and 1 tbsp/15 ml/1 tbsp miso, and finally stir in the sesame oil.
5 Rub the mixture through a sieve to purée. Rinse the yam and cucumber and pat dry. Arrange the beef and vegetables in four small deep bowls and pour the dressing over them. Garnish each dish with a sprig of watercress and a few slices of red chilli (chili) pepper.

Left: Beef salad in hot chilli (chili) dressing.

Right: Sweet-glazed beef.

Beef Salad in Hot Chilli (Chili) Dressing

2 oz/50 g/2 oz Japanese yam (or 4–5 okra, parboiled)	1-in/2.5-cm piece root ginger
½ cucumber	10 oz/275 g/10 oz fillet (tenderloin) of beef
1 young leek or spring onion (scallion)	salt and pepper
	vegetable oil for frying

DRESSING

2 pickled plums (umeboshi)	1 red chilli (chili) pepper, seeded and very finely sliced
1 tbsp/15 ml/1 tbsp miso	1 tbsp/15 ml/1 tbsp sugar
3 tbsp/45 ml/4 tbsp rice vinegar	1 tsp/5 ml/1 tsp sesame oil

1 Wash the vegetables and pat dry. Cut the yam and cucumber into 'poem cards' (see 'Cutting techniques', page 30). Lightly salt and set aside to drain. Sliver the leek or spring onion (scallion) and cut the ginger into threads (see 'needle cut', page 31).
2 Lightly brush a frying pan with oil and fry the beef until both sides are lightly browned. Slice the beef very finely and season with salt and pepper.

Sweet-Glazed Beef

4 oz/100 g/1 cup mushrooms, wiped and trimmed	salt
2 tomatoes	4 sirloin steaks
2 oz/50 g/1 cup beansprouts	vegetable oil
2 oz/50 g/½ cup mange-tout (snow) peas	2 tbsp/30 ml/2 tbsp grated apple

TERIYAKI SAUCE

7 fl oz/200 ml/scant 1 cup soy sauce	3½ fl oz/100 ml/scant ⅔ cup mirin
7 fl oz/200 ml/scant 1 cup sake	2 oz/50 g/¼ cup sugar

1 Prepare the teriyaki sauce: combine the soy sauce, sake, mirin and sugar in a saucepan and stir over medium heat to dissolve the sugar. The sauce may be used immediately or cooled and refrigerated.
2 Cut a neat cross in the top of each mushroom cap. Wash the vegetables and pat dry. Halve the tomatoes, trim the beansprouts and cut the mange-tout (snow) peas diagonally into 1-in/1.5-cm slices. Lightly salt the steaks and set aside for 5 to 20 minutes.
3 Heat a little oil in a frying pan and sauté the vegetables for 2 or 3 minutes or until cooked but still a little crisp. Remove, drain and keep warm.
4 Drain the frying pan and add fresh oil. Heat the oil over medium to high heat, add the steaks and fry until both sides are brown.
5 Pour teriyaki sauce over the steaks. Add grated apple to the pan. Tilt the pan and turn the steaks so that they are well coated with sauce, and heat until the sauce begins to bubble.
6 Serve the meat and vegetables on individual plates. In Japan cast-iron plates are preferred for this dish. Pour the remaining teriyaki sauce in the pan over the steaks and serve immediately.

Fajitas

1 Lay the meat on a cutting board and remove the fat – carefully – with a sharp knife. this is time-consuming.

2 Remove the tough outer membrane. It helps if you have three arms: one to hold the steak, one to lift the membrane, and one to slide the knife along at the point of separation, helping the membrane peel off.

3 Slit the meat with a very sharp knife, working both with and against the grain. Stab it repeatedly with a fork to tenderize it further. You can use a mallet, but it makes for a mushy piece of meat. So do proprietary tenderizers: the marinade should be all the tenderizer you need. The fajita is now ready to marinate.

4 Marinate the meat in large slices, ½-1 in/1.25–2.5 cm thick; after turning it several times to be sure it is evenly coated with marinade, leave it in the refrigerator for 12 to 24 hours. Slice the meat into strips 6 in/15 cm long before you cook it.

5 Take the meat out of the refrigerator an hour or two before you are going to cook it; having the meat at room temperature is one of the secrets of successful cooking, especially barbecuing. Cut the meat into strips 4–6 in/10–15 cm long. Either fry the strips in a heavy iron frying pan or skillet with a minimum of oil, or grill (broil) them on a barbecue – the latter probably tastes better.

6 Serve with warm 6 in/15 cm flour tortillas and any or all of the following accompaniments: salsa; sliced onion; tomato; pepper; sour cream; guacamole or avocado; sliced lettuce; frijoles refritos; Mexican rice.

Margarita Marinade

3 parts lime juice   2 parts tequila
1 part Triple Sec

The lime juice tenderizes the meat, the Triple Sec flavours and sweetens it, and the tequila flavours.

Cooked fajitas.

Lime Marinade

8 fl oz/225 ml/1 cup beef stock
juice of 1 large lime
3 tbsp/45 ml/4 tbsp
Worcestershire sauce

1 or 2 cloves garlic, finely chopped
1 tbsp/15 g/1 tbsp chopped
coriander

Wine Marinade

4 fl oz/110 ml/1 cup really cheap,
nasty red wine (or use half-and-
half red wine and red wine
vinegar)

3 tbsp/45 ml/4 tbsp olive oil
1 or 2 cloves garlic, finely chopped
1 tbsp/15 g/1 tbsp chopped
coriander

VARIATIONS If you are just after unusual tastes, and are using (reasonably) tender meat to start with, mix and match from the following list of possible marinade ingredients:

brandy or whisky (any variety) or
rum
red wine or sherry
beer
vinegar (wine, cider, etc)
juice of any citrus fruit
pineapple juice
hot sauce, or dried red peppers
soaked and pounded

soy sauce or Worcestershire sauce
onion, garlic
fresh coriander, including freshly
crushed seeds
rosemary, basil, sage, thyme,
oregano, cumin
whole peppercorns, black or green

Pork with Cabbage and Corn

Pork with cabbage and corn.

1½ lb/750 g/1½ lb pork ribs, chopped
1 medium onion, cut in rings
2 large tomatoes, cut in rings
2 cloves garlic
pinch of cumin seed

8 peppercorns
2 tbsp/30 ml/2 tbsp vinegar
1 medium caggage, sliced
12 oz/350 g/2¼ cups sweetcorn
salt and pepper

1 Using a heavy flameproof casserole (or Dutch oven), cook the pork in just enough water to cover. When the ribs are tender (at least an hour), add the onion and the tomato. Cook for a few minutes longer.

2 In a blender, combine the garlic, the cumin, the peppercorns and the vinegar. Add to the meat, together with the cabbage and corn. Stir well and season: the meal is ready when the cabbage is cooked. Serve with boiled rice.

Picadillo

2 lb/1 kg/2 lb lean beef
4 tbsp/60 ml/5 tbsp olive oil or lard
1 medium onion
2–4 cloves garlic
1 chayote, peeled and cubed
1 large potato, peeled and cubed
2 large tomatoes, cut in chunks
2 carrots, peeled and sliced
1 courgette (zucchini), sliced

1 oz/25 g/3 tbsp raisins
3 or more canned, sliced jalapeno chillies (chilis)
10 pimiento-stuffed olives, halved
large pinch each of cinnamon and cloves
salt and pepper
6 oz/200 g/1 cup peas
2 oz/50 g/½ cup slivered almonds to garnish

1 Cut the beef into strips ½-in/1-cm wide and 2-in/5-cm long; or chop finely. Fry in a heavy frying pan or skillet until brown; add the onions and garlic. When these are golden, add all the other ingredients except the almonds and peas. Bring to the boil; simmer for 20–30 minutes, according to how well done you like the vegetables. Five minutes (or less) before serving, add the peas and stir them in.
2 Fry the slivered almonds in a little olive oil (or almond oil), shaking the pan constantly to avoid burning. When they are golden-brown, sprinkle them over the picadillo.

Carne de Res Con Nopalitos

3 lb/1.3 kg/3 lb beef, cut in 2-in/5-cm cubes
4 tbsp/60 ml/5 tbsp olive oil or lard
1 large onion, finely chopped
2–4 cloves garlic, finely chopped
1 can or bottle nopalitos
10-oz/300-g/10-oz can tomatillos

6 canned or 3 fresh serrano chillies (chilis), chopped
4 tbsp/60 ml/5 tbsp tomato purée (paste)
8 fl oz/225 ml/1 cup beef stock
one handful fresh coriander, chopped
salt and pepper

1 Fry the beef in the lard or olive oil, a few cubes at a time, until well browned. Transfer to a flameproof casserole (or Dutch oven). In the same fat, fry the onion and garlic until golden. Add to the beef.
2 Drain the nopalitos, and rinse them thoroughly. Add to the beef, onions and garlic with the other ingredients (don't drain the tomatillos). Bring to the boil, and simmer gently until the beef is very tender – 2½ to 3 hours.

Above: Picadillo.

Right: Carne de res con nopalitos.

Shredded Beef Stew

Carne Molida Cruda

2 lb/1 kg/2 lb chuck steak, cubed
1 large onion, sliced
2 cloves garlic, finely chopped
2 tbsp/30 ml/2 tbsp vinegar

16 fl oz/450 ml/2 cups water or stock
1 can or 1 lb/500 g/1 lb fresh tomatoes

1 In a flame-proof casserole (or Dutch oven), bring the meat to a boil with all the other ingredients except the tomatoes.
2 Cover, and simmer over a very low heat for two or three hours. After the first hour or two, add the tomatoes: they should simmer with the meat for at least 45 minutes. When the meat is very tender, fish it out with a fork, and shred it on to a plate. When all the meat is shredded, return it to the stock. Meanwhile, prepare the following:

2 peppers, one red and one green
2 boiled potatoes

2 tbsp/30 ml/2 tbsp olive oil

3 De-seed, de-vein and slice the peppers. Slice the potatoes. Fry them both together in the oil in a frying pan or skillet until the peppers are tender, then add to the meat. Cook very gently until the liquid has almost all evaporated.
4 Serve with boiled rice or tortillas – or boiled potatoes if you're not too much of a traditionalist.

2 jalapeno chillies (chilis), finely chopped
half a small onion

1 lb/450 g/1 lb fillet (tenderloin) steak (other good, lean cuts will do)
salt and pepper to taste

1 In a food processor, chop first the chillies (chilis), then the onion. Remove. Cut the steak into cubes; remove fat and membranes; chop in the food processor. Do not chop too finely: there should still be a meaty texture, rather than beef toothpaste. Mix all the ingredients together, using plenty of fresh-ground black pepper (1 tsp/5 g/1 tsp is not too much), but little salt: raw meat is fairly salty.
2 The longer you leave the meat, the more pronounced the lime flavour will be, and the less obvious the meat flavour. After an hour or so, the lime hides the meat flavour. For carnivores, therefore, serve immediately: for others, leave for an hour. Devotees of steak tartare may prefer the French dish; but the Mexican version is worth trying.

Top left: Shredded beef stew.

Top right: Carne molida cruda.

Carne con chile Colorado.

Carne Con Chile Colorado

8 middle-sized dried chillies (chilis): California or New Mexico type	1½ lb/700 g/1½ lb lean, boneless meat
½ tsp/2.5 g/½ tsp cumin seeds	oil or lard for frying
3 cloves garlic, peeled	16 fl oz/450 ml/2 cups water or stock
1 small onion, chopped	salt to taste
1 tsp/5 g/1 tsp dried oregano	

1 Prepare the dried chillies (chilis) as described on page 37. While they are soaking, grind the cumin seeds in a pestle and mortar or spice grinder.

2 Drain the chillies (chilis), but keep one cup of the soaking liquid. Add the garlic, onion, oregano and fresh-ground cumin.

Purée the lot, with the soaking liquid, in a blender. Blend until smooth, then strain through a wire sieve: this is one of the most time-consuming parts, but it makes for a wonderfully smooth sauce.

3 Cut the meat into approx 1/in/2.5cm cubes, and fry in a heavy, deep frying pan or skillet with a little lard or oil until browned all over – about 10 minutes. Keep turning the meat and scraping the pan.

4 Add the strained sauce; continue to cook, stirring and scraping frequently to avoid burning, for a few minutes (5 at most). The purée should be thick and rather darker than when you started. Add the water or stock; bring to a boil, and simmer over a low heat for at least an hour, stirring occasionally. If the sauce gets too thick, add a little more water or stock. It is ready when the meat is very tender.

Stuffed Peppers

3 rashers (slices) bacon, finely chopped
1 tbsp/15 ml/1 tbsp olive oil
1 small onion, chopped

½ lb/225 g/½ lb minced (ground) beef
1 lb/450 g/generous 2 cups leftover Mexican rice (cooked)
4 very large green peppers

1 Fry the bacon in a little oil; in the bacon fat, fry the onion and beef. When the beef is cooked, add the rice. Warm through.
2 Cut the tops off the peppers. Remove the seeds and veins. Stuff the beef-bacon-rice mixture into the peppers. (Let it mound over the top if need be.) Bake in a moderately hot oven 375°F/200°C (Gas 5) until the peppers are cooked – about 30–40 minutes.

Adobo Sauce

4 medium dried anchos chillies (chilis)
6 medium dried guajillos chillies (chilis)
8 cloves garlic, unpeeled
10 black peppercorns
½-in/12-mm cinnamon bark
2 large bay leaves, torn up

½ tsp/2.5 g/½ tsp dried oregano
½ tsp/2.5 g/½ tsp dried thyme
3 tbsp/45 ml/4 tbsp wine or cider vinegar
2 whole cloves
large pinch cumin seeds
1–2 tsp/5–10 g/1–2 tsp salt

1 Prepare the dried chillies (chilis) as described on page 37 – toasted and soaked. If you can't get guajillos, use all anchos or even pasillas. California or New Mexico chillies (chilis) will, however, give a much lighter flavour.
2 'Dry-fry' the unpeeled garlic in a heavy frying pan with no oil. Turn frequently. After 10–15 minutes, the garlic will be very soft and the blackened, blistered skins can be easily removed – let the cloves cool down before you try!
3 Grind the cinnamon, cloves, peppercorns, bay leaves and cumin in a pestle and mortar or spice-grinder. The aroma of fresh-ground spices is incomparably superior to ready-ground spices.
4 Drain the chillies (chilis), and put them in a blender with the peeled garlic, the herbs and spices, the vinegar, and a very little water – a couple of tablespoons.
5 Now comes the tedious part. Blend this mixture to a smooth paste. You will need to stop every few seconds, and push the mixture down on to the blades; you may even need to add another tablespoon of water. Don't add too much water, though, or the sauce will be weak and watery. It can easily take five or ten minutes to get a reasonably smooth paste, but at least it's easier than doing it the traditional way, with a coarse-grained pestle and mortar.
6 Finally, strain the sauce through a stainless-steel mesh: this is also tedious, as it takes a long time. The easiest way to do it is to use the pestle inside the strainer. You will be left with a smooth, creamy paste and a mass of pungent pulp. Discard the pulp; keep the paste in the refrigerator in a glass jar with a plastic top, as it will corrode metal ferociously.

Above: Stuffed peppers.

Left: Puerco adobado.

Right: Ingredients for adobo sauce.

Puerco Adobado

1 Smear adobo sauce thickly on pork chops.
2 Marinate them overnight (in a plastic bag, for convenience).
3 Fry, grill (broil) or barbecue next day.

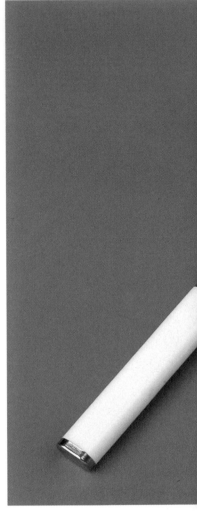

Pork in Chilli (Chili) Sauce

Above: Pork in chilli (chili) sauce.

1½ lb/675 g/1½ lb stewing pork, trimmed and cubed
1 small onion, quartered

1 whole clove garlic, peeled
a bouquet garni

SAUCE

1 tbsp/15 g/1 tbsp chilli (chili) powder
2 oz/50 g/½ cup blanched almonds
2 tbsp/30 ml/2 tbsp oil
2 large tomatoes, seeded and chopped
2 cloves garlic, crushed
1 large onion, chopped

2 canned pimientos (sweet red peppers), quartered
salt and sugar to taste
1 tbsp/15 ml/1 tbsp lime juice
2 sour apples, peeled, cored and chopped
2 thick slices fresh pineapple, cored and chopped

Season with salt and sugar and add the lime juice. Add the pork, the fruit and enough pork cooking liquid to give the sauce a coating consistency. Simmer until the apple is tender, about 10 minutes.

4 Serve with plain boiled rice.

1 Put the pork in a saucepan with just enough water to cover. Add the onion, garlic clove and bouquet garni and simmer until tender, about 30 minutes. Drain, reserving the liquid.

2 Meanwhile, fry the chilli (chili) powder and almonds in the oil until browned. Drain, reserving the oil, and blend or process to a smooth paste with the tomatoes, garlic, onion, pimientos (sweet red peppers) and a little meat stock.

3 Fry the paste in the reserved oil over a high heat until thick.

Green Sauce

10-oz/300-g/10-oz can tomatillos
5 large fresh chillies (chilis)
(Anaheim or poblano)
2 oz/60 g/½ cup chopped onion
3 corn tortillas, torn into small
pieces

1–4 cloves garlic
4 oz/100 g/¼ lb spinach, fresh or
frozen (optional)
24 fl oz/750 ml/3 cups chicken
stock

1 Prepare the chillies (chilis) by peeling, removing the seeds and veins, chopping coarsely.
2 Drain the tomatillos. Add them to the other ingredients, except the stock, in a blender; purée. You may need to do this in batches unless you have a very large blender.
3 Mix the blended purée with the sauce. Simmer the mixture for about an hour. Season to taste; add more stock if the sauce is too thick.

Above: Pork and chicken in green
sauce.

Pork and Chicken in Green Sauce

2–3 lb/1.5 kg/2–3 lb pork
1–2 lb/1 kg/1–2 lb chicken
drumsticks

1 recipe Green Sauce, as on left

1 Country-style ribs are a good choice for this: allow one big slice per person, with perhaps one spare. Alternatively, use any reasonably lean pork, cut into cubes about 2 in/5 cm on a side. You can of course use any other meat, though pork and chicken together are particularly good.
2 Boil the meat until it is very tender indeed, at least an hour: two hours is not too much. If you use ribs, the meat should be falling off the bone. Once it is cooked, fry it briefly in oil to give an attractive brown finish – though this step is more cosmetic than culinary.
3 Cover the meat with the sauce, and heat in a cool oven under 200°F/100°C (Gas ¼), for an hour or more. The important thing is to warm the ingredients through, and blend the flavours, without burning the sauce. This dish is perfect for freezing and re-heating later.

Wild boar curry.

Wild Boar Curry

¼ cup oil

9 oz/250 g/9 oz pork fat (pork fat back), sliced

2 pt/1.2 l/5 cups water

2 tbsp/30 ml/2 tbsp fish sauce

7 oz/200 g/1¼ cups bamboo shoots, diced

5 oz/150 g/5 oz small white aubergines (eggplants)

4 oz/100 g/1 cup French (green) beans

¼ cup rhizome, sliced lengthwise

½ oz/15 g/½ oz fresh red chillies (chilis)

¼ cup basil

CHILLI (CHILI) PASTE

½ oz/15 g/½ oz dry red chilli (chili)

1 oz/25 g/1 oz shallots

1 oz/25 g/1 oz garlic

½ tsp/2.5 g/½ tsp shrimp paste

1 tsp/5 g/1 tsp galanga, chopped

1 tbsp/15 g/1 tbsp lemon grass, chopped

1 tsp/5 g/1 tsp kaffir lime skin

1 tsp/5 g/1 tsp salt

2 pieces coriander root

1 Mix all the chilli (chili) paste ingredients together.

2 Heat the oil in a wok or pot, and fry the chilli (chili) paste for 3 minutes.

3 Add the pork, fry for two minutes; then add the water and bamboo shoots. Cook until the bamboo shoots are tender. Add the aubergines (eggplants), beans, rhizome, fish sauce and red chillies (chilis). Boil once and remove from heat and add basil. Serve with pickled garlic, salted eggs and rice.

Grilled beef tongue.

Grilled (Broiled) Beef Tongue

1 lb/450 g/1 lb beef tongue (whole piece)
1 tsp/5 g/1 tsp salt
½ tsp/2.5 g/½ tsp sugar

¼ tsp/1.25 g/¼ tsp white soya sauce
1 tsp/5 ml/1 tsp Maggi food flavouring

NAM CHIM SAUCE

1 tbsp/15 g/1 tbsp ground dry red chilli (chili)
1 tbsp/15 g/1 tbsp uncooked rice, roasted and pounded fine
½ tbsp/7.5 ml/½ tbsp lemon juice

1 tsp/5 g/1 tsp shallot, sliced
2 tbsp/30 ml/2 tbsp fish sauce
½ tsp/2.5 g/½ tsp spring onions (scallions)
⅛ tsp/1 g/⅛ tsp sugar

1 Mix all the nam chim sauce ingredients together well.
2 Take the beef tongue and mix with the salt, sugar, white soya sauce and Maggi. Leave to sit for one hour.
3 Grill (broil) or roast in a medium-hot oven for 15–20 minutes, or until cooked. Remove, slice and serve with sticky rice and nam chim sauce.

Muslim curry.

Muslim Curry

5 cardamom seeds
1 cinnamon stick
48 fl oz/1.35 l/6 cups thin coconut milk
1 lb 2 oz/500 g/1 lb 2 oz beef (sirloin of stewing) or chicken, cut into ¾ in/ 2 cm cubes
7 oz/200 g/1¾ cup potatoes, peeled and cut into ¾ in/2 cm cubes

1½ oz/40 g/⅓ cup unsalted peanuts
10 shallots
3 bay leaves
3 tbsp/45 g/3 tbsp palm sugar
3 tbsp/45 ml/3 tbsp fish sauce
3 tbsp/45 ml/3 tbsp tamarind sauce

CHILLI PASTE

2 oz/50 g/½ cup shallots, chopped
10 small garlic cloves, chopped roughly
6 dried red chillies, seeded and chopped roughly
5 white peppercorns
½ tsp/2.5 g/½ tsp cloves

1 tbsp/15 g/1 tbsp chopped lemon grass
1 tsp/5 g/1 tsp salt
1 tsp/5 g/1 tsp chopped galangal (ka)
1 tsp/5 g/1 tsp fennel seeds
1 tsp/5 g/1 tsp shrimp paste

1 Mix all the ingredients for the chilli paste together and fry in a dry pan until fragrant. Then pound them with a mortar and pestle or process in a blender until fine. Put to one side.

2 Dry-fry the cardamom seeds and cinnamon stick or dry-roast in a 350°F/180°C/gas 4 oven, for 8 minutes until fragrant.

3 Heat the chilli paste with 16 fl oz/450 ml/4 cups of the coconut milk in a wok or pan for about 5 minutes. Add the beef and fry until cooked, about 8–10 minutes. Add the rest of the coconut milk, bring to a boil and simmer lightly for 10 minutes. Add all the remaining ingredients and cook until the potatoes and meat are tender, about 15 minutes.

4 Serve accompanied by sliced pickled ginger, pickled vegetables and rice.

Raw Meat Salad

Raw meat salad.

7 oz/200 g/1 cup beef, chopped
2 oz/50 g/¼ cup liver, sliced small
and thin
2 tbsp/30 g/2 tbsp uncooked rice,
roasted in oven
1½ tsp/7.5 g/1½ tsp ground dry
chilli (chili)

3 tbsp/45 g/4 tbsp spring onions
(scallions), sliced small
1 tbsp/15 g/1 tbsp Lao parsley,
sliced small
¼ cup mint leaves
3 tbsp/45 ml/4 tbsp lemon juice
½ tbsp/7.5 ml/½ tbsp fish sauce
½ cup beef blood

1 Mix all the ingredients together. Place on plates and serve with morning glory leaves, cabbage, sweet basil and sticky rice.

Beef or Chicken Curry with Coconut Milk

6 pieces dry red chilli (chili), de-seeded	2 oz/50 g/½ cup shallots, chopped
1 tsp/5 g/1 tsp salt	10 pieces small garlic cloves
1 tbsp/15 g/1 tbsp lemon grass, chopped	1 tsp/5 g/1 tsp fennel seed
	5 white pepper corns
1 tsp/5 g/1 tsp galanga, chopped	1 tsp/5 ml/1 tsp shrimp paste

6 cups coconut milk

1 lb/450 g/1 lb beef or chicken, ¾-in/2-cm diced

1 oz/25 g/2 tbsp peanuts

10 pieces shallots, peeled

3 bayleaves

5 cardamom seeds, roasted lightly

1 piece cinnamon stick, roasted

3 tbsp/45 g/4 tbsp palm sugar

7 oz/200 g/1¼ cups potatoes, peeled, ¾-in/2-cm diced

3 tbsp/45 ml/4 tbsp fish sauce

3 tbsp/45 ml/4 tbsp tamarind juice

Above: Beef or chicken curry with coconut milk.

1 To make the chilli (chili) paste, take all ingredients and pan roast until fragrant. Pound all ingredients until fine and set aside.

2 Take chilli (chili) paste and 2 cups of coconut milk, fry together in a wok or pot for about 5 minutes.

3 Add beef or chicken and fry until cooked. Add the rest of the coconut milk and boil lightly for 10 minutes.

4 Add the rest of the ingredients, cook until the potatoes and meat are tender (about 15 minutes). Serve with pickled ginger, pickled vegetables and rice.

Coconut curry beef.

Coconut Curry Beef

¼ cup oil	2 tsp/10 g/2 tsp palm sugar
11 oz/300 g/11 oz beef, sliced	2 pieces fresh red chilli (chili),
3 cups coconut milk	sliced
1 tbsp/15 ml/1 tbsp fish sauce	2 pieces kaffir lime leaf, sliced fine
	⅓ cup basil

CURRY PASTE

6 pieces dry red chilli (chili)	2 pieces fresh coriander root
1 oz/25 g/1 oz shallots	7 pieces white pepper corns
1 oz/25 g/1 oz garlic	2 tsp/10 g/2 tsp salt
1 tsp/5 ml/1 tsp galanga	1 tsp/5 ml/1 tsp shrimp paste
1 tsp/5 g/1 tsp lemon grass	
1 tsp/5 g/1 tsp kaffir lime skin, chopped	

1 Pound all the curry paste ingredients together into a paste.
2 Place oil in pan, fry curry paste for 3–4 minutes and then add the beef. Fry for a further 2 minutes, add the coconut milk, boil until the beef is cooked.
3 Add the fish sauce, sugar and fresh red chilli (chili). Remove from fire, place on plate, sprinkle with kaffir skin and basil. Serve with rice.

Nam Tok Num

11oz/300 g/11 oz beef, steak or loin	15 pieces mint leaves
½ cup pork or chicken stock	¼ cup shallots, sliced
2 tbsp/30 g/2 tbsp browned pounded raw rice	2 tbsp/30 ml/2 tbsp lemon juice
¼ cup spring onions (scallions), sliced fine	½ tbsp/7.5 ml/½ tbsp fish sauce
	1 tsp/5 g/1 tsp sugar
	1 tbsp/15 g/1 tbsp dry pounded red chilli (chili)

1 Season the beef with salt, pepper and some fish sauce.
2 Grill (broil) and slice thinly.
3 Mix all the other ingredients well and add the beef. Check the seasoning, adding more fish sauce, chilli (chili) or lemon juice as you prefer. Serve with fresh cabbage leaf, fresh basil leaf, lettuce, any other raw vegetable and or rice.

Left: Red pork with rice.

Right: Kaeng Hang Ley.

Red Pork with Rice

11 oz/300 g/11 oz pork loin (or butt) fillet

¼ cup tomato purée (paste)

4 cups water

MOO DAENG SAUCE

2 cups reserved cooking liquid

NAM CHIM SAUCE

2 tbsp/30 ml/2 tsp black soya sauce

4 tbsp/60 ml/5 tbsp white vinegar

3 tbsp/45 ml/4 tbsp white soya sauce

3 tbsp/45 g/4 tbsp sugar

3 drops red food colour (optional)

1½ tbsp/22.5 g/1½ tbsp cornflour (cornstarch), mixed with small amount of water

1 tbsp/15 g/1 tbsp fresh red chilli (chili), sliced crosswise

¼ tsp/1 g/¼ tsp sugar

1 To make the marinade, mix together all the ingredients and leave for one hour.

2 Take the pork mixture and place in a pot, bring to a boil then simmer for ½ hour. Remove pork and roast in oven at 350°F/ 180°C (Mark 4) for 10 minutes. Save cooking liquid.

3 Mix the cooking liquid and cornflour (cornstarch). Bring to a boil to thicken and remove from fire.

4 To make the Nam Chim sauce mix together all the ingredients.

5 To serve, slice the pork, place on top of rice spoon. Add the Moo Daeng sauce on top. Serve with sliced cucumber, hard-boiled (hard-cooked) eggs, deep fried pork fat (fresh pork fat back), spring onions (scallions) and Nam Chim sauce.

Pork Fried with Garlic

3 cups oil
11 oz/300 g/11 oz pork, sliced into
¾ × 1-in/2.5-cm rectangles,
¼ in/6 mm thick
2 tbsp/30 g/2 tbsp garlic, chopped
2 tsp/10 g/2 tsp black
peppercorns, crushed lightly

1 tsp/5 ml/1 tsp white soya sauce
1 tsp/5 g/1 tsp salt
¼ cup coriander leaves for garnish
2 pieces fresh red chilli (chili),
julienned lengthwise

1 Place oil in a wok or pot, heat to 350°F/180°C and then fry the pork until lightly brown. Remove all but ½ cup oil, and add garlic, peppercorns, white soya sauce and salt. Stir fry for 2 minutes or until garlic is light brown.
2 Remove pork, drain well, and place on plate. Sprinkle with coriander and chilli (chili). Serve with rice and sliced cucumber.

Kaeng Hang Ley

½ cup lemon grass
1 tbsp/15 ml/1 tbsp galanga
1 tbsp/15 ml/1 tbsp shrimp paste
4 pieces dry red chilli (chili)
2 lb/1 kg/2 lb belly of pork (fresh
pork sides), cut into small strips
1 tbsp/15 g/1 tbsp turmeric
1 tbsp/15 ml/1 tbsp black soy
sauce

3 cups water
¼ cup palm sugar
½ tbsp/7.5 g/½ tbsp marinated
soy beans
2 tbsp/30 g/2 tbsp chopped garlic
¼ cup ginger, pounded
½ cup shallots, sliced
¼ cup tamarind juice

1 Take lemon grass, galanga, shrimp paste and chilli (chili) and pound fine.
2 Mix with sliced pork, turmeric, water and black soy sauce. Cook till tender and then add rest of the ingredients.
3 Boil and remove from heat, season with fish sauce if necessary – serve with rice.

POULTRY DISHES

From India
CHICKEN WITH HONEY 128
CHICKEN BIRIYANI 128
TANDOORI CHICKEN 130
CHICKEN, TANDOORI STYLE 131
CHICKEN WITH SPICES 131
CHICKEN AND TOMATO CURRY 132
CHICKEN CURRY WITH YOGURT 132
CHICKEN KEBABS 133
WHOLE ROAST CHICKEN 134

From China
MELON CHICKEN 134
SHANGHAI QUICK-BRAISED CHICKEN ON THE BONE 135
STEAMED CHICKEN AND GROGS' LEGS WRAPPED IN LOTUS LEAVES 136
ROAST GOOSE 136
BRAISED DUCK 137
ROAST DUCK WITH GARLIC 138
STIR-FRIED SUPREME OF PIGEON, BLACK MUSHROOMS AND BAMBOO SHOOTS 138
CANTONESE ROAST DUCK 139
WHITE CUT CHICKEN 140
KUNG-PO CHICKEN 140
DONG'AN CHICKEN 141
CHILLI (CHILI) CHICKEN CUBES 142
FRAGRANT AND CRISPY DUCK 143
CHICKEN IN VINEGAR SAUCE 144
DUCK AND CABBAGE SOUP 145
FRIED DUCK LIVER AND GIZZARD 145
FU YUNG CHICKEN SLICES 146
CHICKEN CASSEROLE 146

From Japan
SAKE-STEAMED CHICKEN 147
GRILLED (BROILED) CHICKEN 147
SALT-GRILLED (BROILED) CHICKEN 149
SWEET GLAZED CHICKEN 149
GRILLED (BROILED) CHICKEN WITH MISO 150
DEEP-FRIED CHICKEN TATSUTA STYLE 150

From Mexico
CORIANDER CHICKEN 151
TURKEY IN MOLE POBLANO 153
POULTRY WITH CHILLIES (CHILIS) 153
CHICKEN WITH RICE 154
BASIC SPANISH RICE 154

From Thailand
GRILLED CHICKEN 155
NORTHERN GROUND CHICKEN SALAD 156
SWEET AND SOUR CHICKEN 155
CHICKEN FRIED WITH CASHEW NUTS 156
CHICKEN FRIED WITH GINGER 157
RED DUCK CURRY 158
CHICKEN FRIED WITH BASIL 159
CHICKEN WITH RICE 160

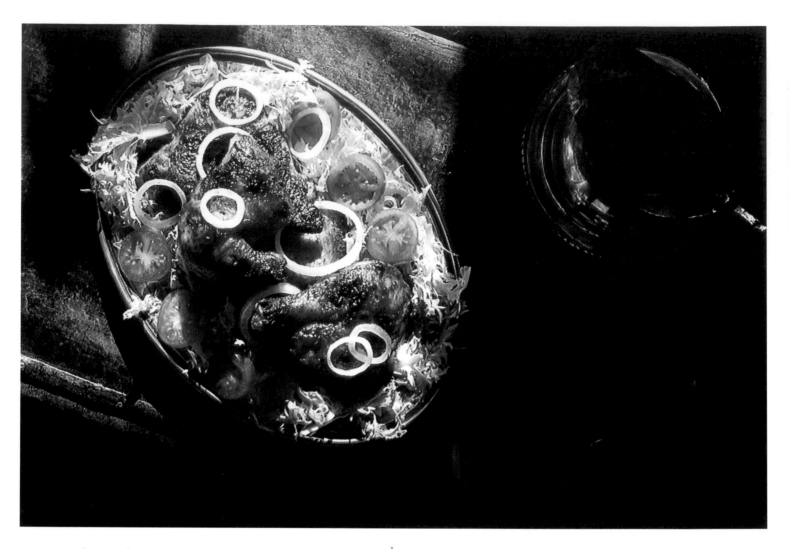

Chicken with Honey

8 chicken legs
½ oz/15 g/½ oz fresh ginger, finely grated
2 cloves garlic, crushed
2 tbsp/30 ml/2 tbsp lemon juice
4 tbsp/60 ml/5 tbsp runny honey
1 tbsp/15 g/1 tbsp paprika

1 tsp/5 g/1 tsp chilli (chili) powder
1 tbsp/15 g/1 tbsp cornflour (cornstarch)
½ tsp/2.5 g/½ tsp salt
2 oz/50 g/¼ cup butter or ghee
1 tbsp/15 ml/1 tbsp lemon juice
leaves from 1–2 sprigs coriander

1 Put the ginger and the next 7 ingredients in a mortar or a blender and pound or blend well to make a smooth paste.
2 Wash the chicken pieces, dry them on absorbent kitchen paper and prick them all over with a sharp, pointed knife.
3 Rub the spice paste all over the chicken and leave for at least 20 minutes to marinate.
4 Lay the chicken pieces on a rack across a roasting tin and cook in the oven at 400°F/200°C (Mark 6) for 45 minutes until the meat is cooked through.
5 Sprinkle over the lemon juice and garnish with coriander leaves.

Chicken Biriyani

FOR THE CHICKEN

3 lb/1.4 kg/3 lb chicken
1 tbsp/15 g/1 tbsp biriyani masala
½ oz/15 g/½ oz fresh ginger, finely grated
2 cloves garlic, chopped
leaves from 2 sprigs coriander
1 tbsp/15 g/1 tbsp chopped mint leaves

1 green chilli (chili)
2 oz/50 g/1½ cup cashew nuts
6 tbsp/90 ml/7 tbsp oil
2 oz/50 g/¼ cup butter or ghee
1 small onion, chopped
8 oz/225 g/1 cup tomatoes, peeled and chopped
salt

FOR THE RICE

4 oz/100 g/½ cup butter or ghee
2 bay leaves
8 oz/225 g/generous 1 cup basmati rice, washed, soaked in water for 20 minutes and drained

1 small onion, chopped
10 cashew nuts
2 oz/50 g/⅓ cup sultanas (golden raisins)

1 Pound, grind or blend in a blender the biriyani masala, green chilli (chili), ginger, garlic, coriander leaves, mint and cashews, adding about 2 tbsp/30 ml/2 tbsp water to make a paste.

Left: *Chicken with honey.*

Right: *Chicken biriyani*

2 Skin the chicken and cut into 8 pieces. Wash in hot water and dry on absorbent kitchen paper.

3 Heat 4 tbsp/60 ml/5 tbsp oil in a pan, add the chicken and fry for about 10 minutes, turning once. Remove the chicken with a slotted spoon and set aside.

4 Add the remaining oil and the butter or ghee to the pan and when hot, add the onion and fry until golden.

5 Add the spice mixture and cook, stirring, until the fat runs clear of the spices.

6 Add the tomato, mashing it with the back of a wooden spoon to make a paste.

7 Add the chicken pieces and salt and pour on 1 pt/600 ml/2½ cups boiling water. Cook for about 1 hour, until the chicken is tender and the sauce has thickened.

8 Meanwhile, for the rice, heat three-quarters of the butter or ghee in a heavy-bottomed saucepan, add the bay leaves and onion and fry until the onion is golden.

9 Pour on the rice and stir well over a low heat for about 10 minutes, until the rice is translucent.

10 Add 1 pt/600 ml/2½ cups boiling water, bring back to the boil and cook on a low heat, covered, for 8–10 minutes. Drain off the water.

11 Mix the rice, chicken and sauce together in an ovenproof casserole, cover with a lid or foil and cook in the oven at 300°F/150°C (Mark 2) for 10–15 minutes, until the rice is completely cooked. This dish should be moist but not too wet.

12 Fry the cashews and sultanas (golden raisins) briefly in the remaining butter or ghee and sprinkle on top of the curry.

Left: Tandoori chicken.

Right: Chicken with spices.

*Below:*Chicken, Tandoori style.

Tandoori Chicken

2 spring (frying) chickens, weighing about 1½ lb/275 g/1½ lb each
1 medium onion, finely chopped
2 cloves garlic, crushed
1 in/2.5 cm piece fresh ginger, grated
2 tsp/10 g/2 tsp chilli (chili) powder
1 tbsp/15 g/1 tbsp garam masala
2 tsp/10 g/2 tsp ground coriander
1 tsp/5 g/1 tsp ground cumin
1 tbsp/15 ml/1 tbsp ghee or oil
¼ pt/125 ml/⅔ cup yogurt
2 tbsp/30 ml/2 tbsp lemon juice
1 tsp/5 g/1tsp salt
lemon wedges

1 Skin the chickens and either halve or quarter them. Score the meat so that the marinade can penetrate more thoroughly.
2 Fry the onions, garlic and spices in the ghee or oil for a minute or two to release the flavours. Stir into the yogurt. Add the lemon juice and salt and pour over the chicken.
3 Rub the marinade well in, cover and leave to marinate for up to 24 hours, overnight is fine.
4 Drain the chicken and grill (broil) or barbecue, with the meat as close as possible to the heat source, until the outside is crisp and browned and the inside is just cooked, but still juicy.
5 Serve with lemon wedges.

Chicken, Tandoori Style

8 chicken legs	1 tsp/5 g/1 tsp chilli (chili) powder
1–2 tbsp/15–30 ml/1–2 tbsp lemon juice	2 tbsp/30 g/2 tbsp paprika
salt	red food colouring (optional)
½ oz/15 g/½ oz fresh ginger, finely grated	1 tsp/5 g/1 tsp garam masala
3 cloves garlic, chopped	½ tsp/2.5 g/½ tsp ground black pepper
1 tsp/5 g/1 tsp ground coriander	5 oz/125 g/⅔ cup yogurt
½ tsp/2.5 g/½ tsp ground cumin	1 lemon, sliced
	1 small onion, sliced

1 Skin the chicken legs, wash thoroughly and dry on absorbent kitchen paper. Slash them with a sharp pointed knife.
2 Rub in the lemon juice and sprinkle with salt.
3 Blend the ginger and garlic in a blender with 1 tbsp/15 ml/1 tbsp water, then mix with the coriander, cumin, chilli (chili) powder, paprika, red food colouring, garam masala and pepper and stir into the yogurt.
4 Smother the chicken legs in the spiced yogurt and leave, covered, in the fridge to marinate overnight.
5 Lay the chicken legs on a rack across a roasting tin and cook in the oven at 400°F/200°C (Mark 6) for about 45 minutes, until tender.
6 Sprinkle with extra salt to taste and garnish with lemon and onion slices.

Chicken with Spices

8 chicken legs	1 tsp/5 g/1 tsp ground cumin
2–3 tbsp/30–45 ml/2–3 tbsp oil	4 tbsp/60 g/5 tbsp cashew nuts
2 cloves garlic, chopped	1 tbsp/15 g/1 tbsp paprika
½ oz/15 g/½ oz fresh ginger, finely grated	1 tsp/5 g/1 tsp chilli (chili) powder
leaves from 1 sprig of coriander	1 tbsp/15 g 1 tbsp lemon juice
½ tsp/2.5 g/½ tsp garam masala	1–2 tbsp/5–10 g/1–2 tbsp salt
1 tsp/15 g/1 tsp ground coriander	5 oz/125 g/⅔ cup yogurt

1 In a liquidizer, blend all the ingredients except the chicken and yogurt to a thick paste, then stir in the yogurt and mix thoroughly.
2 Wash the chicken pieces, dry on absorbent kitchen paper and prick all over with a sharp pointed knife.
3 Smother the chicken in the spice paste and marinate for about 3 hours.
4 Lay the chicken pieces on a rack across a roasting tin and cook in the oven at 400°F/200°C (Mark 6) for 45 minutes until the chicken is tender.
5 Sprinkle on extra salt to taste.

Chicken and Tomato Curry

1 chicken, about 3 lb/1.4 kg/3 lb,
    skinned and jointed
5 oz/125 g/½ cup plus 2 tbsp
    butter or ghee
2 onions, chopped
3 cloves garlic, crushed
½ oz/15 g/½ oz fresh ginger,
    finely grated
1 green chilli (chili), chopped
cardamom seeds from 2 pods,
    crushed
3 cloves
1 in/2.5 cm cinnamon stick
1 bay leaf
8 oz/225 g/1 cup tomatoes, peeled
    and chopped
½ tsp/2.5 g/½ tsp turmeric
½ tsp/2.5 g/½ tsp chilli (chili)
    powder
½ tsp/2.5 g/½ tsp paprika
1 tbsp/15 g/1 tbsp ground
    coriander
½ tsp/2.5 g/½ tsp fennel seeds
8 oz/225 g/1⅓ cups potatoes,
    peeled and diced
¼ tsp/1.25 g/¼ tsp ground
    pepper
¼ tsp/1.25 g/¼ tsp saffron
salt
leaves from 2 sprigs of coriander

1 Heat the butter or ghee in a pan, add the onion, garlic,
ginger, green chilli (chili), cardamom seeds, cloves, cinnamon,
and bay leaf and fry until the onion is golden.
2 Add the tomato, and continue to cook, squashing it under
the back of a wooden spoon to make a paste.
3 Add the turmeric, chilli (chili) powder, paprika, ground
coriander and fennel seeds and fry until the fat runs clear of
the spices.
4 Add the chicken pieces and fry for 5 minutes, then pour on
1½ pt/850 ml/3¾ cups boiling water, add the potato and cook
over a low heat, covered, for 1 hour, until the chicken and
potato are done and the sauce has thickened.
5 Sprinkle on the pepper, saffron, salt and coriander leaves.

Chicken Curry with Yogurt

3 lb/1.4 kg/3 lb chicken, skinned
    and jointed
4 tbsp/60 ml/5 tbsp oil
2 onions, finely chopped
2 cloves garlic, finely chopped
½ oz/15 g/½ oz fresh ginger,
    finely grated
cardamom seeds from 2 pods
1 in/2.5 cm cinnamon stick
2 cloves
½ tsp/2.5 g/½ tsp fennel seeds
1 tsp/5 g/1 tsp paprika
2 tsp/10 g/2 tsp ground coriander
½ tsp/2.5 g/½ tsp ground cumin
½ tsp/2.5 g/½ tsp chilli (chili)
    powder
½ tsp/2.5 g/½ tsp turmeric
5 oz/125 g/⅔ cup yogurt
8 oz/225 g/1⅓ cups potatoes,
    peeled and diced
8 oz/225 g/1 cup tomatoes, peeled
    and chopped
salt
leaves from 2 sprigs of coriander

1 Heat 3 tbsp/45 ml/4 tbsp oil in a pan, add the onion, garlic,
ginger, cardamom seeds, cinnamon, cloves and fennel seeds
and fry until the onion is golden.
2 Add the paprika, ground coriander, cumin, chilli (chili)
powder and turmeric and continue to fry until the oil runs free
from the spice mixture.
3 Drain off the oil, stir in the yogurt and blend in a blender
until smooth.
4 Fry the remaining onion in the remaining oil until golden,
add the chicken and continue to fry for 5 minutes.
5 Add the blended spice mixture, the potato, tomato, ½ tsp/
2.5 g/½ tsp salt and 1½ pt/850 ml/3¾ cups boiling water and
cook on a low heat for about 1 hour, until the meat and vegetables are done.
6 Add extra salt to taste and sprinkle over the coriander leaves.

Far left: Chicken and tomato curry.

Above: Chicken curry with yogurt.

Right: Chicken kebabs.

Chicken Kebabs

1 lb/500 g/1 lb boned chicken, skinned and cubed
2 tbsp/30 ml/2 tbsp soy sauce

2 tbsp/30 ml/2 tbsp oil
1 tsp/5 g/1 tsp ground black pepper

1 Mix the soy sauce, oil and pepper with 1 tbsp/15 ml/1 tbsp water, pour over the chicken, turn to coat and leave to marinate for at least an hour.

2 Thread the chicken cubes onto skewers and grill (broil) slowly for 25–30 minutes, turning and basting occasionally with the marinade, until cooked through.

Whole Roast Chicken

1 chicken, about 3 lb/1.4 kg/3 lb, skinned
½ tsp/2.5 g/½ tsp ground black pepper
salt
2 oz/50 g/½ cup ground almonds
1 oz/25 g/1 oz fresh ginger, finely grated
2 cloves garlic, chopped
leaves from 2 sprigs of coriander

1 onion, finely chopped
1 tsp/5 g/1 tsp garam masala
1 tsp/5 g/1 tsp paprika
1 tsp/5 g/1 tsp chilli (chili) powder
1 tsp/5 g/1 tsp ground coriander
¼ tsp/1 g/¼ tsp saffron
1 tsp/5 g/1 tsp ground cumin
5 oz/25 g/⅔ cup yogurt
1 tbsp/15 ml/1 tbsp lemon juice

1 Skin and wash the chicken and dry with absorbent kitchen paper. Prick all over with a sharp pointed knife, rub in the black pepper and ½ tsp/2.5 g/½ tsp salt and leave to absorb the flavours for about 30 minutes.

2 Pound, grind or blend in a blender the almond, ginger, garlic, coriander leaves, onion, garam masala, paprika, chilli (chili) powder, ground coriander, saffron and cumin, then mix well with the yogurt.

3 Smother the chicken in the spiced yogurt and marinate for at least 4 hours.

4 Put the chicken in a roasting tin and cook in the oven at 400°F/200°C (Mark 6), basting occasionally, for up to 2 hours until tender and the juices run clear when the bird is pierced with a skewer.

5 Sprinkle with lemon juice and salt to taste.

Top left: Whole roast chicken.

Top right: Melon chicken.

Melon Chicken

3 large dried Chinese mushrooms
1 oz/25 g/1 oz dried shrimps
1 large melon, approximately 8 in/20 cm in diameter
3 oz/75 g/3 oz cooked ham
3 oz/75 g/½ cup drained, canned bamboo shoots
2½–3 lb/1.25–1.5 kg/2½–3 lb chicken

2 tbsp/30 ml/2 tbsp vegetable oil
2 slices fresh root ginger
3 oz/75 g/¾ cup button mushrooms
1 tsp/5 g/1 tsp salt
pepper to taste
½ pt/300 ml/1¼ cups good stock
2 tbsp/30 ml/2 tbsp dry sherry

1 Soak the dried mushrooms and dried shrimps separately in hot water to cover for 25 minutes. Slice the top of the melon off and reserve for a lid. Scrape out most of the flesh and reserve about a quarter for cooking with the chicken.

2 Drain and discard the mushroom stalks. Cut the mushroom caps into quarters. Cut the ham and bamboo shoots into cubes.

3 Place the chicken in a steamer and steam for about 1 hour. Leave to cool. When cool enough to handle, remove the meat from the bones and cut into cubes.

4 Heat the oil in a wok or large frying pan. When hot, stir-fry the ginger, dried shrimps and dried mushrooms over high heat for about 2 minutes. Add the ham, half of the chicken, the bamboo shoots, reserved melon, fresh mushrooms, salt and pepper. Stir-fry for a further 3 minutes.

5 Pack all the stir-fried ingredients into the melon. Add any excess to the remaining chicken. Mix the crumbled stock cube with the stock and sherry and pour on to the melon to the brim. Replace melon lid and fasten with a few wooden cocktail sticks. Place on a heatproof plate, steam for 30 minutes.

6 Bring the whole melon to the table to serve. This is a pretty dish and the different savoury flavours in the chicken-ham-mushroom stuffing and the sweetness of the melon give it a unique appeal.

***Above:** Shanghai quick-braised chicken on the bone.*

Shanghai Quick-Braised Chicken on the Bone

3–4 lb/1.5–1.7 kg/3–4 lb chicken
1 tbsp/15 g/1 tbsp cornflour (cornstarch)
4 tbsp/60 ml/5 tbsp vegetable oil
5 slices fresh root ginger
2 tbsp/30 g/2 tbsp sugar
3 tbsp/45 ml/4 tbsp light soy sauce

3 tbsp/45 ml/4 tbsp dark soy sauce
1 tbsp/15 ml/1 tbsp hoisin sauce
1 tbsp/15 ml/1 tbsp oyster sauce
4 tbsp/60 ml/5 tbsp rice wine or dry sherry
¾ pt/450 ml/2 cups good stock
spring onions (scallions)

1 Chop the chicken through the bone into about 30 bite-sized pieces. Bring a large pan of water to the boil, add the chicken and simmer for about 5 minutes. Remove and drain thoroughly. Blend the cornflour (cornstarch) with 3 tbsp/45 ml/4 tbsp water.

2 Heat the oil in a wok or pan. When hot, stir in the ginger for about 1½ minutes. Add the chicken pieces and stir-fry for about 3 minutes.

3 Put in the sugar, soy sauces, hoisin sauce, oyster sauce, wine or sherry and stock. Bring to the boil and continue to stir over the highest heat until the sauce begins to thicken and reduce.

4 Add the blended cornflour (cornstarch) and stir until the sauce is thick and coats the chicken pieces. Garnish with chopped spring onions (scallions).

Steamed Chicken and Frogs' Legs wrapped in Lotus Leaves

1 lb/450 g/1 lb chicken legs	8 oz/225 g/½ lb frogs' legs

MARINADE

1 egg white	½ tsp/2.5 ml/½ tsp sesame seed
1 tsp/5 g/1 tsp salt	oil
1 tbsp/15 ml/1 tbsp light soy	4 oz/100 g/1 cup fresh straw
sauce	mushrooms
1 tsp/5 ml/1 tsp dark soy sauce	2 spring onions (scallions)
1 tsp/5 g/1 tsp sugar	1–2 lotus leaves (depending on
2 tsp/10 ml/2 tsp Chinese yellow	their size)
wine	1 oz/25 g/⅛ cup ham, sliced
1 tbsp/15 g/1 tbsp cornflour	6 slices fresh root ginger
(cornstarch)	

1 Chop the chicken legs into bite-sized pieces and cut the frogs' legs in half, discarding the lower leg. Marinate the chicken and frogs' legs and set aside.

2 Cut the straw mushrooms in half and cut the spring onions (scallions) into 1½-in/4-cm sectors.

3 Blanch the dry lotus leaves in 2 pt/1 l/5 cups boiling water until they are soft, remove, rinse under the tap and pat dry. Put all the ingredients in an even layer on the lotus leaves, wrapping them up firmly and neatly.

4 Place the parcel on a heatproof plate and steam over medium heat for 35 minutes. Unwrap the parcel and trim the lotus leaves to fit the plate. Serve.

Left: Roast goose.

Roast Goose

1 young goose (approximately	1 tbsp/15 ml/1 tbsp Chinese
6 lb/3 kg/6 lb)	yellow wine
1 tbsp/15 ml/1 tbsp soya bean	2½ pt/1.25 l/6¼ cups boiling
paste	water
1 tsp/5 g/1 tsp five-spice powder	2 tbsp/30 g/2 tbsp malt sugar
1 piece star anise	4 tbsp/60 ml/5 tbsp honey or corn
1 tbsp/15 g/1 tbsp sugar	syrup
2 tbsp/30 ml/2 tbsp light soy	4 tbsp/60 ml/5 tbsp vinegar
sauce	8 fl oz/225 ml/1 cup water
2 tsp/10 g/2 tsp garlic, chopped	

1 Cut off the feet and wing tips of the goose. (If a young goose is not available, use a duck.)

2 Blend together the soya bean paste, five-spice powder, star anise, sugar, soy sauce, chopped garlic and yellow wine and rub the mixture all over the inside of the goose. Tightly fasten the neck and tail openings with skewers or string to ensure that the mixture does not run out when the goose is hung.

Right: Braised duck.

Above: Steamed chicken and frogs' legs wrapped in lotus leaves.

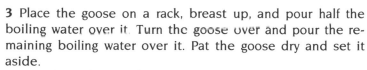

3 Place the goose on a rack, breast up, and pour half the boiling water over it. Turn the goose over and pour the remaining boiling water over it. Pat the goose dry and set it aside.

4 Heat the malt sugar, honey, vinegar and 8 fl oz/225 ml/1 cup water together, stirring to mix well, and brush the mixture all over the goose. Tie a piece of string around the neck of the goose and hang it up in a draughty place for 1 hour to dry.

5 Pre-heat the oven to 450°F/230°C (Mark 8). Place the goose on a rack in a 2-in/5-cm deep roasting pan and roast the goose, breast side up, for 12 minutes until golden. Turn the goose over with a towel (avoid using a fork) and roast for another 12 minutes.

6 Reduce the heat to 350°F/180°C (Mark 4) and, with the goose breast side up again, roast for 20 minutes. Reduce the heat to 300°F/150°C (Mark 2) and roast for a further 10 minutes, then reduce the heat to 250°F/130°C (Mark ½) and roast for a further 10 minutes. Finally, increase the heat to 450°F/230°C (Mark 8) again and roast for 10 minutes. You have to watch closely at this point to avoid burning the goose. Chop the goose into bite-sized pieces and serve.

Braised Duck

1 duckling weighing about 4½ lb/ 2 kg/4½ lb	2 tsp/10 g/2 tsp Chinese cinnamon bark
5½ tbsp/80 g/6 tbsp red fermented rice	1 tsp/5 g/1 tsp fennel seeds
2 fl oz/50 ml/¼ cup soy sauce	2 spring onions (scallions)
1 tsp/5 g/1 tsp salt	2 slices fresh root ginger
2 tbsp/30 ml/2 tbsp rice wine or dry sherry	5½ tbsp/80 g/6 tbsp sugar
5½ tbsp/80 g/6 tbsp crystal sugar, crushed	1½ tbsp/22.5 g/1½ tbsp cornflour (cornstarch)

1 Clean the duck thoroughly; place it in a large pot with its back facing upwards; add enough water to cover it, then add red fermented rice, soy sauce, salt, rice wine or sherry, crystal sugar, cinnamon bark, fennel seeds, spring onions (scallions) and ginger root. Bring it to a rapid boil and keep the heat fairly high for 1 hour; turn the duck over and simmer gently for ½ hour; take it out to cool.

2 Leave about half the juice in the pan (keep the other half for future use), add sugar and when it is dissolved, strain through a sieve to get rid of the spices; mix the cornflour (cornstarch) with a little cold water to thicken the gravy, then leave to cool. Chop the duck into small pieces, pour the gravy over it and serve.

Roast Duck with Garlic

5–6 dried scallops	5 oz/150 g/6 cups spinach
3 oz/75 g/3 oz garlic	½ tsp/25 g/½ tsp salt
9 oz/250 g/9 oz roast duck breast	2 tbsp/30 ml/2 tbsp oil

SEASONING

1 tbsp/15 ml/1 tbsp soy sauce	1 tsp/5 g/1 tsp cornflour
¼ tsp/1 g/¼ tsp sugar	(cornstarch)
1 tbsp/15 ml/1 tbsp oyster sauce	2 tsp/10 ml/2 tsp rice wine or dry
five drops sesame seed oil	sherry

1 Soak the scallops for 3–4 hours and steam for 30 minutes. Fry the garlic until brown. Cut the duck breast into 12 slices (each slice wtih skin attached) and arrange the meat in a big bowl (the skin to the bottom of the bowl), add a layer of scallops and finally the garlic. Steam for 45 minutes.

2 Fry the spinach with a little salt and oil and spread it out on a plate. Put the roast duck, scallops and garlic on top of the spinach and reserve the gravy. Boil the gravy from the bottom of the bowl in a pan. Add the seasonings and stir into a sauce. Pour the sauce over the dish and serve.

Stir-Fried Supreme of Pigeon, Black Mushrooms and Bamboo Shoots

5 oz/150 g/5 oz supreme of pigeon (breast meat)

MARINADE

1 tsp/5 ml/1 tsp light soy sauce	5–6 medium black mushrooms
½ tsp/2.5 g/½ tsp salt	5 oz/150 g/¾ cup bamboo shoots
½ tsp/2.5 ml/½ tsp sesame seed oil	¾ pt/450 ml/2 cups peanut oil
	1 tsp/5 g/1 tsp salt
¼ tsp/1 g/¼ tsp pepper	1 tbsp/15 ml/1 tbsp stock
1 tsp/5 ml/1 tsp Chinese yellow wine	½ tsp/2.5 g/½ tsp garlic, crushed
1 tbsp/15 g/1 tbsp cornflour (cornstarch)	½ tsp/2.5 g/½ tsp fresh root ginger, crushed

SAUCE

1 tbsp/15 ml/1 tbsp oyster sauce	½ tsp/2.5 ml/½ tsp sesame seed oil
1 tsp/5 ml/1 tsp dark soy sauce	
1 tbsp/15 ml/1 tbsp light soy sauce	1 tbsp/15 g/1 tbsp cornflour (cornstarch)
2 tbsp/30 ml/2 tbsp stock	1 tsp/5 ml/1 tsp Chinese yellow wine
1 tsp/5 g/1 tsp sugar	

Above: Roast duck with garlic.

1 Cut the pigeon breasts into thin slices. Mix together the marinade ingredients and marinate the pigeon slices. Set them on one side.

2 Soak the black mushrooms in hot water for about 30 minutes, remove and discard the stalks and cut the caps into thin slices. Cut the bamboo shoots into slices 1½×¾×2-in/30×20×4-mm thick.

3 Heat a pan until very hot, add the oil and after 1 minute add the pigeon pieces. Stir to separate. Remove them from the oil and set aside. Reheat the pan and add the bamboo shoot and mushroom slices. Sauté for 1 minute. Add 1 tsp/5 g/1 tsp of salt and 1 tbsp/15 ml/1 tbsp of stock, cook for 2 minutes and set aside.

4 Heat 2 tbsp/30 ml/2 tbsp of oil in the pan. Add the garlic and ginger and when the fragrance rises add all the cooked ingredients. Stir-fry for 1 minute over high heat before adding the sauce ingredients. Stir rapidly for 15 seconds. Serve.

Right: Cantonese roast duck.

Below: Stir-fried supreme of pigeon, black mushrooms and bamboo shoots.

Cantonese Roast Duck

1 duckling weighing about 4½–5 lb/2–2.5 kg/4½–5 lb	1 tsp/5 g/1 tsp salt

STUFFING

2 slices ginger root, peeled	1 tbsp/15 ml/1 tbsp Hoi Sin sauce
2 spring onions (scallions)	½ tsp/2.5 g/½ tsp five-spice
2 tbsp/30 g/2 tbsp sugar	powder
2 tbsp/30 ml/2 tbsp rice wine or sherry	1 tbsp/15 ml/1 tbsp oil
1 tbsp/15 ml/1 tbsp yellow bean sauce	

COATING

4 tbsp/60 ml/5 tbsp honey	1 tsp/5 g/1 tsp 'red powder' (or
1 tbsp/15 ml/1 tbsp vinegar	cochineal)
	12 fl oz/350 ml/1½ cups water

1 Clean the duck well; pat it dry with a cloth or kitchen paper inside and out. Rub both inside and out with salt, then tie the neck tightly with string so that no liquid will drip out when it is hanging head downward.

2 Heat up the oil in a saucepan, mix in the sugar, rice wine or sherry, bean sauce and Hoi Sin sauce, five-spice powder and finely chopped ginger root and onions. Bring it to the boil, pour it into the cavity of the duck and sew it up securely.

3 Plunge the whole duck into a large pot of boiling water for a few seconds only; take it out and baste it thoroughly with the 'coating' mixture then hang it up to dry for at least 4–5 hours, ideally overnight in a well ventilated place.

4 Roast in a moderately hot oven – 400°F/200°C (Mark 6) hanging on a meat hook with its head down; place a tray of cold water in the bottom of the oven to catch the drippings. After 25 minutes or so, reduce the heat to 350°F/180°C (Mark 4), roast for a further 30 minutes, basting once or twice during the cooking with the remaining coating mixture. When it is done let it cool for a while, then remove the strings and pour the liquid stuffing out. Use as the sauce when serving the duck.

Left: White cut chicken.

Below: Kung-po chicken.

White Cut Chicken

1 young chicken weighing about
3 lb/1.5 kg/3 lb
2 slices ginger root
2 spring onions (scallions)

SAUCE

1 tsp/5 g/1 tsp salt
2 tbsp/30 ml/2 tbsp soy sauce
1 tsp/5 g/1 tsp sugar
1 clove garlic, crushed
1 slice ginger root, peeled
1 spring onion (scallion)
2 tsp/10 ml/2 tsp sesame seed oil

1 Clean the chicken, place it in a large pot with enough water to cover. Add the ginger root and onions; cover the pot with a tight-fitting lid and bring it to the boil. Simmer for 5 minutes, then turn off the heat and let the chicken cook gently in the hot water for 3–4 hours. Do not lift the lid while cooling.
2 To serve, remove the chicken and drain. Chop it into 20–24 pieces, then reassemble on a long dish.
3 Finely chop the garlic, ginger root and onion; mix with salt, sugar, soy sauce, sesame seed oil and a little stock. Either pour it all over the chicken or use as a dip.

Kung-Po Chicken

1 young chicken weighing about
2½ lb/1.25 kg/2½ lb
1 tsp/5 g/1 tsp salt
1½ tbsp/22.5 ml/1½ tbsp soy
sauce
1 tbsp/15 g/1 tbsp cornflour
(cornstarch)
4 tbsp/60 ml/5 tbsp oil
4–5 dried red chillies (chilis),
finely chopped
2 slices ginger root, peeled
2 tbsp/30 ml/2 tbsp crushed
yellow bean sauce
1 tbsp/15 g/1 tbsp sugar
2 spring onions (scallions), cut
into short lengths

1 Bone the chicken, but keep the skin on. Cut the chicken meat into small cubes the size of a cherry; marinate with salt, soy sauce and cornflour (cornstarch).
2 Heat 3 tbsp/45 ml/4 tbsp oil, stir-fry the chicken for about 2 minutes, remove. Heat the remaining oil, put in the red chillies (chilis) and ginger root. When they turn dark, add crushed bean sauce; stir a few times then put the chicken back followed by sugar and onions. Continue stirring until well blended, serve hot.

Dong'an chicken.

Dong'an Chicken

1 young chicken weighing about 2 lb/1 kg/2 lb
3–4 dried red chillies (chilis)
2–3 Chinese dried mushrooms, soaked
2 slices ginger root, peeled
2 spring onions (scallions)
½ tsp/2.5 g/½ tsp Sichuan peppercorns
3 tbsp/45 ml/4 tbsp oil

2 tsp/10 g/2 tsp salt
1½ tbsp/22.5 ml/1½ tbsp vinegar
1 tbsp/15 ml/1 tbsp soy sauce
1 tbsp/15 ml/1 tbsp Kao Liang spirit
1 tbsp/15 g/1 tbsp cornflour (cornstarch)
1 tsp/5 ml/1 tsp sesame seed oil

1 Plunge the chicken into a pot of boiling water for 10 minutes, then rinse it in cold water and leave it to cool. Take the meat off the bone, and cut it into 1 × ½ in/2.5 × 1 cm strips.

2 Cut the mushrooms, dried red chillies (chilis), ginger root and onions into shreds, crush the peppercorns.

3 Warm up the oil, first put in the chillies (chilis), ginger root, onions and pepper, then add the chicken and mushrooms, stir for a few seconds. Now add salt, soy sauce, vinegar and spirit; when the juice starts to bubble, add the cornflour (cornstarch) mixed with a little water; blend well; add the sesame seed oil just before serving.

Chilli (chili) chicken cubes.

Chilli (Chili) Chicken Cubes

½ lb/225 g/½ lb chicken breast
meat, boned
1 egg white
½ tsp/2.5 g/½ tsp salt
1½ tbsp/22.5 g/1½ tbsp
cornflour (cornstarch)
1 slice ginger root, peeled
1 clove garlic
2 spring onions (scallions), white
parts only
1 small green pepper

1 small red pepper
1 tbsp/15 ml/1 tbsp rice wine or
sherry
1 tbsp/15 ml/1 tbsp soy sauce
3 tbsp/45 ml/4 tbsp stock
oil for deep-frying
1 tbsp/15 ml/1 tbsp chilli (chili)
paste
½ tsp/2.5 ml/½ tsp sesame seed
oil

1 Dice the chicken into ½-in/1-cm cubes, mix with the egg white, salt and ½ tbsp/7.5 g/½ tbsp cornflour (cornstarch).
2 Cut the ginger root and garlic into thin slices; cut the onion diagonally into short lengths. Cut the green and red peppers

into small squares roughly the same size as the chicken cubes.
3 Mix together the rice wine or sherry, soy sauce, stock and the remaining cornflour (cornstarch) in a bowl.
4 Heat up the oil and deep-fry the chicken cubes until pale golden; scoop out and drain.
5 Pour off the excess oil leaving about 1 tbsp/15 ml/1 tbsp in the wok; toss in the ginger root, garlic, onions, green and red peppers, the chicken and chilli (chili) paste. Stir a few times.
6 Now add the sauce mixture to the wok; blend well; add the sesame seed oil just before serving.

Fragrant and crispy duck.

Fragrant and Crispy Duck

1 duckling weighing about 3 lb/ 1.5 kg/3 lb
1 tbsp/15 g/1 tbsp salt
2 slices ginger root, crushed
2 cloves garlic, crushed
2 spring onions (scallions), cut into short lengths

3 tbsp/45 ml/4 tbsp rice wine (or sherry)
2 tsp/10 g/2 tsp five-spice powder
1 tsp/5 g/1 tsp Sichuan peppercorns
oil for deep-frying

SERVING:

4 spring onions (scallions), cut into thin strips

6 tbsp/90 ml/7 tbsp Hoi Sin sauce

1 Clean the duck well; rub with salt inside and out; place it in a deep dish; add ginger root, garlic, onions, rice wine or sherry, five-spice powder and Sichuan peppercorns.
2 Steam vigorously for at least 2½ hours; remove and discard the ginger root, garlic, onions and Sichuan peppercorns.

3 Turn the duck over and let it marinate in the juice. After about 2–3 hours take it out to cool until the skin is dry.
4 Heat up the oil and deep-fry the duck until golden and crispy.
5 To serve, either leave it whole or split it in half lengthwise. It is eaten like a Peking duck, wrapped in pancakes or steamed buns with strips of onion and Hoi Sin sauce.

Chicken in Vinegar Sauce

½ lb/225 g/½ lb chicken breast
meat, boned
4 oz/100 g/⅔ cup bamboo shoots
1 egg white
1 tbsp/15 ml/1 tbsp rice wine or
sherry

1 tsp/5 g/1 tsp salt
1 tbsp/15 g/1 tbsp cornflour
(cornstarch)
3–4 dried red chillies (chilis),
soaked
3 tbsp/45 ml/4 tbsp oil

VINEGAR SAUCE:

1 tbsp/15 ml/1 tbsp vinegar
1 tbsp/15 ml/1 tbsp soy sauce
1 tbsp/15 g/1 tbsp sugar
1 slice ginger root, peeled and
finely chopped
1 clove garlic, finely chopped

1 spring onion (scallion), finely
chopped
3 tbsp/45 ml/4 tbsp stock
1 tbsp/15 g/1 tbsp cornflour
(cornstarch)

1 Score the skinless surface of the chicken in a criss-cross pattern; cut it into oblong pieces about the size of a stamp. Marinate it with the egg white, wine or sherry, salt and cornflour (cornstarch).

2 Cut the bamboo shoots to roughly the same size as the chicken; finely chop the soaked red chillies (chilis).

3 Finely chop the ginger root, garlic and onion; mix the sauce in a bowl.

4 Warm up the oil and stir-fry the chicken pieces for about 2 minutes; add chillies (chilis) and bamboo shoots, stir a few times more then add the sauce. Blend well; serve as soon as the sauce thickens.

Above: Chicken in vinegar sauce.   *Right:* Duck and cabbage soup.

Duck and Cabbage Soup

1 duck carcass (plus giblets if available)
1 lb/0.5 kg/1 lb Chinese cabbage

2 slices ginger root
salt and Sichuan pepper

1 Break up the carcass, place it together with the giblets, if you have not already used them for another dish, and any other bits and pieces in a large pot or pan; cover it with water, add the ginger root, bring it to the boil.
2 Skim off the impurities floating on the surface and let it simmer gently with a lid on for at least 45 minutes.
3 About 20 minutes before serving, add the washed and sliced cabbage. Season with salt and pepper, then serve.

Fried Duck Liver and Gizzard

giblets from one duck (the liver and gizzard)

1 lb/0.5 kg/1 lb duck fat (or lard) for deep-frying
salt and Sichuan pepper

1 Clean and trim off all excess fat on the gizzard. Remove the gall bladder from the liver, making sure that it is not broken, otherwise it will leave a sharp, bitter taste. Now cut the gizzard into six small pieces, and the liver into six triangular pieces. Parboil the liver first – testing it by pressing with your finger to see it is still soft to the touch – remove and drain; parboil the gizzard for roughly the same length of time, then also remove and drain.
2 Heat up the fat until you can see blue smoke appearing, then fry the gizzard first for three minutes; remove and drain. Wait for the fat to produce more blue smoke, put both the liver and the gizzard into it and fry for another three minutes, then remove and drain. Serve with salt-pepper mixture as a dip (one part ground pepper mixed with two parts salt).

Left: Fried duck liver and gizzard.

Fu Yung Chicken Slices

4 oz/100 g/½ cup chicken breast
meat (boned and skinned)
4 oz/100 g/½ cup white fish fillet
(sole, haddock, etc.)
2 oz/50 g/½ cup water chestnuts,
peeled
3 egg whites
1 slice ginger root, peeled and
finely chopped

1 spring onion (scallion), finely
chopped
1 tsp/5 g/1 tsp salt
2 tbsp/30 g/2 tbsp cornflour
(cornstarch)
5 tbsp/75 ml/6 tbsp chicken stock
1½ pt/900 ml/3¾ cups oil for
deep-frying

1 Finely chop the chicken meat and fish into pulp. If you can get fresh water chestnuts, peel and boil them in water for a while, then finely chop them; canned water chestnuts have already been boiled, so just drain and finely chop them.
2 Place the chicken, fish and water chestnuts in a mixing bowl, add finely chopped ginger root and onion, ½ tsp/2.5 g/½ tsp salt and 1 tbsp/15 g/1 tbsp cornflour (cornstarch), blend them well, then slowly add the egg whites; do not stir too vigorously but mix gently.
3 Heat up oil in a deep-fryer; before the oil gets too hot, use a spoon to slide the chicken-fish mixture into the oil from the side of the pan – a spoonful at a time. On meeting the hot oil, the mixture will slip out of the spoon and form a slice. Repeat until all the mixture is used up. Turn the slices over and cook for about 10 seconds only, then scoop them out with a perforated spoon.
4 Heat up the chicken stock in a pan together with the remaining salt. When it starts to boil, put in 1 tbsp/15 g/1 tbsp cornflour (cornstarch) mixed with a little water; stir until it thickens; add the chicken slices; blend well, then serve.

Top left: Fu Yung chicken slices.

Top right: Chicken casserole.

Chicken Casserole

1 young chicken weighing about
2½–3 lb/1.25–1.5 kg/2½–3 lb
1 tbsp/15 g/1 tbsp five-spice
powder
2 tbsp/30 g/2 tbsp sugar

1 pt/600 ml/2½ cups soy sauce
1 slice ginger root
1 spring onion (scallion)
2 pt/1.2 l/5 cups vegetable oil
for deep-frying

1 Use a fresh chicken, wash and dry it thoroughly.
2 Put the five-spice powder into a large pot or casserole, add sugar, soy sauce and about 2 pt/1.2 l/5 cups water, bring it to the boil, then reduce the heat and simmer until it turns dark brown. This is the master sauce, which can be used over and over again; the flavour improves each time it is used, though after using it four or five times, you will have to add more five-spice powder.
3 Now parboil the chicken for 2 to 3 minutes, then place it in another pot of clean boiling water; add the ginger root and onion; cook for about 40 minutes over a gentle heat; remove and let it cool for a short while. Cook the chicken in the 'master sauce' for about 15 minutes, turning it over once or twice so that the entire chicken has become dark red. Remove the meat from the sauce and drain.
4 Heat up the oil over a high heat until smoking, then fry the chicken for about 15 minutes until the skin becomes dark brown but not quite burnt; remove. Chop up the chicken with a sharp cleaver and arrange it neatly on a plate and serve.

Sake-Steamed Chicken

11 oz/300 g/11 oz boned chicken breast, skin attached
1 tbsp/15 g/1 tbsp salt
2 tbsp/30 ml/2 tbsp sake
½ cucumber
4 leaves lettuce
4 lemon wedges
wasabi horseradish, freshly made
3 tbsp/45 ml/4 tbsp dark soy sauce
ponzu sauce
red maple radish
1 young leek, shredded and rinsed

1 Put the chicken in a bowl, skin side up, and score the skin with a fork. Sprinkle with salt and sake and set aside for 20 minutes to marinate.
2 Steam the chicken, uncovered, in a preheated steamer over high heat for 15–20 minutes, until just cooked. Allow to cool and slice into ¾-in/2-cm pieces.
3 Cut the cucumber into 2-in/5-cm lengths, and cut lengthwise into paper-thin slices. Salt lightly, knead, rinse and pat dry.
4 Wash the lettuce leaves and pat dry. Lay them on 4 small plates. Arrange the chicken slices on the lettuce leaves, and garnish with cucumber slices and lemon wedges.
5 Prepare the wasabi and serve with soy sauce. Serve the ponzu sauce with red maple radish and shredded leek.

Above: Sake-steamed chicken.

Grilled (Broiled) Chicken

2¼ lb/1 kg/2¼ lb boned chicken thigh
4 young leeks, washed and trimmed

YAKITORI SAUCE:
14 fl oz/400 ml/1¾ cups dark soy sauce
7 fl oz/200 ml/⅞ cup sake
7 fl oz/200 ml/⅞ cup chicken stock
4 oz/100 g/½ cup sugar
3½ fl oz/100 ml/scant ½ cup mirin

1 Combine the yakitori sauce ingredients in a saucepan. Bring it to the boil, and simmer gently for 5 minutes. Remove from the heat and cool to room temperature. Transfer the sauce to a deep jar. (This amount of yakitori sauce can be used for several meals, and should be stored tightly sealed in the refrigerator.)
2 Cut the chicken into 1-in-2.5-cm pieces, and cut the leeks into 1½-in/4-cm lengths. Thread the chicken and leeks alternately onto bamboo skewers.
3 Grill (broil) over the hottest flame, turning frequently to avoid burning. When the juices begin to drip, dip the skewered chicken into the sauce and return to the grill (broiler). Repeat this several times until the chicken is lightly cooked. Be careful not to overcook the chicken; it should remain moist.
4 Serve the chicken piping hot, on the skewers, and spoon over a little of the yakitori sauce. Traditionally, yakitori is sprinkled with a little dash of Seven spice pepper, and eaten with the fingers straight from the skewer.

Salt-Grilled (Broiled) Chicken

8 small-boned chicken thighs, skin	salt
intact	lemon wedges
2 tbsp/30 ml/2 tbsp sake	

1 Sprinkle the chicken thighs with sake and leave to stand for 5 to 10 minutes to tenderize. Thread onto skewers.
2 Sprinkle both sides liberally with salt.
3 Grill (broil) over a hot flame for 10 minutes, turning occasionally, until the skin is golden, and the flesh is cooked but still moist. Garnish with lemon wedges. Serve hot or at room temperature.

Sweet Glazed Chicken

2 chicken legs, boned	teriyaki sauce (see page 106)
vegetable oil	

1 Pierce the skin of the chicken with a fork to allow the sauce to penetrate. Brush a frying pan with oil and fry the chicken over high heat, turning, until well browned.
2 Remove the chicken from the heat and rinse with boiling water. Return the chicken pieces to the pan and pour over the teriyaki sauce. Cook until the sauce is glossy, turning the chicken so that it is well coated in sauce. Remove from heat when the sauce is well reduced and thick.
3 Cut the chicken into ½-in/1.5-cm slices, and arrange the slices on individual plates. Serve hot.

Left: Sweet glazed chicken.

Above: *Three versions of the ever-popular yakitori: (top right) grilled (broiled) chicken (yakitori) garnished with parsley; (centre) salt grilled (broiled) chicken (shio yakitori) garnished with parsley and lemon; (bottom right) grilled (broiled) chicken with red and white miso toppings (miso yakitori) garnished with parsley (see page 150).*

Grilled (Broiled) Chicken with Miso

2¼ lb/1 kg/2¼ lb boned chicken thigh

4 young leeks, washed and trimmed

MISO TOPPING

4 oz/100 g/½ cup miso

1½ oz/40 g/3 tbsp sugar

3 tbsp/45 ml/4 tbsp sake

2 tbsp/30 ml/2 tbsp mirin

1 Combine the miso topping ingredients in a saucepan. Heat until the sugar dissolves and set aside. (This amount of miso topping can be used for several meals.)

2 Cut the chicken into 1-in/2.5-cm pieces and cut the leeks into 1½-in/4-cm lengths. Thread the chicken and leeks alternately onto bamboo skewers. Grill (broil) over the hottest flame, turning frequently, until nearly cooked.

3 Brush evenly with miso topping and continue grilling (broiling). Turn the miso topped side towards the fire, and brush the other side with miso topping. Repeat this process two or three times with each skewer. Serve immediately.

Above: Deep-fried chicken tatsuta style.

Deep-Fried Chicken Tatsuta Style

1½ lb/700 g/1½ lb boned chicken, skin attached

MARINADE

4 tbsp/60 ml/5 tbsp soy sauce

2 tbsp/30 ml/2 tbsp sake

1 tbsp/15 g/1 tbsp sugar

1 tbsp/15 ml/1 tbsp ginger juice

2 oz/50 g/½ cup cornflour (cornstarch)

vegetable oil for deep frying

1 lemon, washed, dried and quartered

4 sprigs parsley, washed and patted dry

1 Cut the chicken into large bite-sized chunks. Mix the marinade ingredients and pour over the chicken. Mix well so that the chicken is evenly covered. Set aside to marinate for 30 minutes.

2 Drain the chicken and coat with cornflour (cornstarch). Wait for a few minutes so that the coating can set.

3 In a small saucepan, heat oil for deep frying to 350°F/180°C. Carefully place the chicken in the oil, a few pieces at a time, and deep-fry for about 3 minutes, until crisp and brown.

4 Remove piece by piece and drain. Arrange a few pieces of chicken on a neatly-folded paper napkin. Garnish with lemon quarters and sprigs of parsley.

Coriander chicken.

Coriander Chicken

4 small, boned, skinless chicken
breasts
1 small onion
at least 1 clove garlic
2 tbsp/30 g/2 tbsp chopped
coriander leaves

4 tbsp/60 ml/5 tbsp olive oil or
butter (or a mixture of the two)
salt and pepper

1 Chop the onion and garlic, and fry them together in the olive oil and/or butter until the onion is, in the Spanish term, 'crystalline' (tender and transparent).
2 Cut the chicken into 1-in/2.5-cm cubes. Fry with the onion and garlic until the chicken is cooked through: this should take no more than 5–10 minutes, depending on the temperature and the size of the cubed chicken. The meat should be browned slightly on the outside, but only in places.
3 Add the chopped coriander leaves; stir for a few seconds to coat; serve. The pan juices are the usual sauce: for a much stronger-flavoured (and darker-coloured) sauce, deglaze the pan with half a glass of dry white wine or vermouth.
4 Serve with plain boiled rice: enough for 4 to 6 people, depending on what else you are serving.

Above: Cooking mole in Mexico style.

Right: Poultry with chillies.

Turkey in Mole Poblano

8 lb/3.5 kg/8 lb turkey, cut into serving pieces
1 dozen ancho or pasilla chillies (chilis)
4 tbsp/60 g/5 tbsp sesame seeds
½ tsp/2.5 g/½ tsp coriander seeds
2 onions, chopped
4 cloves garlic, peeled and chopped
1 cup blanched almonds
½ cup raisins
½ tsp/2.5 g/½ tsp ground cloves
½ tsp/2.5 g/½ tsp ground cinnamon
3 sprigs fresh coriander
½ tsp/2.5 g/½ tsp anise
1 tortilla
3 medium tomatoes, peeled, de-seeded and chopped
4 tbsp/60 g/5 tbsp lard
2 oz/50 g/⅓ cup dark (unsweetened) chocolate
salt and pepper

1 Boil the turkey, in just enough salted water; simmer for one hour. Save 2 cups of the stock. Dry the turkey pieces (paper towels are useful) and fry them, a few at a time, in the lard.
2 Prepare the chillies (chilis) as described on page 37. Ideally, you should use 6 anchos, 4 pasillas and 4 mulatos, but you will be doing well to get anchos or pasillas in most places.
3 Toast the sesame seeds in a dry pan, shaking constantly. In a mortar, grind half of them to break their shells. Also toast and grind the coriander seeds.
4 In a blender, purée together the ground sesame seeds and the following: onions, garlic, almonds, raisins, cloves, cinnamon, coriander (seeds and leaves), anise, tortilla, chillies (chilis) and tomatoes.
5 Cook this purée in the lard remaining in the frying pan or skillet (you may need to add another tablespoon of fat). Stir constantly, over a fairly high heat, for five minutes; then add the broth, the chocolate (broken into small pieces, or grated), and pepper and salt to taste. Cook over a low heat until the chocolate melts. The sauce should be quite thick – like American heavy cream, or somewhere between English single and double cream.
6 Arrange the turkey in a flameproof casserole (or Dutch oven); pour over the sauce; and cook at about 200°F/90°C (Gas ¼) inside the oven, or over the lowest possible heat on top, for half to three-quarters of an hour. Garnish with the remaining toasted sesame seeds. With tortillas, beans and rice, this serves a dozen people, or six very hungry ones.

Poultry with Chillies (Chilis)

1 lb/500 g/1 lb cooked chicken or turkey
4 poblano chillies (chilis)
1 large red onion, chopped
2–3 tbsp/30–45 ml/2–3 tbsp lard or olive oil
8 fl oz/225 ml/1 cup sour cream
6–8 oz/200–250 g/1½–2 cups grated cheddar (or jack) cheese
salt and pepper

1 You can use any leftover cooked poultry, diced or shredded; the super-de-luxe version of this dish, shown here, uses shredded chicken breasts.
2 Blister and peel the chillies (chilis) as described on page 37. Remove veins and seeds; dice.
3 Cook the onion in the oil or lard until it is translucent. Add the chicken and the chillies (chilis). Cook until both are warm, stirring frequently – about 5 minutes.
4 Add the sour cream and grated cheese. Season to taste. Stir constantly until the cheese melts – about 2 or 3 minutes.

Chicken with Rice

3½–4 lb/1.5 kg/3½–4 lb chicken

Basic Spanish Rice ingredients, as below

1 Cut the chicken into serving pieces. Fry until golden; drain and set aside. In the same oil, fry the chopped or sliced onion together with the garlic. Drain, and add to the chicken, together with the tomatoes, stock and spices. Bring to the boil; simmer for about half an hour.

2 Meanwhile, still in the same oil – adding a little more if necessary – fry the rice until it is golden, stirring frequently. Add the rice to the chicken; mix well; bring back to the boil; and proceed as for Basic Spanish Rice, below. You can omit the peas.

Above: *Chicken with rice.*

Basic Spanish Rice

2 medium onions, chopped finely
at least 2 cloves garlic, chopped
at least 2 serrano chillies (chilis), chopped (fresh or canned)
1 lb/450 g/1 lb peeled and de-seeded tomatoes or 1 can tomatoes
2 fl oz/50 ml/¼ cup olive oil
1 lb/450 g/generous 2 cups rice

¼ tsp/1 g/¼ tsp whole cumin seed
¼ tsp/1 g/¼ tsp saffron
32 fl oz/1 1/4 cups chicken stock
salt and pepper
6 oz/200 g/1 cup peas, fresh or frozen

1 Purée the onion, garlic, serranos and tomatoes in a blender.
2 Heat the oil in a large, heavy frying pan or skillet and fry the rice, stirring frequently, until it is golden. Add the tomato mixture, the spices and the chicken stock; bring to the boil, stirring frequently. When the rice has absorbed all the visible liquid (10–20 minutes), add the peas; stir briefly; then cover tightly and simmer over a very low heat for another 20 minutes.

Grilled chicken.

Grilled (Broiled) Chicken

3 lb/1.5 kg/3 lb whole chicken, split in half

¼ cup garlic, chopped fine

1 tsp/5 g/1 tsp salt

2 tbsp/30 g/2 tbsp crushed black pepper

2 tbsp/30 ml/2 tbsp white soy sauce

2 tbsp/30 g/2 tbsp sugar

2 tbsp/30 ml/2 tbsp brandy or sherry

SAUCE

½ cup sugar

1 cup vinegar

2 fresh red chillies (chilis), pounded

½ tbsp/7.5 g/½ tbsp salt

3 cloves garlic or canned marinated garlic

1 Mix all the ingredients and marinate for 3 to 4 hours. Then grill (broil) over charcoal, or roast in the oven until done.

2 Mix all the ingredients and boil until thick. Cool and serve with roasted chicken. Accompany with sticky rice or steamed rice.

Sweet and Sour Chicken

4 cups oil

1 lb/450 g/1 lb chicken breast, sliced

½ cup onion, sliced

½ cup green pepper, sliced

½ cup tomato quarters

½ cup tomato purée (paste)

½ cup pineapple, diced to ½-in/1.25-cm pieces

2 tsp/10 ml/2 tsp white soya sauce

1 tsp/5 g/1 tsp sugar

1 tsp/5 ml/1 tsp white vinegar

½ cup chicken stock

1 Heat oil in wok or pot, flour chicken in bread flour and fry light brown. Remove, drain and remove all oil except for ⅓ cup.

2 Add onion and pepper to pan, and then add tomato purée (paste). Mix well, add rest of the ingredients and stir fry.

3 Finally, add the chicken and cook until the onions are tender. Serve with rice.

Northern Ground Chicken Salad

1 lb/0.5 kg/1 lb chicken meat, minced (ground) or chopped fine
4 tbsp/60 g/5 tbsp uncooked rice, baked in oven till brown and pounded fine
¼ cup sliced shallot
3 tbsp/45 ml/4 tbsp fish sauce

4 tbsp/60 ml/5 tbsp lemon juice
1 tbsp/15 g/1 tbsp dry red chillies (chilis)
¼ cup fresh coriander, sliced small
½ tsp/2.5 g/½ tsp sugar
fresh mint leaves

1 Cook chicken in a non-stick pan – no water or oil.
2 Place in a bowl and add all the ingredients except mint. Mix well, check seasoning and, if necessary, add more lemon, fish sauce or chilli (chili). Sprinkle fresh mint over the top and serve with fresh cabbage, spring onions (scallions) and un-cooked French (green) beans.

Chicken fried with Cashew Nuts

11 oz/300 g/11 oz chicken breast, sliced
2 cups oil
4 pieces whole dry red chilli (chili), fried and sliced
1 tbsp/15 g/1 tbsp garlic, chopped
⅓ cup cashew nuts, roasted unsalted
3 oz/75 g/¾ cup onion, sliced

1 cup spring onions (scallions) with white part cut into 2-in/5-cm pieces
2 tbsp/30 ml/2 tbsp oyster sauce
1 tbsp/15 ml/1 tbsp white soya sauce
1 tbsp/15 g/1 tbsp sugar
few drops black soya sauce

1 Flour chicken and fry in oil. Remove from pan, add sliced chilli (chili), add garlic and the rest of the ingredients. Fry until cooked, place on plates and serve with rice.

Left: *Northern ground chicken salad.*

Right: *Chicken with ginger.*

Below: *Chicken fried with cashew nuts.*

Chicken fried with Ginger

⅓ cup oil	2 tsp/10 ml/2 tsp brandy
1 tbsp/15 g/1 tbsp garlic, chopped	¼ tsp/1 g/¼ tsp salt
11 oz/300 g/11 oz chicken breast, sliced	½ cup spring onions (scallions) cut into 1-in/2.5-cm pieces
1 oz/25 g/¼ cup fresh mushrooms	3 pieces fresh red chilli (chili), sliced into six pieces lengthwise
1 oz/25 g/¼ cup ginger, sliced into small juliennes	½ tsp/2.5 g/½ tsp sugar
1 tbsp/15 ml/1 tbsp white soya sauce	2 oz/50 g/½ cup sliced onion

1 Place oil in wok or pot, heat, add the garlic and mix well. Then add the chicken, mix well and add mushrooms. Then add the rest of the ingredients. Stir-fry well until chicken is cooked. Place on plates and serve with rice.

Red Duck Curry

7 cups coconut milk
1 roast duck, de-boned and sliced,
skin on
15 cherry tomatoes
5 pieces fresh large red chillies
(chilis), sliced lengthwise

3 pieces kafir lime leaves, chopped
2 tbsp/30 ml/2 tbsp fish sauce
1 tsp/5 g/1 tsp salt
3 tbsp/45 g/3 tbsp sugar
1 cup fresh basil

CURRY PASTE

7 pieces dry red chillies (chilis)
3 tbsp/45 g/4 tbsp garlic, chopped
¼ cup lemon grass, sliced
¼ cup galanga, chopped
1 tsp/5 g/1 tsp kaffir leaf, chopped

1 tsp/5 g/1 tsp coriander root,
chopped
1 tbsp/15 ml/1 tbsp shrimp paste
1 tsp/5 g/1 tsp white peppercorns
½ tsp/2.5 g/½ tsp coriander seed

1 To make the curry paste pound together all the ingredients into a fine paste with a mortar and pestle.
2 To make the curry, take 2 cups coconut milk, place in a wok or pot and heat. Then add the curry paste and fry together for 5 minutes.
3 Add the rest of the coconut milk, boil, add the duck, cherry tomatoes and red chilli (chili). Boil, then add the rest of the ingredients and boil for a further 5 minutes and serve with rice.

Red duck curry.

Chicken fried with basil.

Chicken fried with Basil

¼ cup oil
8 pieces garlic clove
8 pieces green chilli (chili)
11 oz/300 g/11 oz chicken breast,
sliced
2 pieces fresh red chilli (chili),
quartered lengthwise

1 tbsp/15 ml/1 tbsp oyster sauce
¼ tsp/1 ml/¼ tsp black soy sauce
½ tsp/2.5 ml/½ tsp fish sauce
⅓ cup basil leaf

1 Place wok on fire, heat until hot, add oil, garlic and green chilli (chili). Fry for 1 minute. Add chicken, fry, add red chilli (chili), oyster sauce, black soy sauce and fish sauce. Fry further and then add basil. Mix well, place on plate and eat with rice.

Chicken with rice.

Chicken with Rice

11 oz/300 g/11 oz chicken breast, boneless

5 cups water

2 tsp/10 g/2 tsp salt

3 pieces coriander root

1 cup uncooked white rice, rinsed

2 tsp/10 g/2 tsp ginger, sliced and crushed

10 cloves garlic, chopped

3 tbsp/45 ml/3 tbsp oil

1 cup cucumber, sliced

¼ cup coriander leaf

CAW MON SAUCE

2 tbsp/30 g/2 tbsp pickled soy beans

1 tsp/5 g/1 tsp sugar

1 tsp/5 ml/1 tsp black soya sauce

5 pieces small green chillies (chilis), chopped

½ tbsp/7.5 g/½ tbsp ginger, chopped

½ tbsp/7.5 ml/½ tbsp vinegar

¼ tsp/1 g/¼ tsp garlic, chopped

1 For caw mon sauce, mix all the ingredients together.
2 Boil the chicken in water with salt and coriander root, until the chicken is soft. Remove and place on side.
3 Strain cooking liquid. Place in pot, add the rice, ginger, garlic, and oil. Cook the rice until tender but not soft.
4 Place rice on plates, slice chicken and place on top of rice. Place cucumber on the sides of the plate and sprinkle with coriander. Serve with chicken stock (broth) if desired and caw mon sauce.

Chicken with Green Pepper

¼ cup oil
1 tbsp/15 g/1 tbsp garlic, chopped
11 oz/300 g/11 oz chicken breast, sliced
1 cup green pepper, sliced
5 pieces fresh red chilli (chili), sliced lengthwise
½ cup onion, sliced
1 tsp/5 ml/1 tsp fish sauce
½ tbsp/7.5 ml/½ tbsp white soya sauce
¼ tsp/1 ml/¼ tsp black soya sauce
1 tbsp/15 ml/1 tbsp oyster sauce
½ cup fresh sweet basil leaf

1 Heat oil in wok, add the garlic and chicken. Fry well and add green pepper and chilli (chili). Mix, add the onion, and then one by one add the rest of the ingredients with basil the last. Remove from heat immediately and serve with rice.

Chicken with green pepper.

FISH DISHES

From India

FISH KOFTA 164

FISH MOLIE 164

FISH CURRY 165

SARDINES IN A THICK SPICY SAUCE 166

PRAWN (SHRIMP) BIRIYANI 167

CHILLI (CHILI) FRIED PRAWNS (SHRIMP) 167

FISH CURRY WITH YOGURT 168

FRIED SPICED FISH 168

BAKED FISH STUFFED WITH MUSHROOMS 169

FRIED SPICED PRAWNS (SHRIMP) 170

PRAWN (SHRIMP) VINDALOO 170

From China

FISH-HEAD CASSEROLE 171

FRIED BASS IN SWEET AND SOUR SAUCE 171

SLICED ABALONE IN OYSTER SAUCE WITH LETTUCE 172

STEAMED WHOLE FISH WRAPPED IN LOTUS LEAVES 172

ABALONE STEAK IN OYSTER SAUCE 173

BRAISED WHOLE FISH IN HOT VINEGAR SAUCE 174

PEPPERY PRAWNS (SHRIMP) 175

STEAMED SCALLOPS WITH BLACK BEAN SAUCE 175

STEAMED BASS IN SALTED BLACK BEANS 176

STIR-FRIED CRAB IN CURRY SAUCE 176

FRIED BASS IN SWEET AND SOUR SAUCE 177

SQUID AND PEPPERS WITH PRAWN (SHRIMP) BALLS 178

FISH IN HOT SAUCE 179

FRIED SQUID WITH PEPPERS 179

CRAB WITH SPRING ONIONS (SCALLIONS) AND GINGER 179

BRAISED PRAWNS (SHRIMP) 180

SWEET-SOUR CRISP FISH 180

BEAN-CURD FISH IN CHILLI (CHILI) SAUCE 181

CHRYSANTHEMUM FISH POT 182

FU YUNG CRAB MEAT 184

WEST LAKE FISH IN VINEGAR SAUCE 185

SWEET AND SOUR CARP 186

BRAISED FISH 186

CRAB BALLS 187

SWEET AND SOUR PRAWNS (SHRIMP) 187

From Japan

CRAB AND CUCUMBER ROLLS 189

SALMON STEAMED WITH ROE 189

SHINSHU-STYLE STEAMED SEA TROUT 190

SWEET GLAZED SALMON 191

DEEP-FRIED PRAWNS (SHRIMP) IN THICKENED STOCK 191

DEEP-FRIED SOLE 192

SOLE SIMMERED IN SAKE 193

MIXED SASHIMI 194

PONZU SAUCE 194

RIVERBANK OYSTER CASSEROLE 195

From Mexico

ESCABECHE 196

PESCADO IN ESCABECHE 196

SEVICHE 197

PAELLA 197

From Thailand

FRIED CAT FISH SALAD 198

FRIED FISH WITH PORK AND GINGER 199

PLAA LAD PHRIK 200

SPICY SEAFOOD SALAD 201

STUFFED CRABSHELL 201

FISH STEAMED WITH LEMON AND CHILLI (CHILI) 202

NAM PHRIK PLAATOO 202

STEAMED FISH CURRY 203

Fish Kofta

12 oz/350 g/¾ lb cooked firm white fish
1 small onion, grated
1 tsp/5 g/1 tsp ground coriander
½ tsp/2.5 g/½ tsp ground turmeric
½ tsp/2.5 g/½ tsp ground cumin
½ tsp/2.5 g/½ tsp chilli (chili) powder
pinch ground ginger
1 tbsp/15 ml/1 tbsp lime juice
salt to taste
2 eggs, lightly beaten
breadcrumbs
oil for frying

1 Mash or process together all the ingredients except the eggs, breadcrumbs and oil.
2 Form into small balls, roll in the beaten egg and then in the breadcrumbs, and deep or shallow fry until golden.
3 Drain on kitchen paper (paper towels) and serve hot, with cocktail sticks (toothpicks) and perhaps a choice of dips.

Fish Molie

1 lb/500 g/1 lb white fish, boned and skinned
salt
flesh of 1 coconut, grated (shredded)
3 tbsp/45 ml/3 tbsp oil
1 onion, finely chopped
½ oz/15 g/½ oz fresh ginger, finely grated
2 green chillies (chilis), chopped
¼ tsp/1 g/¼ tsp turmeric
2 tsp/10 g/2 tsp ground coriander
1 tsp/5 g/1 tsp cornflour (cornstarch)
2 tbsp/30 ml/2 tbsp white wine vinegar
4–6 curry leaves

1 Rub the fish with salt, leave for 5 minutes and then rinse under cold running water. Cut into large chunks and set aside.
2 Blend the coconut in a blender with 1–2 tbsp/15–30 ml/1–2 tbsp boiling water. Transfer to a sheet of muslin (cheesecloth) and squeeze the milk into a bowl. Return the coconut to the blender and repeat the process.
3 Heat the oil in a pan, add the onion, ginger, green chilli (chili), turmeric and coriander and fry until the onion is golden.
4 Mix the cornflour (cornstarch) with the coconut milk, add to the pan and bring to the boil.
5 Add the fish and ½ tsp/2.5 ml/½ tsp salt and cook gently for 10 minutes, until the fish is tender.
6 Add the vinegar, cook for a further minute, then take the curry from the heat and sprinkle on the curry leaves.

Top left: Fish kofta.

Top right: Fish molie.

Fish Curry

6 Meanwhile, fry the remaining onion in the remaining oil until golden. Add to the curry when the fish is cooked.
7 Sprinkle on the curry leaves and add extra salt to taste.

1 lb/500 g/1 lb white fish, boned and skinned
4 tbsp/60 ml/4 tbsp oil
1 onion, finely chopped
½ tsp/2.5 g/½ tsp fennel seeds
2 oz/50 g/⅔ cup grated (shredded) coconut
1 tsp/5 g/1 tsp chilli (chili) powder
¼ tsp/1 g/¼ tsp turmeric

3 tbsp/45 ml/4 tbsp tamarind juice
½ oz/15 g/½ oz fresh ginger, finely grated
2 oz/50 g/¼ cup tomatoes, peeled and chopped
1 green chilli (chili), chopped
salt
4–6 curry leaves

1 Cut the fish into 2-in/5-cm squares and wash well
2 Heat 3 tbsp/45 ml/4 tbsp oil in a pan, add three-quarters of the onion, the fennel seeds and coconut and fry until the onion is golden.
3 Add the chilli (chili) powder and turmeric and continue to cook for 4–5 minutes, then pound, grind or blend in a blender.
4 Heat the tamarind juice in a small pan over a low heat and mix in the blended spices, the ginger, tomato and green chilli (chili).
5 Heat until the mixture bubbles then add the fish and ½ tsp/2.5 g/½ tsp salt and cook gently for 10 minutes, until the fish is tender.

Fish curry.

Sardines in a Thick Spicy Sauce

1 lb/500 g/1 lb fresh sardines, cleaned	1–2 tbsp/15–30 ml/1–2 tbsp tamarind juice
3 tbsp/45 ml/4 tbsp oil	1 green chilli (chili) chopped
2 tbsp/30 ml/2 tbsp coriander seeds	½ oz/15 g/½ oz fresh ginger, finely grated
3 red chillies (chilis), cut into pieces	1 onion, finely chopped
2–3 oz/50–75 g/⅔–1 cup grated (shredded) coconut	¼ tsp/1 g/¼ tsp turmeric
	salt
	4–6 curry leaves

1 Heat half the oil in a pan, add the coriander seeds and red chilli (chili) and fry for 3–4 minutes until the fragrance emerges, then grind, pound or blend with the coconut.

2 Return to the pan and continue to fry, adding the tamarind, green chilli (chili), ginger, half the onion and the turmeric, for a further 5–7 minutes, until they make a thick paste.

3 Lay the sardines on a plate, smother them in the paste and leave to marinate for 15 minutes.

4 Meanwhile, heat the remaining oil and fry the remaining onion until golden.

5 Add the marinated sardines to the pan with 2 tbsp/30 ml/2 tbsp water, cover and cook on a low heat for 5–8 minutes, until tender.

6 Add salt to taste and sprinkle on the curry leaves.

Above: Sardines in a thick spicy sauce.

Opposite top: Prawn (shrimp) biriyani.

Right: Chilli (chili) fried prawns (shrimp).

Prawn (Shrimp) Biriyani

FOR THE PRAWNS

1 lb/500 g/1 lb shelled prawns (shrimp)
1 green chilli (chili)
½ oz/15 g/½ oz fresh ginger, grated
1 clove garlic, chopped
2 oz/50 g/⅔ cup grated (shredded) or desiccated coconut
4 cashew nuts

2 tsp/10 g/2 tsp biriyani masala
2 oz/50 g/¼ cup butter or ghee
1 small onion, chopped
salt
1 tbsp/15 ml/1 tbsp lemon juice
cashew nuts and sultanas (golden raisins), fried in a little butter or ghee, for decoration

FOR THE RICE

2 oz/50 g/¼ cup butter or ghee
1 small onion, chopped
2 bay leaves

8 oz/225 g/generous 1 cup basmati rice, washed, soaked in water for 20 minutes and drained
salt
4 oz/100 g/⅔ cup fresh peas

1 Grind, pound or blend in a blender the chilli (chili), ginger, garlic, coconut, cashews and biriyani masala to make a thick paste.

2 Heat the butter or ghee in a pan, add the onion and fry until golden.

3 Add the blended spice paste and fry for a further 5–8 minutes, stirring.

4 Add the prawns (shrimp) and ½ tsp/2.5 g/½ tsp salt and cook on a low heat for 3–4 minutes, stirring until the prawns (shrimp) are hot through and coated in the spice mixture.

5 For the rice, heat the butter or ghee in a pan, add the onion and bay leaves and fry until the onion turns golden.

6 Pour on the rice, stir and fry for about 10 minutes, until translucent.

7 Add ½ tsp/2.5 g/½ tsp salt, the peas and enough water to cover and simmer on a low heat for 10–15 minutes, until the rice is almost cooked.

8 Stir the prawns (shrimp) and rice together in an ovenproof casserole, cover with a lid or foil and cook in the oven at 300°F/150°C (Mark 2) for 10–15 minutes.

9 Sprinkle over the lemon juice, cashews and sultanas (golden raisins) and add extra salt to taste.

Chilli (chili) Fried Prawns (shrimp)

8 oz/225 g/1⅓ cups peeled prawns (shrimp)
½ tsp/2.5 g/½ tsp turmeric
1 tsp/5 g/1 tsp chilli (chili) powder

salt
2 tbsp/30 ml/2 tbsp oil
1 lemon, sliced, for garnish

1 Wash the prawns (shrimp) well and dry them on absorbent kitchen paper.

2 Mix them with the turmeric, chilli (chili) powder and ½ tsp/2.5 g/½ tsp salt and leave to marinate for 10 minutes.

3 Heat the oil, add the prawns (shrimp) and fry gently for 5 minutes.

4 Transfer the prawns (shrimp) to a serving dish and decorate with lemon slices.

Fish Curry with Yogurt

1 lb/500 g/1 lb white fish, boned,
skinned and cubed
3 tbsp/45 ml/4 tbsp oil
6 cloves garlic, finely chopped
½ tsp/2.5 g/½ tsp fenugreek
seeds
1 onion, finely chopped
2 tsp/10 g/2 tsp chilli (chili)
powder

1 tsp/5 g/1 tsp ground coriander
salt
8 oz/225 g/1 cup tomatoes, peeled
and chopped
5 oz/125 g/⅔ cup yogurt
4–6 curry leaves

1 Heat the oil in a pan, add the garlic and fry until golden.
2 Add the fenugreek seeds and continue to cook until lightly
browned. Remove garlic and fenugreek with a slotted spoon
and keep aside.
3 Add the onion to the pan and fry until golden, then return
the garlic and fenugreek to the pan and cook for a further 3–4
minutes.
4 Add the chilli (chili) powder and coriander and cook for 3–4
minutes until their fragrance emerges.
5 Pour on about ½ pt/300 ml/1¼ cups water and bring to the
boil. Add ½ tsp/2.5 g/½ tsp salt, then add the fish and tomato
and cook gently for 10–15 minutes, until the fish is tender and
the sauce is thick.
6 Stir in the yogurt and curry leaves, taking care not to break
up the fish. Heat through for 2–3 minutes and then add extra
salt to taste.

Fried Spiced Fish

1 lb/500 g/1 lb white fish, boned,
skinned and cubed
1 onion, finely chopped
½ oz/15 g/½ oz fresh ginger,
finely grated

6 curry leaves
salt
¼ tsp/1 g/¼ tsp turmeric
1 tsp/5 g/1 tsp chilli (chili) powder
4 tbsp/2.5 g/5 tbsp oil

1 Pound, grind or blend in a blender the onion, ginger, curry
leaves, ½ tsp/2.5 g/½ tsp salt, the turmeric and chilli (chili)
powder to make a thick paste.
2 Spread the paste over the fish and leave to marinate for
about 2 hours.
3 Heat the oil in a large pan that the fish will fit in one layer,
add the fish and fry for about 10 minutes, until tender.
4 Add extra salt to taste.

Above: Baked fish stuffed with mushrooms.

Far left: Fish curry with yogurt.

Left: Fried spiced fish.

Baked Fish Stuffed with Mushrooms

---

1 1½ lb/500–850 g/1–1½ lb whole fish, such as cod, cleaned
1 onion, sliced and separated into rings
½ oz/15 g/½ oz fresh ginger, finely grated
1 tsp/5 g/1 tsp chopped mint leaves, fresh or bottled

8 oz/225 g/1 cup tomatoes, peeled and chopped
½ tsp/2.5 g/½ tsp chilli (chili) powder
salt
8 oz/225 g/2 cups mushrooms, peeled and sliced
2 tbsp/30 ml/2 tbsp lemon juice

1 Heat 2 tbsp/30 ml/2 tbsp oil in a pan, add the onion, ginger and mint and fry until the onion is golden.
2 Add the tomato, chilli (chili) powder and ½ tsp/2.5 g/½ tsp salt and cook, mashing the tomato into a thick paste with the back of a wooden spoon.
3 Add the mushroom and continue to cook for 6–7 minutes.
4 Use this mixture to stuff the fish. Lay it in a greased oven-proof dish, sprinkle with the remaining oil and the lemon juice, cover with foil and bake in the oven at 350°F/175°C (Mark 4) for 30–35 minutes, until tender.
5 Remove skin and serve.

Fried Spiced Prawns (Shrimp)

8 oz/225 g/1⅓ cups peeled
prawns (shrimp)
2 tsp/10 g/2 tsp ground coriander
1 tsp/5 g/1 tsp chilli (chili) powder
½ tsp/2.5 g/½ tsp turmeric
2–3 oz/50–75 g/⅔–1 cup grated
(shredded) coconut
4 oz/100 g/½ cup tomatoes,
peeled and chopped

1 onion, finely chopped
½ oz/15 g/½ oz fresh ginger,
finely grated
salt
4 tbsp/60 ml/5 tbsp oil
4–6 curry leaves
1 tbsp/15 ml/1 tbsp lemon juice
leaves from 1 sprig of coriander

1 Grind, pound or blend in a blender the ground coriander, chilli (chili) powder, turmeric and coconut.
2 Mix with the tomato, half the onion, the ginger and ½ tsp/ 2.5 g/½ tsp salt. Coat the prawns (shrimp) in this mixture and leave to marinate for 10–15 minutes.
3 Heat the oil, add the remaining onion and the curry leaves and fry until the onion is golden.
4 Add the prawns (shrimp) and cook gently for 10 minutes.
5 Take the curry from the heat, add extra salt to taste and sprinkle over the lemon juice and coriander leaves.

Top left: Fried spiced prawns (shrimp).

Top right: Prawn (shrimp) vindaloo.

Prawn (Shrimp) Vindaloo

1 lb/500 g/1 lb shelled prawns
(shrimp) (or langoustines)
½ tsp/2.5 g/½ tsp cumin seeds
10 oz/25 g/¼ cup fresh ginger,
finely grated
1–2 cloves garlic, finely chopped
1 tsp/5 g/1 tsp mustard seeds
3 tbsp/45 ml/4 tbsp oil
2 onions, finely chopped
6 curry leaves

4 oz/100 g/½ cup tomatoes,
peeled and chopped
2 tsp/10 g/2 tsp chilli (chili)
powder
½ tsp/2.5 g/½ tsp turmeric
3 tbsp/45 ml/4 tbsp white wine
vinegar
1 tsp/5 g/1 tsp cornflour
(cornstarch) (optional)
salt
½ tsp/2.5 g/½ tsp sugar (optional)

1 Crush the cumin seeds with the ginger, garlic and mustard seeds.
2 Heat the oil in a pan, add the onion and curry leaves and fry until the onion is golden.
3 Add the tomato, chilli (chili) powder, turmeric and 1–2 tbsp/ 15–30 ml/1–2 tbsp water and cook, mashing the tomato under the back of a wooden spoon to make a thick paste.
4 Add the crushed spices and continue to fry for 5 minutes, then add the prawns (shrimp) and 4 tbsp/60 ml/5 tbsp water and simmer for 10 minutes.
5 Pour on the vinegar. The sauce may be thickened, if necessary, by mixing the cornflour (cornstarch) with 1 tsp/5 ml/1 tsp water. Add salt to taste and sugar, if liked.

Left: Fish-head casserole.

Below: Fried bass in sweet and sour sauce.

Fish-Head Casserole

1 fish-head weighing about 1 lb/ 450 g/1 lb	1 tsp/5 g/1 tsp salt
2 oz/50 g/¼ cup lean pork	2 tbsp/30 ml/2 tbsp rice wine or dry sherry
3–4 dried Chinese mushrooms, soaked	1 tbsp/15 g/1 tbsp sugar
2 cakes fresh bean curd	2 tbsp/30 ml/2 tbsp soy sauce
2 slices fresh root ginger	2 tbsp/30 g/2 tbsp flour
2 spring onions (scallions)	½ tsp/300 ml/1¼ cups stock
	oil for deep frying

GARNISH

spring onions (scallions)	fresh coriander
red chilli (chili)	

1 Discard the gills from the fish-head; rub some salt both inside and out; coat the head with flour.

2 Cut the pork, mushrooms, bean curd and root ginger into small slices; cut the onions into short lengths.

3 Deep-fry the fish-head over a moderate heat for 10 minutes or until golden. Remove.

4 Heat a little oil in a sand-pot or casserole. Put in the root ginger and onions, followed by pork, mushrooms and bean curd; stir for a while, then add rice wine or sherry, sugar, soy sauce, stock and the fish-head; bring it to the boil; add a little salt; reduce heat; simmer for 7 minutes.

5 Garnish with onions, red chilli (chili) and fresh coriander. Serve in a sand-pot or casserole.

Fried Bass in Sweet and Sour Sauce

1 sea bass weighing about 1½–2 lb/0.75–1 kg/1½–2 lb	2 tbsp/30 g/2 tbsp flour
1 tsp/5 g/1 tsp salt	oil for deep-frying

SAUCE

2 tbsp/30 g/2 tbsp sugar	½ tbsp/7.5 g/½ tbsp cornflour (cornstarch)
2 tbsp/30 ml/2 tbsp vinegar	
1 tbsp/15 ml/1 tbsp soy sauce	2 tbsp/30 ml/2 tbsp stock or water

GARNISH

2 spring onions (scallions)	1 small red pepper
2 slices fresh root ginger, peeled	fresh coriander

1 Clean and scale the fish, slash both sides diagonally at intervals. Rub salt both inside and out, then coat with flour.

2 Thinly shred the onions, root ginger and red pepper.

3 Deep-fry the fish in hot oil until golden; place it on a long dish.

4 Pour off the excess oil from the wok, put in the sauce mixture and stir until smooth, then pour it over the fish. Garnish with shredded onions, root ginger, red pepper and coriander.

Sliced Abalone in Oyster Sauce with Lettuce

1¼ lb/550 g/1¼ lb canned abalone
5 fl oz/140 ml/⅔ cup peanut oil
1 tbsp/15 g/1 tbsp salt
1¼ lb/550 g/1¼ lb lettuce
2–3 slices fresh root ginger
1–2 cloves garlic
1 tbsp/15 ml/1 tbsp Chinese yellow wine
2 tbsp/30 ml/2 tbsp oyster sauce

1 tsp/5 ml/1 tsp dark soy sauce
1 tsp/5 ml/1 tsp sesame seed oil
1 tsp/5 g/1 tsp sugar
4 tbsp/60 ml/5 tbsp chicken stock
4 tbsp/60 ml/5 tbsp abalone stock
1 tsp/5 ml/1 tsp Chinese yellow wine
1 tbsp/15 g/1 tbsp cornflour (cornstarch)

1 Stand the unopened can of abalone in plenty of water and boil for 3 hours. Remove the abalone from the can, saving 4 tbsp/60 ml/5 tbsp of juice to make the sauce. Trim the abalone into thin slices and set aside.

2 Heat 4 tbsp/60 ml/5 tbsp of oil and the salt with 1½ pt/900 ml/3¾ cups water in a pan. Bring to the boil and blanch the lettuce leaves for 1 minute. Remove, drain thoroughly and place on a serving dish.

3 Heat 6 tbsp/90 ml/7 tbsp of oil in the pan and add the ginger and garlic. Remove and discard the garlic when it has turned brown. Add the abalone slices and 1 tbsp/15 ml/1 tbsp of Chinese yellow wine and sauté them lightly.

Add the remaining ingredients, stir and cook for 30 seconds over medium heat. Transfer to the serving dish with lettuce.

Above: Sliced abalone in oyster sauce with lettuce.

Steamed Whole Fish wrapped in Lotus Leaves

1 whole fish, about 2 lb/1 kg/2 lb
1½ tbsp/22.5 ml/1½ tbsp dark soy sauce

2 lotus leaves
3 tbsp/45 ml/4 tbsp vegetable oil

GARNISH AND SAUCE

3–4 oz/75–100 g/¾ cup canned snow pickles
3 slices fresh root ginger
2 spring onions (scallions)
2 fresh chillies (chilis)

2 tbsp/30 ml/2 tbsp light soy sauce
2 tbsp/30 ml/2 tbsp rice wine or dry sherry
6 tbsp/90 ml/7 tbsp good stock
2 tsp/10 g/2 tsp sugar

Abalone Steak in Oyster Sauce

2 cans abalone	1 tbsp/15 ml/1 tbsp Chinese
3–4 tbsp/45–60 ml/4–5 tbsp	yellow wine
peanut oil	2 tbsp/30 ml/2 tbsp oyster sauce
3–4 slices fresh root ginger	1 tsp/5 g/1 tsp sugar
1–2 cloves garlic	2 tbsp/30 g/2 tbsp cornflour
	(cornstarch)

1 Boil the abalone in the tins for 5 hours over a low heat in 6–7 pt/3–4 l/7–8 pt of water before opening the cans. Cut the abalone in slices ½-in/1-cm thick. Save 8 tbsp/120 ml/½ cup of liquid in the cans as a base for the sauce. Heat 3–4 tbsp/45–60 ml/4–5 tbsp of oil in a pan and add the ginger and garlic, frying them until browned. Remove and discard.

2 Add the Chinese yellow wine and liquid from the abalone to the pan and stir in the oyster sauce, sugar and cornflour (cornstarch) mixed with 2 tbsp/30 ml/2 tbsp of water. Finally, add the abalone slices, stir well to mix with the sauce and serve.

Above: Steamed whole fish wrapped in lotus leaves.

Top right: Abalone steak in oyster sauce.

1 Clean the fish and dry well. Rub inside and out with the soy sauce. Shred the pickles, ginger, spring onions (scallions) and fresh chillies (chilis), discarding seeds. Soak the lotus leaves in warm water for 10 minutes to soften. Drain.

2 Heat the oil in a wok or frying pan. When hot, stir-fry pickles, spring onions (scallions), ginger and chillies (chilis) over medium heat for 1 minute. Add the soy sauce, rice wine or sherry, stock and sugar, bring to the boil and stir for 30 seconds.

3 Place the fish on the lotus leaves. Pour half the contents of the wok or pan over the length of the fish. Turn the fish over and pour over the remainder. Wrap the fish completely in the lotus leaves. Secure by tying with string. Place in a steamer and steam for 25 minutes.

Braised Whole Fish in Hot Vinegar Sauce

2 slices fresh root ginger
1 whole fish, 1½–2lb/700–900 g/
1½–2 lb

SAUCE

3 slices fresh root ginger
1½ oz/40 g/⅓ cup canned
bamboo shoots, drained
½ red pepper
1 small carrot
1 green chilli (chili)
2 dried chillies (chilis)
2 spring onions (scallions)

1 tsp/5 g/1 tsp salt
pepper to taste
4 tbsp/60 ml/5 tbsp vegetable oil

1 oz/25 g/2 tbsp lard
2 tbsp/30 ml/2 tbsp light soy
sauce
3 tbsp/45 ml/4 tbsp good stock
6 tbsp/90 ml/7 tbsp vinegar
½ tbsp/7.5 ml/½ tbsp cornflour
(cornstarch) blended with 2 tbsp/
30 ml/2 tbsp water

1 Finely chop the 2 slices of ginger. Clean the fish and dry well. Rub evenly inside and out with salt, pepper, chopped ginger and 1 tbsp/15 ml/1 tbsp of the oil. Leave to season for 30 minutes. Shred the 3 slices of ginger, bamboo shoots, red pepper, carrot, chillies (chilis), discarding seeds, and spring onions (scallions).

2 Heat the remaining oil in a wok or frying pan. When hot, fry the fish for 2½ minutes on each side. Remove and drain. Add the shredded ginger, bamboo shoots, red pepper, carrot, chillies (chilis) and spring onions (scallions) to the remaining oil and stir-fry over medium heat for 1 minute. Add the lard, soy sauce, stock and half the vinegar and cook for another minute.

3 Lay the fish back in the wok or pan and cook gently for 2 minutes on both sides, basting. Transfer the fish to a serving dish. Stir the remaining vinegar into the wok, then add the blended cornflour (cornstarch) stirring over high heat until the sauce thickens.

Pour the sauce from the wok over the length of the fish and garnish with the shredded vegetables.

Peppery Shrimps

1½ lb/700 g/1½ lb shrimps	1 tsp/5 g/1 tsp red chilli (chili),
¾ pt/450 ml/2 cups peanut oil	minced
2 tsp/10 g/2 tsp salt	1 tsp/5 ml/1 tsp Chinese yellow
½ tsp/2.5 g/½ tsp sugar	wine
1 tsp/5 g/1 tsp garlic, chopped	

1 Trim and de-vein the shrimps but leave the shells on. Pat them dry and set aside. Heat the peanut oil in a pan and add the shrimps to fry for 2 minutes. Turn off the heat and let them sit in the oil for another 2 minutes. Drain and set aside.
2 Reheat the pan and add the salt, stirring over a low heat until it is slightly browned. Transfer the salt to a saucer and mix with ½ tsp/2.5 g/½ tsp of sugar. Set aside.
3 Heat 1 tbsp/15 ml/1 tbsp of oil in pan. Add the garlic and chilli (chili) and return the shrimps. Stir-fry them over a high heat for 1 minute and add the Chinese yellow wine, stirring for 20 seconds. Sprinkle the salt and sugar mixture over the shrimps, stir-fry for a further 30 seconds and serve.

Top left: *Braised whole fish in hot vinegar sauce.*

Above: *Peppery shrimps.*

Top right: *Steamed scallops with black bean sauce.*

Steamed Scallops with Black Bean Sauce

12 fresh scallops, with shells

SAUCE

1½ tbsp/22.5 g/1½ tbsp salted	1 tsp/5 g/1 tsp pounded Sichuan
black beans	peppercorns
4 tbsp/60 ml/5 tbspp vegetable oil	1 tbsp/15 g/1 tbsp spring onion
1 tbsp/15 g/1 tbsp fresh root	(scallions), finely chopped
ginger, finely chopped	2 tbsp/30 ml/2 tbsp soy sauce
½ tbsp/7.5 g/½ tbsp red chilli	1 tbsp/15 ml/1 tbsp rice wine or
(chili), finely chopped	dry sherry
½ tbsp/7.5 g/½ tbsp garlic,	2 tbsp/30 ml/2 tbsp good stock
crushed	1 tsp/5 ml/1 tsp sesame seed oil

1 Scrub the scallops under running cold water, then remove the flat shell. Soak black beans in hot water for 5 minutes. Drain and crush.
2 Put the scallops on a large heat-proof dish, place in a steamer and steam for 8–9 minutes.
3 Meanwhile, heat the vegetable oil in a small wok or saucepan. When hot, stir-fry the ginger, chilli (chili), garlic, peppercorns, spring onion (scallions) and black beans for 30 seconds. Add the soy sauce, sherry and stock and continue to stir-fry for another 15 seconds. Sprinkle on the sesame seed oil.
4 Drip about 2 tsp/10 ml/2 tsp of the sauce over each scallop and serve them in the shells. The diners should be able to remove the scallops from their shells, then drink the remaining sauce from the shells.

Steamed Bass in Salted Black Beans

1 bass weighing about 1½ lb/0.75 kg/1½ lb
1 oz/25 g/2 tbsp pork fat
1 oz/25 g/⅙ cup bamboo shoots
2–3 Chinese dried mushrooms, soaked
2 cloves garlic

2 slices ginger root, peeled
2 spring onions (scallions)
2 tbsp/30 ml/2 tbsp salted black beans
1 tbsp/15 ml/1 tbsp lard or oil
½ tbsp/7.5 g/½ tbsp cornflour (cornstarch)

SAUCE

1 tbsp/15 ml/1 tbsp soy sauce
2 tsp/10 g/2 tsp sugar

1 tbsp/15 ml/1 tbsp rice wine or sherry
2 tbsp/30 ml/2 tbsp stock

GARNISH

shredded spring onion (scallion)   fresh coriander

1 Scale and gut the fish, clean well then plunge it into a pot of boiling water; take it out as soon as the water starts to boil again. Place it on a plate.
2 Dice the pork fat, bamboo shoots and mushrooms into small cubes.
3 Crush one clove garlic with the salted black beans. Finely chop the remaining garlic with ginger root and onions. Mix the sauce in a jug or bowl.
4 Heat up the lard or oil; first fry the garlic, ginger root and onions. When they start to turn golden, add the crushed garlic and black beans followed by the pork, bamboo shoots, mushrooms and the sauce mixture. Bring it to the boil, then add the cornflour (cornstarch) mixed with a little cold water; stir to make into a smooth sauce; pour it all over the fish.

Place the fish in a steamer and steam vigorously for 20 minutes.

Above: Steamed bass in salted black beans.

Above: Stir-fried crab in curry sauce.

Stir-Fried Crab in Curry Sauce

2 lb/1 kg/2 lb crab
2 tbsp/30 g/2 tbsp cornflour (cornstarch)
¾ pt/450 ml/2 cups peanut oil
6 slices fresh root ginger
2 tsp/10 g/2 tsp garlic, chopped
4 oz/100 g/1 cup spring onions (scallions) cut into 2-in/5-cm pieces

1 tbsp/15 g/1 tbsp curry paste
½ pt/300 ml/1¼ cups chicken stock
2 tsp/10 g/2 tsp sugar
1 tsp/5 g/1 tsp salt
1 tsp/5 ml/1 tsp Chinese yellow wine

1 Place the crab on a chopping board, belly side up, and cut through the middle with a cleaver, but avoid cutting into the top shell. Chop off the claws, lightly crush the shell and set them aside. Lift off the top shell and clean the crab, discarding the 'dead men's fingers'. Chop the body into 4 or 6 pieces, depending on the size, and lightly coat the crab meat with cornflour (cornstarch).

Fried Bass in Sweet and Sour Sauce

1 sea bass weighing about 1½–2 lb/0.75–1 kg/1½–2 lb	2 tbsp/30 g/2 tbsp flour
	oil for deep-frying
1 tsp/5 g/1 tsp salt	

SAUCE

2 tbsp/30 g/2 tbsp sugar	½ tbsp/7.5 g/½ tbsp cornflour
2 tbsp/30 ml/2 tbsp vinegar	(cornstarch)
1 tbsp/15 ml/1 tbsp soy sauce	2 tbsp/30 ml/2 tbsp stock or water

GARNISH

2 spring onions (scallions)	1 small red pepper
2 slices ginger root, peeled	fresh coriander

1 Clean and scale the fish, slash both sides diagonally at intervals. Rub salt both inside and out, then coat with flour.
2 Thinly shred the onions, ginger root and red pepper.
3 Deep-fry the fish in hot oil until golden; place it on a long dish.
4 Pour off the excess oil from the wok, put in the sauce mixture and stir until smooth, then pour it over the fish. Garnish with shredded onions, ginger root, red pepper and coriander.

2 Heat the oil in a pan and fry the crab for 2 minutes over a very high heat. Remove, drain and set aside.
3 Heat 2 tbsp/30 ml/2 tbsp of oil in the pan. Add the ginger, garlic, spring onion (scallions) and curry paste, stir and cook for 1½ minutes.
4 Return the crab to the pan, stirring, and add the chicken stock, sugar and salt. Cover the pan and cook over medium heat for 10 minutes, turning the contents once or twice to ensure that they are evenly cooked. Sprinkle with Chinese yellow wine and serve.

Right: Fried bass in sweet and sour sauce.

Squid and Peppers with Prawn (Shrimp) Balls

1 lb/0.5 kg/1 lb squid
½ lb/225 g/½ lb green peppers
1 tsp/5 g/1 tsp salt
1 tsp/5 g/1 tsp sugar
1 tbsp/15 ml/1 tbsp crushed black
bean sauce
2 green chillies (chilis)
1 slice ginger root, peeled

1 spring onion (scallion)
1 tbsp/15 ml/1 tbsp rice wine (or
sherry)
1 tbsp/15 ml/1 tbsp soy sauce
oil for deep-frying
20 deep-fried prawn (shrimp)
balls

1 Discard the soft bone, head and ink bag of the squid; peel off the skin and make a criss-cross pattern on the outside, then cut into slices not much bigger than a matchbox.

2 Cut the green peppers into slices roughtly the same size as the squid; finely chop the ginger root, onion and green chilli (chili).

3 Deep-fry the squid for 1 minute; remove and drain. Pour off the excess oil leaving about 2 tbsp/30 ml/2 tbsp in the wok. Toss in the ginger root, onion and chillies (chilis) followed by green peppers; add salt and sugar; stir for a short while then add the squid together with the crushed black bean sauce, rice wine or sherry and soy sauce. Cook for about 1½ minutes and blend everything well. Serve with deep-fried prawn (shrimp) balls decorating the edge of the plate.

Left: Squid and pepper with prawn (shrimp) balls.

Right: Fish in hot sauce (top) and 'pock-marked woman' bean-curd (bottom).

Opposite, left: Fried squid with peppers.

Opposite, right: Crab with spring onions (scallions) and ginger.

Fish in Hot Sauce

1 freshwater fish weighing about 1½ lb/0.75 kg/1½ lb	8 fl oz/250 ml/1 cup stock
2 tbsp/30 ml/2 tbsp chilli (chili) paste	2 slices ginger root, peeled and finely chopped
1 tbsp/15 ml/1 tbsp tomato purée (paste)	1 clove garlic, finely chopped
1 tbsp/15 ml/1 tbsp soy sauce	1 tbsp/15 ml/1 tbsp vinegar
2 tbsp/30 ml/2 tbsp rice wine or sherry	2 spring onions (scallions), finely chopped
½ tbsp/7.5 g/½ tbsp sugar	1 tbsp/15 ml/1 tbsp cornflour (cornstarch)
	oil for deep-frying

1 Scale and gut the fish, clean well. Slash each side diagonally four or five times as deep as the bone.
2 Heat up the oil, deep-fry the fish until golden, turning it over once or twice; remove and drain.
3 Pour off the excess oil leaving about 1 tbsp/15 ml/1 tbsp in the wok; put in the chilli (chili) paste, tomato purée (paste), soy sauce, rice wine or sherry, sugar, stock, finely chopped ginger root and garlic. Bring it to the boil, put the fish back; reduce heat and cook gently for a few minutes turning it over two or three times.
4 Place the fish on a serving dish. Increase the heat, add vinegar and onions to the sauce, thicken it with the cornflour (cornstarch) then pour it over the fish and serve.

Fried Squid with Peppers

¾ lb/350 g/¾ lb squid	½ tsp/2.5 g/½ tsp fresh ground black pepper
1 red pepper	
2 slices ginger root, peeled	1 tsp/5 ml/1 tsp vinegar
1 tsp/5 g/1 tsp salt	1 tsp/5 ml/1 tsp sesame seed oil
1 tbsp/15 ml/1 tbsp rice wine or sherry	oil for deep-frying
1 tbsp/15 ml/1 tbsp soy sauce	fresh coriander for garnish

1 Discard the head, transparent backbone and ink bag of the squid. Peel off the thin skin and score a criss-cross pattern on the outside, then cut into small pieces the size of a matchbox.
2 Thinly shred the red pepper and ginger root.
3 Deep-fry the squid in oil over a moderate heat for 30 seconds; scoop out and drain. Pour off the excess oil, leaving about 1 tbsp/15 ml/1 tbsp in the wok; toss in the ginger root and red pepper followed by the squid; add salt, rice wine or sherry, soy sauce, black pepper and vinegar. Stir-fry for about 1 minute, add sesame seed oil and serve. Garnish with coriander.

Crab with Spring Onions (Scallions) and Ginger

1 lb/0.5 kg/1 lb crab	1 tbsp/15 g/1 tbsp cornflour (cornstarch)
4–5 spring onions (scallions), finely chopped	2 tbsp/30 ml/2 tbsp soy sauce
4–6 slices ginger root, peeled and finely chopped	1 tbsp/15 g/1 tbsp sugar
2 tbsp/30 ml/2 tbsp rice wine or sherry	1 tbsp/15 ml/1 tbsp vinegar
	4 tbsp/60 ml/5 tbsp oil
	greens to garnish

1 Separate the legs and claws of the crabs. If the crabs are large, break the body into two or three pieces. Heat up the oil and fry the crab pieces until golden. Remove and drain.
2 Toss in the finely chopped onions and ginger root in what is left of the oil in the wok; add soy sauce, sugar, rice wine or sherry and vinegar. Thicken with cornflour (cornstarch) mixed with a little cold water, then return the crab pieces to be coated by this sauce. Blend well and serve.

Decorate the plate with greens or other garnishes.

Braised Prawns (Shrimp)

½ lb/225 g/½ lb prawns (shrimp), unshelled
1 tbsp/15 ml/1 tbsp rice wine or sherry
4 tbsp/60 ml/5 tbsp stock
4 dried red chillies (chilis), soaked and finely chopped
1 tbsp/15 ml/1 tbsp chilli (chili) paste
½ tbsp/7.5 ml/½ tbsp Kao Liang spirit
1 slice ginger root, peeled and finely chopped
1 spring onion (scallion), finely chopped
1 tsp/5 g/1 tsp salt
½ tsp/2.5 g/½ tsp Sichuan pepper
2 tbsp/30 ml/2 tbsp tomato purée (paste)
1 tbsp/15 g/1 tbsp cornflour (cornstarch)
oil for deep-frying
½ tsp/2.5 g/½ tsp sesame seed oil

1 Clean the prawns (shrimp), cut them into two or three pieces and keep the shells on.
2 Heat up the oil and deep-fry the prawns (shrimp) until they turn bright pink. Scoop them out and pour off the excess oil. Put the prawns (shrimp) back in the pan, together with the rice wine or sherry and a little stock; cook for about 1 minute; remove.
3 Heat about 1 tbsp/15 ml/1 tbsp oil in the wok; add the red chillies (chilis), chilli (chili) paste, Kao Liang spirit, ginger root, onions, salt and pepper, the remaining stock and the prawns (shrimp). Reduce heat and braise for 2 minutes, then add the tomato purée (paste) and the cornflour (cornstarch) mixed with a little water. Blend well; add sesame seed oil and serve.

Above: Braised prawns (shrimp).

Right: Sweet-sour crisp fish.

Below right: Bean-curd fish in chili sauce.

Sweet-Sour Crisp Fish

1 carp (or freshwater fish) weighing 1½ lb/0.75 kg/1½ lb
2 tbsp/30 ml/2 tbsp rice wine or sherry
4 tbsp/60 ml/5 tbsp soy sauce
2 oz/50 g/½ cup cornflour (cornstarch)
1 clove garlic
2 spring onions (scallions)
2 slices ginger root, peeled
2 dried red chillies (chilis), soaked
1 oz/25 g/⅙ cup bamboo shoots
2–3 Chinese dried mushrooms, soaked
oil for deep-frying
1½ tbsp/22.5 g/1½ tbsp sugar
1½ tbsp/22.5 ml/1½ tbsp vinegar
4 fl oz/100 ml/½ cup stock

1 Clean the fish; make six or seven diagonal cuts as deep as the bone on each side of the fish. Marinate in rice wine or sherry and 2 tbsp/30 ml/2 tbsp soy sauce for 5 minutes; remove and wipe dry. Make a paste with 1½ oz/40 g/⅜ cup cornflour (cornstarch) and water and coat the entire fish evenly.
2 Finely chop the garlic, 1 onion and 1 slice ginger root. Cut the other onion and ginger root into thin shreds. Cut the soaked red chillies (chilis) (discarding the seeds), bamboo shoots and mushrooms all into thin shreds.
3 Heat up the oil to boiling point, pick up the fish by the tail, lower it head first into the oil, turn it around and deep fry for about 7 minutes or until golden; remove and drain.
4 Pour off the excess oil leaving about 2 tbsp/30 ml/2 tbsp in the wok; add finely chopped onion, ginger root, garlic and red chilli (chili), bamboo shoots and mushrooms followed by the remaining soy sauce, sugar, vinegar and stock. Stir a few times, then add the remaining cornflour (cornstarch) mixed with a little water; blend well to make a slightly thick smooth sauce.
5 Place a cloth over the fish, press gently with your hand to soften the body, then put it on a serving dish and pour the sauce over it; garnish with onion and ginger root shreds.

Bean-Curd Fish in Chilli (Chili) Sauce

1 lb/0.5 kg/1 lb mullet or mackerel
2 spring onions (scallions), white parts only
1 clove garlic
2 slices ginger root, peeled
2 cakes bean-curd
1 tsp/5 g/1 tsp salt
4 tbsp/60 ml/5 tbsp oil
2 tbsp/30 ml/2 tbsp chilli (chili) paste
1 tbsp/15 ml/1 tbsp soy sauce
2 tbsp/30 ml/2 tbsp rice wine (or sherry)
1 tbsp/15 g/1 tbsp cornflour (cornstarch)
12 fl oz/350 ml/2 cups stock

1 Cut the heads off the fish and remove the backbone; crush the garlic, cut it and the ginger root into small pieces; cut the onion whites into short lengths.
2 Cut each bean-curd into about 10 pieces. Blanch them in boiling water; remove and soak them in stock with salt.
3 Heat up the oil until hot; fry the fish until both sides are golden; put them to one side; tilt the wok, and put in the chilli (chili) paste. When it starts to bubble, return the wok to its original position, push the fish back, add soy sauce, rice wine or sherry, onion, ginger root, garlic and a little stock – about 4 fl oz/100 ml/½ cup. At the same time add the bean-curd taken from the stock and cook with the fish for about 10 minutes.
4 Now pick out the fish with chopsticks and place them on a serving dish, then quickly mix the cornflour (cornstarch) with a little cold water. Add to the wok to make a smooth sauce with the bean-curd; pour it all over the fish and serve.

Chrysanthemum Fish Pot

4 oz/100 g/4 oz fish maw
4 oz/100 g/½ cup chicken breast
    meat, boned and skinned
2 chicken gizzards
½ lb/225 g/½ lb pig's tripe
4 oz/100 g/4 oz Beche-de-mer
4 oz/100 g/⅔ cup mange-tout
    (snow) peas
½ lb/225 g/½ lb spinach leaves

2 oz/50 g/1½ cups fresh coriander
2 slices ginger root, peeled
2–3 spring onions (scallions)
2 tsp/10 g/2 tsp salt
1 tsp/5 g/1 tsp freshly ground
Sichuan pepper
3½ pts/2 l/9 cups stock
1 large chrysanthemum (white or
yellow)

1 Cut the fish maw, chicken gizzards, Beche-de-mer and tripe
into slices.
2 Wash the cabbage, mange-tout (snow) peas, spinach and
coriander; cut them into small pieces.
3 Finely chop the ginger root and onions; place them with salt
and pepper in a small bowl. These are the 'four seasonings'.
4 Bring the stock to a rolling boil in the fire-pot; arrange the
meat and vegetables in the moat. They will only need to be
cooked for about five minutes. Everybody just helps themselves from the pot with chopsticks, and dips their helping in
the 'four seasonings' before eating it.

Chrysanthemum fish pot.

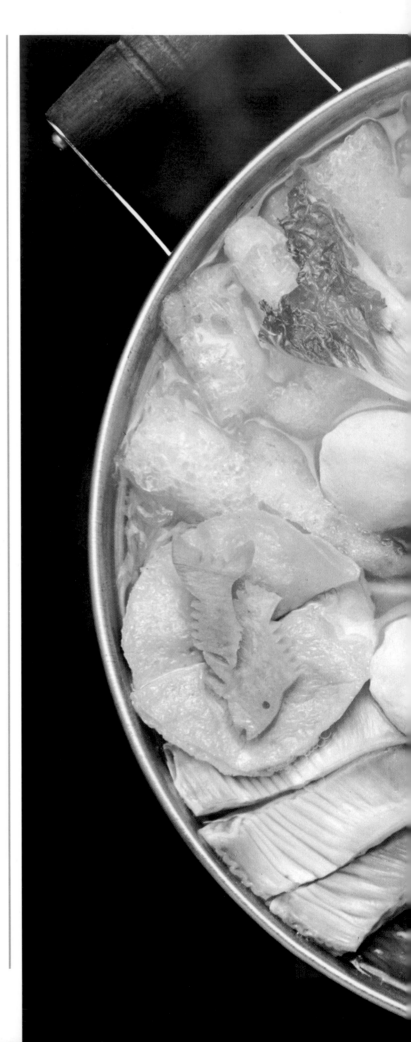

Fu Yung Crab Meat

10 oz/275 g/1¼ cups crab meat
3 tbsp/45 ml/4 tbsp lard
2 tbsp/30 ml/2 tbsp rice wine or
sherry
1 tbsp/15 ml/1 tbsp soy sauce
1 tbsp/15 ml/1 tbsp wine vinegar
1 tbsp/15 g/1 tbsp sugar
6 egg whites
1 tsp/5 g/1 tsp cornflour
(cornstarch)

2 cloves garlic, finely chopped
1 slice ginger root, peeled and
finely chopped
2 spring onions (scallions), finely
chopped
2 large crab shells (or 4 small
ones)
3 tbsp/45 ml/4 tbsp stock

1 Warm up about 2 tbsp/30 ml/2 tbsp lard; fry about half of the finely chopped ginger root and onions followed by the crab meat. Add rice wine or sherry, continue stirring until all the liquid has evaporated, then put the crab meat into the empty shells.

2 Beat the egg whites with salt and a little water until foamy; pour on top of the crab meat and steam the stuffed shells vigorously for 6 minutes. By then the egg whites will have become solid. Remove and place them on a long serving dish.

3 Heat the last 1 tbsp/15 ml/1 tbsp lard, add the finely chopped garlic together with the remaining onion and ginger root, followed by soy sauce, vinegar, sugar and stock. When it starts to bubble, add the cornflour (cornstarch) mixed with a little cold water. When it is smooth and thickened pour it over the crab meat and serve.

Above: Fu yung crab meat.

Right: West lake fish in vinegar sauce.

West Lake Fish in Vinegar Sauce

1 *mirror carp weighing about 1 ½ lb/0.75 kg/1 ½ lb*	2 *tbsp/30 ml/2 tbsp soy sauce*
2 *slices ginger root, peeled and finely chopped*	2 *tbsp/30 g/2 tbsp sugar*
1 *tbsp/15 ml/1 tbsp Shaoxing wine or sherry*	1 *tbsp/15 ml/1 tbsp vinegar*
	1 *tbsp/15 g/1 tbsp cornflour (cornstarch)*
	2–2½ *pt/about 1 l/6 cups water*

1 Scale and gut the fish; clean well. Split it in half lengthways with its back bone still attached to one half, known as the male side (the half without the bone is known as the female side).

2 Score the 'male' side through the skin five times not quite as deep as the bone, but cut all the way down at the third cut so it becomes two halves. Then score the 'female' side through the flesh not quite as deep as the skin.

3 Bring the water to the boil, put in the fish opened out with skin side up and the tail piece on top, but try to keep the head out of the water. Place the lid on and boil rapidly for 5 minutes; ladle out most of the water leaving about ¼ pt/150 ml/⅔ cup in the pan.

4 Add soy sauce, wine and half the ginger root, then immediately scoop the fish out; place it on a plate still with skin side up and the tail piece restored to its original position. Add sugar and the remaining ginger root together with the corn-flour (cornstarch) mixed with the vinegar; stir to make a thickish smooth gravy. Pour it all over the fish and serve. This is the traditional way of cooking West Lake fish, which is supposed to resemble crab in its flavour.

Above: *Sweet and sour carp (see page 186).*

Sweet and Sour Carp

(see picture on page 185)

1 Yellow River carp weighing
about 1 ½ lb/0.75 kg/1 ½ lb
a little salt
a little flour
oil for deep-frying
5–6 wooden ears, soaked

4–5 water chestnuts, peeled
2 oz/50 g/⅓ cup bamboo shoots
2–3 spring onions (scallions)
2 slices ginger root, peeled
1 clove garlic, finely chopped

FOR THE SAUCE:

3 tbsp/45 ml/4 tbsp wine vinegar
3 tbsp/45 ml/4 tbsp sugar
2 tbsp/30 ml/2 tbsp soy sauce
2 tbsp/30 ml/2 tbsp rice wine or
sherry

2 tsp/10 g/2 tsp cornflour
(cornstarch)
¼ pt/150 ml/⅔ cup clear stock

1 Scale and gut the carp and clean thoroughly. Score the fish on both sides diagonally in a crisscross pattern down to the bone. Lift the fish up by the ends so the cuts open up, spread a little salt into them followed by a little flour, then coat the whole fish from head to tail with flour.

2 Cut the wooden ears into thin slices together with the bamboo shoots and water chestnuts. Shred the onions and ginger root into the size of matches, and finely chop the garlic.

3 Heat up the oil in a wok until it smokes. Holding the fish by the tail, gently lower it into the hot oil, bending the body so that the cuts open up; use a spatula beneath the body to prevent it from sticking to the wok.

4 After 2 minutes turn the fish on its side with its stomach facing up, still holding the tail to make sure the body is kept curved. Cook for 2 more minutes, then turn the fish over so that its stomach is now facing down; after 2 minutes cook the fish on its flat side again, tilting the wok so that the head is in the oil. When the fish has been cooked for 8 minutes in all, take it out (carefully!) and place it on a long dish.

5 Pour off the excess oil and leave about 2 tbsp/30 ml/2 tbsp oil in the wok. Fry the onions, ginger root and garlic; add the vinegar followed by the rest of the ingredients, together with the sauce mixture; stir and bring to the boil; pour it all over the fish and serve.

Braised Fish

1 Yellow River carp weighing
about 1 ½ lb/0.75 kg/1 ½ lb
2 tbsp/30 ml/2 tbsp soy sauce
½ tbsp/7.5 g/½ tbsp sugar
1 pt/600 ml/2½ cups clear stock
1 ½ tbsp/22.5 ml/1 ½ tbsp rice
wine or sherry

1 tbsp/15 ml/1 tbsp crushed
yellow bean sauce
2 spring onions (scallions), finely
chopped
1 slice ginger root, peeled and
finely chopped
oil for deep-frying

1 Should you find the Yellow River a little too far for you to catch your carp, then by all means use any freshwater fish, only do not expect the same result. No other fish has quite the same taste and I think it is an experience everyone has the right to at least once in their lifetime.

2 Scale and gut the fish and clean it thoroughly. Score both sides of the fish diagonally down to the bone at intervals of about ¼ in/6 mm. There are two reasons for doing this; since the fish is to be cooked whole, it prevents the skin from bursting; and it allows the heat to penetrate quickly and at the same time helps to diffuse the flavour of the seasoning and sauce.

3 Heat up about 1¾ pt/1 l/4¼ cups oil in a wok or deep-fryer, fry the fish until golden, take it out and drain.

4 Leave about 1 tbsp/15 ml/1 tbsp oil in the wok, put in the finely chopped onions, ginger root and sugar; stir to dissolve the sugar, then add the bean sauce, followed by the rice wine or sherry, soy sauce, stock and the fish. Bring to the boil, then reduce the heat and cook until the juice is reduced by half; turn the fish over and continue cooking until the juice is almost completely evaporated.

5 Be careful not to break up the fish when lifting it out of the wok; it does not look right unless the fish is served whole with both head and tail intact.

Above: Braised fish.

Opposite, left: Crab balls.

Opposite, right: Sweet and sour prawns (shrimp).

Crab Balls

½ lb/225 g/1 cup crab meat
2 oz/50 g/¼ cup pork fat
2 oz/50 g/½ cup water chestnuts, peeled
2 eggs
2 tbsp/30 ml/2 tbsp rice wine or sherry
1 tsp/5 ml/1 tsp monosodium glutamate
1 tsp/5 g/1 tsp salt

2 tbsp/30 g/2 tbsp cornflour (cornstarch)
1 slice peeled ginger root, finely chopped
1 spring onion (scallion), finely chopped
4 fl oz/100 ml/½ cup chicken stock
1 lb/0.5 kg/2 cups lards for deep-frying
1 oz/25 g/2 tbsp cooked ham

1 Finely chop the crab meat, pork fat and water chestnuts and add 2 eggs, 1 tbsp/15 ml/1 tbsp wine or sherry, ½ tsp/2.5 ml/½ tsp monosodium glutamate, ½ tsp/2.5 g/½ tsp salt, and 1 tbsp/15 g/1 tbsp cornflour (cornstarch) together with the finely chopped ginger root and onion. Blend well, then make into small balls about the size of walnuts.
2 Heat up the lard over high heat for about 3–4 minutes, then reduce the heat to moderate and deep-fry the crab balls for about 5 minutes until pale golden. Scoop them out with a perforated spoon and serve them hot or cold. Alternatively place them in a bowl with a little chicken stock – not quite enough to cover them – then place the bowl in a steamer and steam for 15 minutes.
3 Now mix the remaining sherry, monosodium glutamate, salt and cornflour (cornstarch) with the chicken stock and make a white sauce over a moderate heat, then pour it over the crab balls. Garnish with finely chopped ham and serve.

This dish is delicious as well as being very pretty to look at.

Sweet and Sour Prawns (Shrimp)

1 lb/0.5 kg/1 lb unshelled, uncooked Pacific prawns (shrimp)
1 egg white
2 tbsp/30 g/2 tbsp sugar
2 slices ginger root, peeled
1½ tbsp/22.5 g/1½ tbsp cornflour (cornstarch)

1½ tbsp/22.5 ml/1½ tbsp vinegar
1 spring onion (scallion)
2 tbsp/30 ml/2 tbsp chicken stock
oil for deep-frying

1 Shell the prawns (shrimp), make a shallow incision down the back of each prawn (shrimp) and remove the black intestinal parts. Wash and clean, then cut each prawn (shrimp) in half lengthwise.
   Make a criss-cross pattern on each half and marinate them with the egg white and ½ tbsp/7.5 g/½ tbsp cornflour (cornstarch).
2 Finely chop the onion and ginger root. Heat up about 1¾ pt/1 l/4¼ cups oil in a wok and, before the oil gets too hot, put in the prawns (shrimp) piece by piece; fry until golden, take them out and drain.
3 Leave about 1 tbsp/15 ml/1 tbsp oil on the wok; stir-fry the finely chopped onion and ginger root until their colour changes, then put in the prawns (shrimp), stir and add sugar and continue stirring until all the sugar has dissolved. Add the remaining cornflour (cornstarch) mixed with the chicken stock, blend well, then serve.

   You will find this dish quite different from the ones you have tasted in ordinary Chinese restaurants; the secret is in the method of cooking.

Crab and Cucumber Rolls

½ cucumber
½ tsp/2.5 g/½ tsp salt
2 large or 4 small rectangular egg sheets (omelettes)
6 oz/175 g/¾ cup crab meat
3 tbsp/45 ml/4 tbsp rice vinegar
2 tbsp/30 g/2 tbsp fresh root ginger, grated

1 Cut the cucumber into 2-in/5-cm lengths and slice thinly. Dissolve ½ tsp/2.5 g/½ tsp of salt in 3½ fl oz/100 ml/scant ½ cup of cold water, add the cucumber and leave to soak for 20 minutes. Squeeze gently to remove excess moisture and pat dry with absorbent kitchen paper.

2 Arrange all the ingredients in preparation for the roll. Lay one egg sheet on a bamboo rolling mat. Arrange a wide band of crab meat along the near end; lay a line of cucumber slices along the crab meat.

3 Holding the crab meat and cucumber firmly in place with your fingers, roll the bamboo mat over with your thumbs to enclose them, making sure that they remain in the centre of the roll (this may be a little tricky the first time). Gently press the mat around the roll to shape it. Leaving the mat behind, continue to roll up the egg sheet until the roll is nearly complete.

4 Brush a little vinegar along the edge of the roll and finish rolling, pressing gently to seal. Leave the roll to rest for a few minutes with the sealed edge underneath. Repeat with the remaining ingredients to make another large or 3 small rolls.

5 Wet a very sharp knife and cut each roll into slices 1–2 in/2–5 cm long, wetting the knife several times as you cut. Arrange 2 or 3 slices in individual dishes and serve.

Salmon Steamed with Roe

12 oz/350 g/¾ lb salmon fillets, boned and skinned
salt
vegetable oil
2 oz/50 g/2 oz salmon roe

2 tbsp/30 ml/2 tbsp sake
2 oz/50 g/½ cup grated daikon radish, drained
1 egg

SAUCE

½ pt/300 ml/1¼ cups dashi
3 tbsp/45 ml/4 tbsp mirin
2 tbsp/30 ml/2 tbsp rice vinegar
2 tbsp/30 ml/2 tbsp light soy sauce
2 tsp/10 g/2 tsp cornflour (cornstarch) mixed with 2 tsp/10 ml/2 tsp water
1 lemon
1 young leek, shredded and rinsed

1 Salt the salmon and slice it thinly. Place in a lightly oiled frying pan and fry for 1–2 minutes on each side. Immediately remove to a sieve and rinse with cold water.

2 Mix the roe with the sake in a small bowl to clean the roe; strain and discard the liquid. Mix the radish with the egg and season with a little salt. Stir the roe into the radish and egg mixture.

3 Divide the salmon pieces evenly among 4 small bowls, and spoon the roe mixture over the salmon. Cover with cling film (plastic wrap) or tin foil, sealing the edges tightly. Place in a preheated steamer; steam for 5 minutes over high heat.

4 While the salmon is steaming, prepare the sauce. In a small saucepan, bring the dashi, mirin, vinegar and soy sauce to a simmer. Turn the heat to low, add the cornflour (cornstarch) solution and stir continuously until the sauce thickens.

5 Remove the bowls from the steamer, uncover, and spoon the thickened sauce over the salmon pieces. Squeeze a little lemon juice onto each portion, top with a few shreds of leek and serve.

Left: Crab and cucumber rolls.

Above: *Salmon steamed with roe.*

Shinshu-Style Steamed Sea Trout

1 sea trout, weighing about 1 lb 2
oz/500 g/1 lb 2 oz
salt
4 dried mushrooms, reconstituted
1 young leek, shredded and rinsed
4 oz/100 g/4 oz buckwheat
noodles

4 × 2 in/5 cm pieces kombu
seaweed, wiped
sake
wasabi horseradish, freshly made

SAUCE

1½ pt/900 ml/3¾ cups dashi
⅓ pt/200 ml/⅞ cup dark soy
sauce

¼ pt/150 ml/⅔ cup mirin

1 Fillet the fish. Cut the fish into 4 slices; or use 4 ready-cut fillets. Slice each fillet and open it out like a book. Lightly salt both sides and set aside for 40 minutes to 1 hour.

2 Simmer the mushrooms in their soaking water for 20 minutes until tender, and prepare the leek.

3 Separate the noodles into 4 bunches and tie each bunch securely at the base. Put into plenty of rapidly boiling salted water. Boil for 10 minutes until the noodles are tender; do not add cold water. Remove the noodles and immediately place in cold water.

4 Rinse the fish slices and pat dry. Lay the free end of the noodles over the open fish slice, and fold over the fish to enclose the noodles like a sandwich.

5 Fold the tied end of the noodles over the fish, then cut away the tied end. Repeat with the remaining slices of fish.

6 Divide the kombu pieces among 4 ovenproof bowls, and carefully place the fish and noodles on the kombu. Place a drained mushroom in each bowl. Sprinkle a little sake over each piece of fish. Cover the bowls tightly with cling film (plastic wrap) or foil, and steam in a pre-heated steamer for 10 minutes.

7 Combine the dashi, soy sauce and mirin in a small saucepan and bring to the boil. Remove the fish from the steamer and ladle the hot sauce over the fillets. Garnish with shredded leek and a little wasabi, and serve immediately.

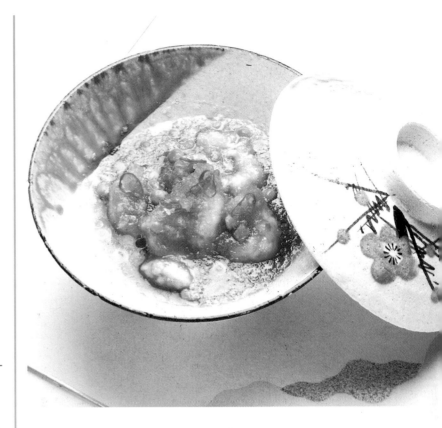

Left: Shinshu-style steamed sea trout.

Below: Sweet glazed salmon.

Right: Deep-fried prawns (shrimp) in thickened broth.

Sweet Glazed Salmon

4 salmon fillets   teriyaki sauce

1 Cut the fillets in 1-in/2.5-cm slices and skewer, being careful not to pierce the skin. Grill (broil) the salmon over very high heat, cooking the flesh side first.

2 Turn the salmon to grill (broil) the skin side, and brush with teriyaki sauce. Serve immediately and spoon over a little more teriyaki sauce.

Deep-Fried Prawns (Shrimp) in Thickened Stock

14 oz/400 g/scant 2 cups prawns (shrimp)	1/3 pt/200 ml/7/8 cup dashi
cornflour (cornstarch) or potato flour	4 tbsp/60 ml/5 tbsp mirin
vegetable oil for deep-frying	4 tbsp/60 ml/5 tbsp light soy sauce
4 oz/100 g/1 cup daikon radish, grated	1 dried red chilli (chili) pepper, seeded and very finely sliced
	1 1/2 oz/40 g/1/4 cup fresh peas

1 Peel the prawns (shrimp) leaving just the tails attached. To de-vein, insert a cocktail stick (toothpick) under the vein in the centre of the back and pull up gently. Rinse the prawns (shrimp) and pat dry. Sprinkle cornflour (cornstarch) or potato flour over the prawns (shrimp).

2 Preheat plenty of oil to 325°F/170°C. Carefully lower the prawns (shrimp) into the oil by spoonfuls and deep-fry for 2–3 minutes, until golden. Remove and drain on absorbent kitchen paper.

3 Place the grated radish in a sieve and rinse in cold water. Squeeze the radish firmly and shape into a ball.

4 In a small saucepan, bring the dashi to a simmer. Add the mirin, soy sauce and the ball of grated radish with sliced chilli (chili) pepper on top. Parboil the peas and add together with the prawns (shrimp). Bring back to a simmer and serve immediately in individual bowls.

Deep-Fried Sole

Deep-fried sole.

4 × 3 oz/80 g/3 oz fillets of sole
salt
vegetable oil for deep frying
1 oz/25 g/¼ cup kuzu or cornflour
(cornstarch)

4 tbsp/60 g/5 tbsp grated daikon
radish
2 tbsp/30 g/2 tbsp freshly grated
root ginger
ponzu sauce (see below)

1 Lay the fish fillets on a cutting surface, dark side uppermost. With a sharp knife, make a shallow cross, about ¼-in/0.5-cm deep, in the top of each fillet. Sprinkle with a little salt and set aside to drain for at least one hour. Prepare the condiments while the fish is draining. Rinse in cold water and pat dry.
2 Heat plenty of oil in a small heavy saucepan to 340°F/170°C. Coat both sides of each fillet evenly with kuzu or cornflour (cornstarch). Set the fish aside for a few minutes so that the coating can set.
3 Deep-fry the fillets one at a time for 4–5 minutes. Remove and drain on absorbent paper.
4 Arrange each fillet on a small plate on a folded napkin, and serve the condiments and sauce separately. The condiments are combined into the sauce, and then the fish dipped into the sauce before eating.

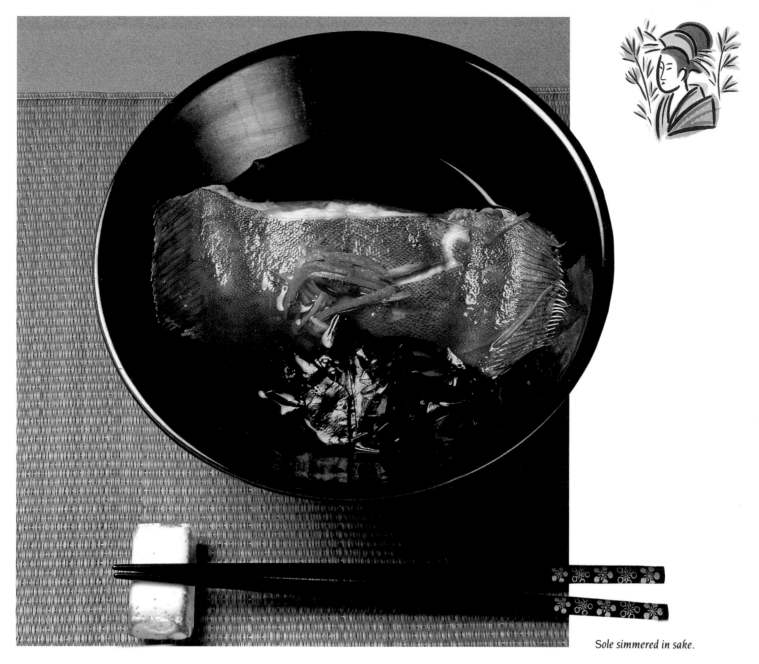

Sole simmered in sake.

Sole Simmered in Sake

4 × 3 oz/75 g/3 oz fillets of sole
salt
⅓ oz/10 g/⅓ oz fresh root ginger
⅓ pt/200 ml/2 cups dashi
4 tbsp/60 ml/5 tbsp sake
4 tbsp/60 ml/5 tbsp dark soy
sauce

4 tbsp/60 ml/5 tbsp mirin
1 tsp/5 g/1 tsp salt
⅓ oz/10 g/⅓ oz piece dried
wakame seaweed, reconstituted

1 Lay the fish fillets on a cutting surface with the dark side uppermost. With a sharp knife make a shallow cross, about ¼-in/5-mm deep, in the top of each fillet, to allow the fish to absorb the flavour of the simmering liquid more thoroughly.
2 Arrange the fillets on a strainer and sprinkle with a little salt;

set aside to drain for at least 1 hour.
   Rinse in cold water and then pat dry. Peel the ginger and slice thinly.
3 Combine the dashi, sake, soy sauce, mirin and salt in a large saucepan and bring to the boil. Arrange the fish in a single layer in the simmering stock, with the dark side on top.
4 Add the ginger. Return to the boil, carefully skim the surface, cover with a drop lid and cook over medium heat, occasionally ladling the simmering stock over the fish pieces, until the stock is reduced by half.
5 Cut the reconstituted wakame into 1-in/2.5-cm pieces and add to the simmering stock. Continue to simmer for a few more minutes until the stock is thick and much reduced. Turn off the heat and leave the fish for a few minutes in the hot stock before serving.
   With a fish slice, remove the fish. Arrange in individual bowls and distribute the wakame and ginger evenly. Pour over a little of the simmering stock and serve.

Mixed Sashimi

1½–2 lb/700–900 g/1½–2 lb fresh raw fish (sea bream, sea bass, salmon, squid, tuna etc)
4 oz/100 g/1 cup thread-cut daikon radish
1 lemon, washed, dried and thinly sliced
3–4 sprigs parsley, washed and patted dry
¼ cucumber, finely sliced
2 tbsp/30 g/2 tbsp grated wasabi, or wasabi paste
soy sauce or dipping sauce

1 Clean, fillet and slice the fish into thick or thin slices, depending on the variety of fish. Make some decorative squid rolls and tuna roses. Prepare garnishes, condiments and dipping sauce. Put out small individual bowls for dipping.
2 Arrange a bed of thread-cut daikon on a tray or attractive platter, and carefully set the sashimi on it. Arrange it decoratively.
3 Use the garnishes to fill the display, taking care not to disturb the fish. Add a fresh green leaf to complete the display. Serve immediately.

Ponzu Sauce

½ pt/300 ml/1¼ cups lemon juice
½ pt/300 ml/1¼ cups soy sauce
3 tbsp/45 ml/4 tbsp mirin
3 tbsp/45 ml/4 tbsp sake
1 piece kombu seaweed 4 in sq
1 tbsp/15 g/1 tbsp dried bonito flakes

Combine the ingredients and leave for 24 hours. Strain through muslin (cheesecloth) into a jar and refrigerate. Use as required. Keeps for up to 3 months.

Above: Mixed sashimi.

Opposite: Riverbank oyster casserole.

Riverbank Oyster Casserole

18 oz/500 g/1 lb 2 oz large
oysters, opened
4 spring onions (scallions) or
young leeks

salt
7 oz/200 g/1¾ cups Chinese
cabbage
7 oz/200 g/1⅞ cup tofu

MISO 'RIVERBANK'

2 oz/50 g/1¼ cup red miso
9 oz/250 g/1 cup white miso
5 tbsp/75 ml/6 tbsp mirin

1 piece kombu seaweed, 4 in/10
cm sq
2 pt/1.1 l/5 cups dashi
4 eggs

1 Gently wash the oysters in lightly-salted water. Rinse separately under cold running water and drain. Wash and trim the vegetables. Cut the spring onions (scallions) or leeks into 2-in/5-cm lengths, separating the white and the green parts. Halve the Chinese cabbage lengthwise and cut into 2-in/5-cm chunks. Cut the tofu into 1¼-in/4-cm squares.

2 Mix together the two misos and the mirin to make a thick but spreadable paste – you may need to dilute the mixture with a little dashi. Spread the paste to coat the inside of a flameproof casserole, making a thick bank all around the edge.

3 Wipe the combu and make a few slashes in it; lay in the casserole. Arrange the oysters, vegetables and tofu attractively on the kombu.

4 Bring the casserole to table and set over a low flame. Heat for a few minutes to roast the miso. Add enough dashi to cover the ingredients and bring to the boil. Continue to simmer. The diners help themselves to the cooked ingredients directly from the casserole, dipping each ingredient into a small bowl of beaten raw egg. The oysters are ready when they swell and the edges curl; oysters become tough if they are overcooked.

Escabeche

6 pickled wax peppers, sliced and de-seeded
2 large peppers, sliced, de-seeded and de-veined
2 large white onions, sliced
2 or more cloves garlic, finely chopped

16 fl oz/450 ml/2 cups vinegar
1 tsp/5 g/1 tsp salt
½ tsp/2.5 g/½ tsp oregano
2 bay leaves
¼ tsp/1 g/¼ tsp freshly ground black pepper
pinch cumin

1 Fry the peppers, onion and garlic together until they are soft. Add all the other ingredients, and bring to a boil. As soon as it starts to boil, remove it from the heat and set it aside to cool. This is a typical escabeche for fish: for meat or poultry, reduce the oil to 2 tbsp/30 ml/2 tbsp.

Pescado in Escabeche

6 large fish fillets   escabeche sauce (above)
olive oil for frying

1 Any firm fish is appropriate; huachinango or red snapper is excellent; sole or sea bass is good, too, but cheap, frozen fish can be greatly improved with this technique.
2 Fry the fish fillets in a little oil until they are thoroughly cooked – this takes three or four minutes on each side, starting with fish at room temperature (not chilled, and certainly not frozen).
3 Marinate the fish in a glass dish in the refrigerator, turning occasionally, for up to three days: at the very least, leave it overnight.

Paella

1 Instead of – or in addition to – chicken or other poultry, paella contains some or all of the following: prawns (shrimp) (whole or shelled); clams, oysters or other bivalves; conch or snail; pork, cut up finely; small crabs; crayfish; chunks of fish; and whatever else you like. Everything is added to the fried rice, along with the stock, and cooked fairly slowly. You need to cover and uncover the dish from time to time, in order to stop it drying out on the one hand or becoming excessively soupy on the other.

1 Put the fish into a pretty glass bowl, pour over it the lime juice, cover and leave to marinate for 4 to 6 hours or overnight.
2 Half an hour or so before serving, stir in the remaining ingredients, except for the avocado, and season to taste.
3 Chill briefly, and serve decorated with avocado slices, if you like.

Seviche

1 lb/450 g/1 lb firm white fish fillets, skinned and cubed
4 fl oz/100 ml/½ cup lime juice
1 small onion, finely chopped
1 large tomato, peeled, seeded and chopped

1–2 fresh green chillies (chilis), seeded and thinly sliced
3 tbsp/45 ml/4 tbsp olive oil
salt
1 small ripe avocado, peeled, pitted and sliced (optional)

Left: Pescado in escabeche.

Above: Paella.

Right: Seviche.

Fried cat fish salad.

Fried Cat Fish Salad

1 lb/500 g/1 lb cat fish, whole
5 cups oil
¼ cup green mango, finely julienned
7 pieces small green chillies (chilis), chopped

¼ cup unsalted peanuts
3 tbsp/45 g/4 tbsp shallots
3 tbsp/45 ml/4 tbsp fish sauce
1 tbsp/15 g/1 tbsp coriander leaves and stem, cut into 1-in/2.5-cm pieces

1 Steam the cat fish for 15 minutes until well cooked. Remove all flesh and finely chop. Place oil in a wok or pot, heat well and then sprinkle chopped fish into hot oil. Fry until light brown. Remove and drain well.
2 Mix all ingredients except coriander with the cat fish salad place on plates and sprinkle with coriander. Serve with rice or liquor.

Fried Fish with Pork and Ginger

11 oz/300 g/¾ lb whole pomfret
fish, cleaned and gutted
½ tsp/2.5 g/½ tsp salt
3 oz/75 g/½ cup finely sliced pork
belly or fresh fat back
2 salted preserved plums or 1 tbsp
pickled lemon juice
1½ oz/40 g/¼ cup sliced ginger

10 small garlic cloves, crushed
2 oz/50 g/½ cup celery with its
leaves, cut into 1 in/2.5 cm pieces
4 spring onions (scallions), cut
into 1 in/2.5 cm pieces
2 fresh red chillies, cut into
lengthwise strips

1 Wash and dry the fish and rub it inside and out with the salt.
Place half the pork fat on a heatproof plate that fits a steamer,
put the fish on top and cover with the rest of the pork fat.
Roughly chop the salted plum and sprinkle it (or the juice)
over the top together with the ginger and garlic.

2 Steam for 15 minutes, then add the celery, spring onion
(scallion) and chilli and steam for 5 more minutes, until the
fish is firm but tender.

3 Serve accompanied by rice.

Fried fish with pork and ginger.

Plaa lad phrik.

Plaa Lad Phrik

2 lb/1 kg/2 lb sea perch or bass, whole
3 cups oil
8 cloves garlic
5 fresh yellow chillies (chilis)
1 tbsp/15 ml/1 tbsp tamarind juice or vinegar

1 tsp/5 ml/1 tsp fish sauce
2 tsp/10 g/2 tsp palm sugar
4 fl oz/120 ml/½ cup chicken stock
2 pieces fresh red chilli (chili) cut into quarters lengthwise
½ cup fresh basil leaf

1 Fry fish well in oil, remove the fish and all except ½ cup of oil.
2 Mix together the garlic and chilli (chili), add to the fish and then add the rest of the ingredients except for the basil. Boil lightly.
3 Fry the basil in hot oil and garnish fish with this. Serve with rice.

Spicy seafood salad.   **Right:** Stuffed crab shell.

Spicy Seafood Salad

7 pieces small green chilli (chili)
2 tbsp/30 ml/2 tbsp fish sauce
½ tsp/2.5 g/½ tsp sugar
5 garlic cloves
2 pieces coriander root
2 tbsp/30 ml/2 tbsp lemon juice
5 oz/150 g/5 oz sea bass or perch
sliced thin

5 oz/150 g/¾ cup prawns
(shrimp), shelled
5 oz/150 g/5 oz squid, sliced
½ cup spring onions (scallions),
sliced ¼-in/1-cm long
4 oz/100 g/1 cup onion, sliced
2 oz/50 g/½ cup celery and leaf,
sliced

1 Take the chilli (chili), fish sauce, sugar, garlic and coriander and pound well together.
2 Meanwhile, cook the fish in salted water. Drain and place in a bowl. Add all other ingredients, mix and serve.

Stuffed Crab Shell

⅓ cup crabmeat
½ cup prawns (shrimp), minced
(ground)
1 cup pork, minced (ground)
2 tbsp/30 g/2 tbsp onion, chopped
fine
1 tsp/5 g/1 tsp ground white
pepper
¼ tsp/1 g/¼ tsp salt
¼ tsp/1 g/¼ tsp white soya sauce

1 tsp/5 g/1 tsp sugar
1 tbsp/15 g/1 tbsp spring onions
(scallions), sliced fine
4 blue crab shells, cleaned well
3 eggs
¼ cup coriander leaves
5 cups oil
2 pieces fresh red chilli (chili),
finely julienned lengthwise

1 Mix together the first ten ingredients well.
2 Take crab shells and stuff with the pork mixture.
3 Mix the eggs well in bowl. Heat the oil in a pot to approx. 350°F/180°C. Dip the stuffed crabs in the eggs and fry in the oil until thoroughly cooked. Remove and drain well. Place on plates and sprinkle with coriander and chilli (chili). Serve as hors d'oeuvres or with rice and Chinese plum sauce (available at most supermarkets).

Fish Steamed with Lemon and Chilli (Chili)

1 lb/45 g/1 lb sea bass or sea perch per person
½ cup lemon juice
2 tbsp/30 g/2 tbsp small green chillies (chilis), crushed lightly
2 tbsp/30 g/2 tbsp garlic, peeled and chopped
½ tbsp/7.5 g/½ tbsp salt
2 tbsp/30 ml/2 tbsp fish sauce
1 tsp/5 g/1 tsp sugar
¼ cup coriander leaf and stem cut into ½-in/2.5-cm pieces

1 Wash the fish well and steam for 15 minutes. Remove and add the lemon juice mixed with the chillies (chilis), garlic, salt, fish sauce and sugar over the top. The fish must be hot when the sauce is poured over. Sprinkle with coriander and serve with rice.

Nam Phrik Plaatoo

1 tbsp/15 g/1 tbsp garlic, sliced
½ tbsp/7.5 ml/½ tbsp shrimp paste, pan roasted in foil for 5 minutes
2 tbsp/30 g/2 tbsp dry shrimp, pounded fine
2 pieces small green aubergines (eggplants), meat only, no skin
6 pieces aubergine (eggplant), pea sized, or fresh green peas
15 pieces fresh small green or red chillies (chilis)
2 tbsp/30 ml/2 tbsp lemon juice
½ tbsp/7.5 g/½ tbsp palm sugar
1 tbsp/15 ml/1 tbsp fish sauce
1 piece fresh large red chilli (chili) sliced into small circles

1 Take the garlic, shrimp paste, dried shrimp and aubergines (eggplants) and pound together. Add the chillies (chilis), pound lightly, and then add the rest of the ingredients, except the sliced red chillies (chilis). Mix well. Place in bowl and sprinkle with the reserved chillies (chilis). Serve with fresh vegetables and lightly boiled cabbage, French (green) beans and fried fish.

Fish steamed with lemon and chilli (chili).

Nam phrik plaatoo.

Steamed fish curry.

Steamed Fish Curry

11 oz/300 g/11 oz fish fillet, sliced small	3 tbsp/45 ml/4 tbsp fish sauce
	1 cup basil leaves
1 pt/600 ml/2½ cups coconut milk	1 cup cabbage, finely julienned
	2 kaffir lime leaves, fine julienned
2 eggs	1 fresh red chilli (chili), de-seeded and julienned

CURRY PASTE

5 pieces dry red chilli (chili)	½ tsp/2.5 g/½ tsp salt
½ tsp/2.5 g/½ tsp kaffir lime, skin chopped fine	3 pieces shallots
	10 pieces small garlic cloves
2 pieces coriander root	1 tsp/5 g/1 tsp galanga, sliced
5 white peppercorns	1 tsp/5 g/1 tsp lemon grass

1 To make the curry paste, pound all the ingredients together until very fine.
2 Take the fish and mix with the curry paste, add 2 cups of the coconut milk, egg, and fish sauce. Mix well.
3 Take 6 ovenproof cups – divide the basil and cabbage between cups and cook in a pressure cooker, or in an oven in a half pan filled with hot water and covered for 10 minutes.
4 Meanwhile, take remaining ½ cup of coconut milk, boil, and add a pinch of cornflour (cornstarch) to thicken slightly. After the fish mix has cooked for 10 minutes, spoon the coconut mix on top and sprinkle with the kaffir leaf and chillies (chilis). Then steam for 5 more minutes. Serve with rice.

VEGETABLES & VEGETARIAN DISHES

From India

OMELETTE CURRY 206
DEVILLED EGGS 206
EGG CURRY 206
CABBAGE ROLLS 208
CABBAGE WITH COCONUT 208
FRIED EGG CURRY 209
WHITE RADISH 210
CABBAGE WITH PEAS 210
FRIED OKRA WITH ONIONS 211
MASALA AUBERGINE (EGGPLANT) 212
OKRA WITH YOGURT 214
DRY DODDY 214
SPINACH WITH COTTAGE CHEESE 215
SPICY BITTER GOURD 217
PANIR BHIYIA 217
COTTAGE CHEESE WITH PEAS 217
FRIED LENTIL CAKE CURRY 218
SPICY AUBERGINE (EGGPLANT) 219
BEANS WITH COCONUT 219
AUBERGINE (EGGPLANT) WITH SOUR CREAM 220
ROASTED AUBERGINE (EGGPLANT) 220
ANGLED LOOFAH WITH POPPY SEEDS 221
POTATOES WITH GREEN PEPPERS AND COCONUT 222
POTATO CURRY 222
CAULIFLOWER AND POTATO CURRY 223
DRY POTATOES 224
CAULIFLOWER WITH POTATOES AND PEAS 224
ROASTED CAULIFLOWER 225
DRY POTATO AND CAULIFLOWER 226
VEGETABLE CURRY 226

From China

SWEET AND SOUR CUCUMBER SALAD 227
HOT AND SOUR CUCUMBER – SICHUAN STYLE 228
SPICY CABBAGE – SICHUAN STYLE 228
CELERY SALAD 229

CHINESE CABBAGE SALAD 230
FIVE-SPICE BEAN CURD 230
PICKLED VEGETABLES 230
AUBERGINE (EGGPLANT) WITH SICHUAN 'FISH SAUCE' 232
FRENCH (GREEN) BEANS A LA SICHUAN 232
VEGETARIAN 'LION'S HEAD' CASSEROLE 233
'POCK MARKED WOMAN' BEAN CURD 234

From Japan

WHITE SALAD 235
DEEP-FRIED BEAN CURD IN BROTH 237
RED AND WHITE SALAD 237
CUCUMBER AND WAKAME SALAD 238

From Mexico

CABBAGE SALAD 239
BASIC GUACAMOLE 240
FANCY GUACAMOLE 240
STUFFED PEPPERS 241
TOMATO SALAD 241
MEXICAN OMELETTE 242

From Thailand

SON TAM THAI 243
ISSAAN SHREDDED BAMBOO SHOOT 243
AJAAD SALAD 244
MIXED FRIED VEGETABLES 245
ROAST AUBERGINE (EGGPLANT) SALAD 245

Omelette Curry

6 eggs
½ tsp/2.5 g/½ tsp salt
6 tbsp/90 ml/7 tbsp oil
1 large potato, cut into 1-in/2.5-cm pieces
4 tbsp/60 g/5 tbsp onion mixture

1 tsp/5 g/1 tsp ground turmeric
½ tsp/2.5 g/½ tsp chilli (chili) powder
¾ tsp/4 g/¾ tsp salt
12 fl oz/325 ml/1½ cups water

1 Whisk the eggs and the salt together.
2 Heat 1 tbsp/15 ml/1 tbsp of the oil in a large frying pan and make an omelette with half the beaten eggs. Set aside and cut into four pieces. Similarly, make another omelette.
3 Heat the rest of the oil and fry the potatoes until lightly browned. Set aside. Add the onion mixture and fry for 2–3 minutes. Add the turmeric, chilli (chili), and salt and stir well with the onion mixture.
4 Add the water and bring it to boil. Put in the potatoes, cover, lower heat and simmer for 10 minutes. Place the pieces of omelette in the pan, cover again and cook until the potatoes are tender, about another 10 minutes.

Devilled Eggs

4 hard-boiled eggs, cut in half – lengthwise
1½ tbsp/22.5 g/1½ tbsp onions, finely chopped
2 green chillies (chilis), finely chopped
1 tbsp/15 g/1 tbsp coriander leaves, chopped

½ tsp/2.5 g/½ tsp salt
2 tbsp/30 g/2 tbsp mashed potatoes
oil for deep frying
1 tbsp/15 g/1 tbsp plain flour
2 fl oz/50 ml/¼ cup water

1 Remove the yolks and mix with the onions, chillies (chilis), coriander leaves, salt and mashed potatoes. Put the mixture back into the egg whites. Chill for 30 minutes.
2 Heat the oil in a karai over high heat. While the oil is heating up make a batter with the flour and water. Be careful not to allow the oil to catch fire.
3 Dip eggs into the batter and gently put into the hot oil. Fry until golden, turning once.

Egg Curry

4 tbsp/60 ml/5 tbsp oil
1 large onion, finely sliced
2 tbsp/30 g/2 tbsp onion mixture
½ tsp/2.5 g/½ tsp ground turmeric
½ tsp/2.5 g/½ tsp chilli (chili) powder

¾ tsp/4 g/¾ tsp salt
a big pinch of sugar
8 hard-boiled (hard-cooked) eggs
4 fl oz/100 ml/½ cup water

1 Heat the oil in a frying pan over medium high heat and fry the sliced onion for 3–4 minutes until lightly browned.
2 Add the onion mixture, turmeric, chilli (chili), salt and sugar and, stirring constantly, fry for another 2–3 minutes. Add the eggs and mix until well covered with the spices.
3 Add the water, bring it to the boil, lower heat, cover and cook for about 10 minutes until the gravy thickens.

Opposite, top: Devilled eggs.

Right: Egg curry.

Below: Omelette curry.

Cabbage Rolls

8 large cabbage leaves, parboiled
for 5 minutes and drained
3 tbsp/45 ml/4 tbsp oil
2 medium onions, finely chopped
7 oz/200 g/generous 1 cup panir,
drained
½ tsp/2.5 g/½ tsp ground
turmeric

½ tsp/2.5 g/½ tsp chilli (chili)
powder
½ tsp/2.5 g/½ tsp garam masala
1–2 green chillies (chilis), chopped
½ tsp/2.5 g/½ tsp salt
1 tbsp/15 g/1 tbsp coriander
leaves, chopped
oil for shallow frying

1 Heat the 3 tbsp/45 ml/4 tbsp of oil in a frying pan over medium high heat and fry the onions till lightly browned.
2 Add the panir, turmeric, chilli (chili), garam masala, green chillies (chilis), and salt and stir fry for 5–6 minutes. Sprinkle with the coriander leaves and remove from the heat.
3 Place 2 tbsp/30 g/2 tbsp of the mixture on a cabbage leaf and roll up, folding the two sides in. Tie with the string. Make all the rolls in the same way.
4 Heat oil for shallow frying over medium heat and fry the rolls, turning once, till browned.

Cabbage with Coconut

2 tbsp/30 ml/2 tbsp oil
2 bay leaves
¾ tsp/4 g/¾ tsp whole cumin
seeds
1–2 green chillies (chilis), chopped
1½ lb/700 g/9 cups cabbage,
shredded

¾ tsp/4 g/¾ tsp salt
⅓ tsp/3 g/⅓ tsp sugar
3 tbsp/45 g/4 tbsp desiccated
(shredded) coconut
½ tsp/2.5 g/½ tsp ground cumin

1 Heat oil in a karai over medium high heat and add the bay leaves, cumin seeds and the green chillies (chilis) and let them sizzle for a few seconds.
2 Add the cabbage, salt and sugar and mix. Cover, lower heat to medium and cook for about 15 minutes until half done.
3 Add the coconut and ground cumin and fry, stirring constantly for 10–15 minutes until all the moisture has evaporated.

Above: *Cabbage with coconut.*

Fried Egg Curry

3 medium onions	6 cardamoms
5 cloves garlic	2–3 green chillies (chilis)
1-in/2.5-cm root ginger	1½ tsp/7.5 g/1½ tsp ground
1 tbsp/15 ml/1 tbsp white vinegar	turmeric
8 tbsp/120 ml/¼ cup mustard oil	½ tsp/2.5 g/½ tsp chilli (chili)
8 eggs	powder
3 bay leaves	1 tsp/5 g/1 tsp salt
2-in/5-cm stick cinnamon	¼ tsp/1 g/¼ tsp sugar

1 Blend the onions, garlic, ginger and vinegar in a blender until you have a fine paste.

2 Heat the oil in a large frying pan over a medium heat, fry the eggs one at a time and set aside.

3 To the remaining oil add the bay leaves, cinnamon and cardamoms and let them sizzle for a few seconds.

4 Add the blended paste and the green chillies (chilis) and fry for 6–8 minutes, stirring constantly. Add the turmeric, chilli (chili) powder, salt and sugar and continue frying for another minute.

5 Carefully add the eggs and, stirring gently, cover them with some of the spices.

6 Cover and cook for 5 minutes. Serve hot with a pillau.

Left: *Cabbage rolls.*

Above: *Fried egg curry.*

White Radish

2 tbsp/30 ml/2 tbsp oil
½ tsp/2.5 g/½ tsp kalonji
1–2 green chillies (chilis), chopped

1 lb/450 g/4 cups white radish,
peeled and grated
½ tsp/2.5 g/½ tsp salt
¼ tsp/1 g/¼ tsp sugar

1 Heat the oil in a karai, add the kalonji and green chillies (chilis) and let them sizzle for a few seconds.
2 Add the radish and stir fry for 2–3 minutes. Cover, lower the heat and cook for about 15 minutes, stirring occasionally.
3 Add the salt and sugar, increase the heat to medium high and, stirring constantly, cook till dry and brown.

Cabbage with Peas

3 tbsp/45 ml/4 tbsp oil
2 bay leaves
¾ tsp/4 g/¾ tsp whole cumin seeds
1½ lb/700 g/9 cups cabbage, finely shredded
½ tsp/2.5 g/½ tsp chilli (chili) powder

1 tsp/5 g/1 tsp ground turmeric
1½ tsp/7.5 g/1½ tsp ground cumin
1 tsp/5 g/1 tsp ground coriander
2 tomatoes, chopped
¾ tsp/4 g/¾ tsp salt
½ tsp/2.5 g/½ tsp sugar
4 oz/100 g/⅔ cup peas

Top left: White radish.   ***Above:*** Cabbage with peas.

1 Heat the oil in a karai over medium high heat and add the bay leaves and the cumin seeds. Let them sizzle for a few seconds.
2 Add the cabbage and stir for 2–3 minutes.
3 Add the turmeric, chilli (chili), cumin, coriander, tomatoes, salt and sugar and mix with the cabbage.
4 Lower heat, cover and cook for 15 minutes. Add the peas and cover again. Continue to cook for a further 15 minutes, stirring occasionally.
5 Remove the cover, turn heat up to medium high and, stirring continuously, cook until it is dry.

Above: *Fried okra with onions.*

Fried Okra with Onions

1 lb/450 g/1 lb okra
3 tbsp/45 ml/4 tbsp oil

2 large onions, finely chopped
1 tsp/5 g/1 tsp salt

1 Wash the okra and pat dry with paper towels.
2 Cut into ½-in/1-cm pieces.
3 Heat oil in a karai over medium heat and fry the onions until soft.
4 Add the okra and salt, and, stirring gently, continue frying until the okra is cooked, about 10–12 minutes. Serve with rice and lentils or paratha.

Masala Aubergine (Eggplant)

1 large aubergine (eggplant), cut into large pieces
½ tsp/2.5 g/½ tsp salt
big pinch of turmeric
8 tbsp/120 ml/¼ cup mustard oil
½ tsp/2.5 g/½ tsp kalonji
¾ tsp/4 g/¾ tsp ground turmeric
½ tsp/2.5 g/½ tsp chilli (chili) powder

½ tsp/2.5 g/½ tsp salt
¼ tsp/1 g/¼ tsp sugar
4 tbsp/60 ml/5 tbsp yogurt
2 fl oz/50 ml/¼ cup water
2–3 green chillies (chilis)
1 tsp/5 g/1 tsp ground roasted cumin

1 Rub the aubergine (eggplant) pieces with the ½ tsp/2.5 g/½ tsp salt and a big pinch of turmeric and set aside for 20 minutes.
2 Heat the oil in a karai over high heat and fry the aubergines (eggplants) until brown. Drain on paper towels.
3 Lower the heat to medium and add the kalonji. After 4–5 seconds add the turmeric, chilli (chili) powder, salt, sugar and yogurt. Stir fry for 1 minute.
4 Add the water; when it starts to boil add the aubergines (eggplants) and green chillies (chilis) and cook for 5 minutes.
5 Before removing from the heat sprinkle with the ground roasted cumin. Serve with rice.

Masala aubergine (eggplant).

Okra with Yogurt

1 lb/450 g/1 lb okra
4 tbsp/60 ml/5 tbsp oil
½ tsp/2.5 g/½ tsp panch phoron
½ in/1 cm root ginger, grated
2 green chillies (chilis), cut
lengthwise

big pinch of turmeric
½ tsp/2.5 g/½ tsp salt
5 fl oz/125 ml/⅔ cup yogurt
8–10 curry leaves

1 Wash the okra and pat dry on kitchen towels. Cut into 1-in/ 2.5-cm pieces.
2 Heat oil in a karai over medium high heat, add the panch phoron, ginger and chillies (chilis). Let them sizzle for a few seconds.
3 Add the okra, and stirring gently fry for 5 minutes. Lower heat to medium low.
4 Add the turmeric, salt and yogurt and mix gently with the okra. Cover and cook for 10 minutes.
5 Add the curry leaves and cook a further 5 minutes. Serve with rice.

Dry Doddy

2 tbsp/30 ml/2 tbsp ghee
¾ tsp/4 g/¾ tsp whole cumin
seeds
2 bay leaves
1½ lb/675 g/1½ lb doddy, peeled
and grated

½ tsp/2.5 g/½ tsp salt
pinch of sugar
½ tbsp/7.5 g/½ tbsp coriander
leaves, chopped

1 Heat the ghee in a karai over medium heat and add the cumin seeds and bay leaves and let them sizzle for a few seconds. Add the doddy and fry for 3–4 minutes stirring constantly.
2 Cover, lower heat and cook for 20–25 minutes, stirring occasionally so that it does not stick to the bottom.
3 Remove the cover, turn the heat up to medium high, add the salt and sugar and, stirring constantly, fry till the doddy is browned and dry.
4 Serve sprinkled with the chopped coriander leaves.

Right: Dry doddy.

Above: *Okra with yogurt.*

Opposite: *Spinach with cottage cheese.*

Spinach with Cottage Cheese

4 tbsp/60 ml/5 tbsp oil
6 oz/175 g/1 cup panir, drained
and cut into ½-in/1-cm cubes
1 large onion, finely sliced
4 cloves garlic, crushed
½-in/1-cm root ginger, grated
12 oz/350 g/1½ cups frozen
spinach, chopped

½ tsp/2.5 g/½ tsp ground
turmeric
⅓ tsp/2 g/⅓ tsp chilli (chili)
powder
1 tsp/5 g/1 tsp ground coriander
¾ tsp/4 g/¾ tsp salt

1 Heat oil in a karai over medium high heat and fry the panir until brown. Set aside.
2 Add the onion, garlic, and ginger in the remaining oil and fry until golden.
3 Add the spinach, turmeric, chilli (chili), coriander and salt and fry for 2–3 minutes.
4 Lower heat to medium, cover and cook a further 10 minutes.
5 Add the panir and, stirring constantly, cook until dry.

Spicy Bitter Gourd

2 large bitter gourds, finely sliced
1 tbsp/15 ml/1 tbsp oil
1 clove garlic, crushed
4–6 curry leaves
1–2 green chillies (chilis), chopped
½ tsp/2.5 g/½ tsp ground turmeric
¼ tsp/1 g/¼ tsp chilli (chili) powder
½ tsp/2.5 g/½ tsp salt

1 Wash the slices of bitter gourd and pat dry.
2 Heat oil in a karai over medium high heat, add the garlic, curry leaves and green chillies (chilis) and fry for 10 seconds.
3 Add the bitter gourd, turmeric, chilli (chili) and salt and fry for 10–15 minutes, stirring occasionally until tender.

Panir Bhiyia

2 tbsp/30 ml/2 tbsp oil
1 medium onion, finely chopped
1 clove garlic, crushed
10 oz/275 g/1⅔ cups panir, drained
½ tsp/2.5 g/½ tsp ground turmeric
½ tsp/2.5 g/½ tsp salt
1 small green pepper, seeded and cut into ½-in/1-cm pieces
1 large tomato, chopped
1–2 green chillies (chilis), chopped
1 tbsp/15 g/1 tbsp coriander leaves, chopped

1 Heat the oil in a karai over medium heat and fry the onions and garlic for 5 minutes.
2 Add the panir, turmeric and salt and stir-fry for 5 minutes.
3 Add the green pepper and tomato and cook for 8–10 minutes, stirring occasionally.
4 Sprinkle with the green chillies (chilis) and coriander leaves and remove from the heat.

Above: Panir bhiyia.

Left: Spicy bitter gourd.

Below: Cottage cheese with peas.

Cottage Cheese with Peas

6 tbsp/90 ml/7 tbsp oil
10 oz/275 g/1⅔ cups panir, drained and cut into ½-in/1-cm pieces
6 tbsp/90 ml/7 tbsp onion mixture
1 tsp/5 g/1 tsp ground turmeric
½ tsp/2.5 g/½ tsp chilli (chili) powder
1 tsp/5 g/1 tsp ground coriander
¾ tsp/4 g/¾ tsp salt
6 oz/175 g/1 cup peas
8 fl oz/225 ml/1 cup water
1 tbsp/15 g/1 tbsp coriander leaves, chopped (optional)

1 Heat the oil in a karai over medium high heat and fry the panir pieces until golden brown. Remove and drain on paper towels.

2 In the remaining oil add the onion mixture and fry for 3 minutes, stirring constantly. Add the turmeric, chilli (chili), coriander and salt and continue to fry for a further 2–3 minutes.
3 Add the peas and mix thoroughly. Add the water and bring to the boil. Cover, lower heat to medium low and simmer for 5 minutes. Gently add the pieces of fried panir and simmer a further 10 minutes. Garnish with the coriander leves and serve hot.

Fried Lentil Cake Curry

5 oz/125 g/⅔ cup channa dal, washed
30 fl oz/825 ml/3¾ cups water
¾ tsp/4 g/¾ tsp salt
½ tsp/2.5 g/½ tsp ground turmeric
½ in/1 cm root ginger, grated
2 tbsp/30 g/2 tbsp desiccated (shredded) coconut
2 green chillies (chilis)
5 fl oz/125 ml/⅔ cup water
14 tbsp/210 ml/⅞ cup oil
3 medium potatoes, cut into 1-in/ 2.5-cm pieces

½ tsp/2.5 g/½ tsp whole cumin seeds
2 bay leaves
1 tsp/5 g/1 tsp ground turmeric
½ tsp/2.5 g/½ tsp chilli (chili) powder
1½ tsp/7.5 g/1½ tsp ground cumin
1 tsp/5 g/1 tsp ground coriander
½ tsp/2.5 g/½ tsp salt
2 tomatoes, chopped
12 fl oz/325 ml/1½ cups water
1 tsp/5 g/1 tsp ghee
½ tsp/2.5 g/½ tsp garam masala

1 Soak the dal in 30 fl oz/825 ml/3¾ cups water overnight. Drain.

2 Mix the drained dal with the salt, turmeric, ginger, coconut, green chillies (chilis) and 5 fl oz/125 ml/⅔ cup water in a blender until you have a smooth creamy mixture.

3 In a karai, heat 8 tbsp/120 ml/½ cup of the oil over medium heat and fry the dal mixture until it leaves the side and a ball forms. Spread ½-in/1-cm thick on a greased plate. Cool. Cut into 1-in/2.5-cm squares.

4 Heat the rest of the oil in a karai over medium high heat and fry the dal squares a few at a time until golden brown. Set aside.

5 Fry the potatoes until lightly browned. Set aside.

6 Lower heat to medium, add the whole cumin seeds and bay leaves and let them sizzle for a few seconds.

7 Add the turmeric, chilli (chili), coriander, salt and tomatoes and fry for 2 minutes. Add the water and bring to boil.

8 Add the potatoes, cover and cook for 10 minutes. Add the fried dal squares, cover again and cook until the potatoes are tender.

9 Add the ghee and sprinkle on the garam masala. Remove from the heat. Serve hot with rice or pillau.

Below: Fried lentil cake curry.

Beans with Coconut

3 tbsp/45 ml/4 tbsp oil
½ tsp/2.5 g/½ tsp kalonji
2–3 dried red chillies (chilis)
1 lb/450 g/1 lb green beans
washed and cut into 1-in/2.5-cm
lengths
2 tbsp/30 g/2 tbsp desiccated
(shredded) coconut
½ tsp/2.5 g/½ tsp salt

1 Heat oil in a karai over medium high heat, add the kalonji and chillies (chilis) and let them sizzle for a few seconds.
2 Add the beans and stir fry for 10 minutes.
3 Add the coconut and salt and mix in thoroughly with the beans, and stirring constantly to avoid sticking cook a further 5–7 minutes.

Above: Spicy aubergine (eggplant).

Spicy Aubergine (Eggplant)

1 lb/450 g/1 lb aubergines (eggplants)
3 tbsp/45 ml/4 tbsp oil
1 large onion, finely chopped
3 tomatoes, chopped
1 tbsp/15 g/1 tbsp coriander leaves, chopped
1–2 green chillies (chilis), chopped
½ tsp/2.5 g/½ tsp ground turmeric
½ tsp/2.5 g/½ tsp chilli (chili) powder
¾ tsp/4 g/¾ tsp ground coriander
¾ tsp/4 g/¾ tsp salt

1 Place the aubergines (eggplants) under a pre-heated grill (broiler) for about 15 minutes, turning frequently until the skin turns black and the flesh soft. Peel off the skin and mash the flesh.
2 Heat the oil in a karai over medium heat and fry the onions until soft. Add the tomatoes, coriander leaves and green chillies (chilis) and fry another 2–3 minutes.
3 Add the mashed aubergine (eggplant), turmeric, chilli (chili), coriander and salt and stir.
4 Fry for another 10–12 minutes and serve with chappatis.

Right: Beans with coconut.

Aubergine (Eggplant) with Sour Cream

1 large aubergine (eggplant) cut
into ½-in/1-cm slices
½ tsp/2.5 g/½ tsp salt
½ tsp/2.5 g/½ tsp ground
turmeric
pinch of sugar
8 tbsp/120 ml/½ cup oil
pinch of asafetida

2 tbsp/30 g/2 tbsp onion mixture
1 tsp/5 g/1 tsp ground cumin
1 tsp/5 g/1 tsp ground coriander
½ tsp/2.5 g/½ tsp chilli (chili)
powder
big pinch of sugar
½ tsp/2.5 g/½ tsp salt
5 fl oz/125 g/⅔ cup sour cream

1 Rub the aubergine (eggplant) slices with ½ tsp/2.5 g/½ tsp salt, turmeric and a pinch of sugar and set aside for 30 minutes.
2 Heat the oil in a large frying pan over medium high heat and fry the aubergine slices until brown. Drain on paper towels.
3 Lower heat to medium and add the asafetida to the remaining oil. Fry for 3–4 seconds and then add the onion mixture, cumin, coriander, chilli (chili), sugar and salt and fry for 2 minutes.

4 Add the sour cream and mix with the spices. Add the fried aubergine (eggplant) slices. Cover and cook for 10 minutes.

Roasted Aubergine (Eggplant)

1 large aubergine (eggplant)
1 small onion, finely chopped
1–2 green chillies (chilis), finely
chopped

½ tsp/2.5 g/½ tsp salt
2–3 tbsp/30–45 ml/2–3 tbsp
mustard oil

1 Place the aubergine (eggplant) under a pre-heated grill (broiler) for about 15 minutes, turning frequently, until the skin becomes black and the flesh soft.
2 Peel the skin and mash the flesh.
3 Add the rest of the ingredients to the mashed aubergine (eggplant) and mix thoroughly.

Angled Loofah with Poppy Seeds

2 tbsp/30 g/2 tbsp poppy seeds
1–2 green chillies (chilis)
4 tbsp/60 ml/5 tbsp oil
½ tsp/2.5 g/½ tsp kalonji
1–2 dried red chillies (chilis)

2 lb/900 g/2 lb jhinge, peeled and sliced into ½-in/1-cm pieces
½ tsp/2.5 g/½ tsp ground turmeric
¾ tsp/4 g/¾ tsp salt

1 Grind the poppy seeds and green chillies (chilis) to a paste.
2 Heat oil in a karai over medium high heat and add the kalonji and red chillies (chilis) and let them sizzle for a few seconds.
3 Add the jhinge, turmeric and salt and stir for a few minutes.
4 Cover, lower heat to medium and cook for about 10–15 minutes. Add the paste.
5 Increase heat to medium high and, stirring constantly, fry until dry.

Opposite: Aubergine (eggplant) with sour cream.

Right: Angled loofah with poppy seeds.

Below: Roasted aubergine (eggplant).

Potato Curry

6 tbsp/90 ml/7 tbsp oil	½ tsp/2.5 g/½ tsp chilli (chili)
4 tbsp/60 ml/5 tbsp onion mixture	powder
1½ lb/674 g/1½ lb small	¾ tsp/4 g/¾ tsp salt
potatoes, peeled and boiled	big pinch of sugar
½ tsp/2.5 g/½ tsp ground	6 fl oz/175 ml/¾ cup water
turmeric	½ tsp/2.5 g/½ tsp garam masala

1 Heat the oil in a karai over medium high heat and add the onion mixture and fry for 5 minutes, stirring frequently.
2 Add the potatoes, turmeric, chilli (chili), salt and sugar and fry a further 2–3 minutes, stirring constantly so that it does not stick.
3 Add the water; when it starts to boil, cover, lower heat and simmer for about 10 minutes until you have a thick gravy.
4 Before removing from the heat sprinkle with the garam masala.

Left: Potato curry.

Below: Potatoes with green peppers and coconut.

Potatoes with Green Peppers and Coconut

3 tbsp/45 ml/4 tbsp oil	1 green pepper, seeded and cut
½ tsp/2.5 g/½ tsp whole mustard	into ½-in/1-cm pieces
seeds	3 tbsp/45 g/4 tbsp desiccated
pinch of asafetida	(shredded) coconut
6–8 curry leaves	½ tsp/2.5 g/½ tsp salt
1 lb/450 g/1 lb potatoes, boiled,	2 green chillies (chilis), chopped
peeled and diced into ½-in/1-cm	1 tbsp/15 g/1 tbsp coriander
cubes	leaves, chopped

1 Heat the oil in a karai over medium heat, add the mustard seeds, asafetida and curry leaves and let them sizzle for 3–4 seconds.
2 Add the potatoes and green pepper and stir fry for 5 minutes.
3 Add the coconut and salt and, stirring occasionally, cook for another 5–7 minutes.
4 Before removing from the heat, sprinkle with the chillies (chilis) and coriander leaves.

Cauliflower and Potato Curry

6 tbsp/90 ml/7 tbsp oil	1 ½ tsp/7.5 g/1 ½ tsp ground cumin
1 lb/450 g/1 lb potatoes, peeled and quartered	¾ tsp/4 g/¾ tsp salt
1 small cauliflower, cut into large florets	big pinch of sugar
pinch of asafetida	2 tomatoes, chopped
¾ tsp/4 g/¾ tsp ground turmeric	10 fl oz/275 ml/1 ¼ cups water
½ tsp/2.5 g/½ tsp chilli (chili) powder	2 tsp/10 g/2 tsp ghee
	½ tsp/2.5 g/½ tsp garam masala

1 Heat the oil in a karai over medium high heat.

2 Fry the potatoes a few pieces at a time until slightly brown. Remove and set aside.

3 Fry the cauliflower pieces a few at a time until brown spots appear on them. Remove and set aside.

4 Lower heat to medium, add the asafetida and after 3–4 seconds add the turmeric, chilli (chili), cumin, salt and sugar. Mix the spices together, add the tomatoes and fry for 1 minute with the spices.

5 Add the water and bring to the boil. Put in the potatoes, cover and cook for 10 minutes.

6 Add the cauliflower, cover again and cook a further 5–7 minutes until the potatoes and cauliflower are tender.

7 Add the ghee and sprinkle with the garam masala. Remove from the heat and serve hot with rice and red lentils.

Above: Cauliflower and potato curry.

Dry Potatoes

6 tbsp/90 ml/7 tbsp mustard oil
¾ tsp/4 g/¾ tsp kalonji
1½ lb/675 g/1½ lb potatoes, cut
into thin strips

½ tsp/2.5 g/½ tsp ground
turmeric
1 tsp/5 g/1 tsp salt
3–4 green chillies (chilis)

1 Heat oil in a karai over medium high heat. Add the kalonji and let it sizzle for a few seconds.
2 Add the potatoes and fry for 2–3 minutes.
3 Add the turmeric, salt and chillies (chilis) and mix in with the potatoes.
4 Cover, lower heat to medium low and, stirring occasionally, cook for another 15–20 minutes until the potatoes are tender.

Above: Dry potatoes.

Opposite, top: Cauliflower with potatoes and peas.

Right: Roasted cauliflower.

Cauliflower with Potatoes and Peas

4 tbsp/60 ml/5 tbsp oil
2 medium onions, finely chopped
1 lb/450 g/1 lb potatoes, diced into
¾-in/2–cm pieces
1 small cauliflower, cut into ¾-in/
2-cm pieces
½ tsp/2.5 g/½ tsp ground
turmeric

⅓ tsp/2 g/⅓ tsp chilli (chili)
powder
1 tsp/5 g/1 tsp ground cumin
2 tomatoes, chopped
1 tsp/5 g/1 tsp salt
¼ tsp/1 g/¼ tsp sugar
7 oz/200 g/generous 1 cup peas
½ tsp/2.5 g/½ tsp garam masala

1 Heat the oil in a karai over medium high heat.
2 Add the onions and fry for 3–4 minutes until light brown.
3 Add the potatoes and cauliflower and stir. Add the turmeric, chilli (chili), cumin, tomatoes, salt and sugar. Stir and fry for 2–3 minutes.
4 Add the peas, cover and lower heat to medium low and cook for about 20 minutes until the potatoes and cauliflower are tender. During the cooking period stir the vegetables a few times to stop them sticking.
5 Sprinkle with garam masala before serving.

Roasted Cauliflower

4 medium tomatoes	½ tsp/2.5 g/½ tsp garam masala
1 large onion	6 oz/175 g/1 cup peas
3 cloves garlic	½ tsp/2.5 g/½ tsp salt
½-in/1-cm root ginger	1 medium-sized cauliflower,
2 tbsp/30 ml/2 tbsp ghee	blanched
¾ tsp/4 g/¾ tsp ground turmeric	
½ tsp/2.5 g/½ tsp chilli (chili) powder	

1 Blend the tomatoes, onion, garlic and ginger in a blender until you have a paste.

2 Heat the ghee in a frying pan over medium heat and add the paste, turmeric, chilli (chili) and garam masala and stir fry until the ghee and spices separate which should be no more than about 5–6 minutes.

3 Add the peas and salt and cook a further 5 minutes, stirring constantly. Remove from the heat.

4 Place the cauliflower in a large oven-proof dish and pour the spices over it. Place in a preheated oven 375°F/190°C (Mark 5) for 30–35 minutes. Serve on a flat plate with the peas and spices poured over.

Dry Potato and Cauliflower

3 tbsp/45 ml/4 tbsp oil
¾ tsp/4 g/¾ tsp kalonji
3–4 green chillies (chilis), split in half

1 small cauliflower, cut into ¾-in/2-cm pieces
1 lb/45 g/1 lb potatoes, diced into ¾-in/2-cm pieces
¾ tsp/4 g/¾ tsp salt

1 Heat oil in a karai over medium high heat and add the kalonji and green chillies (chilis). Let them sizzle for a few seconds.

2 Add the cauliflower and potatoes and stir for 1–2 minutes.

3 Lower heat to medium low, cover and cook for 15–20 minutes, stirring occasionally to stop it sticking to the bottom of the karai.

4 Add the salt, turn up the heat and, stirring constantly, fry until the potatoes and cauliflower are tender.

Vegetable Curry

1–2 fresh green chillies (chilis), seeded and chopped
2 cloves garlic, crushed
2 tbsp/30 ml/2 tbsp ghee or oil
1 tsp/5 g/1 tsp ground turmeric
1 tbsp/15 g/1 tbsp garam masala
1 tsp/5 g/1 tsp mustard seed, crushed
1 tsp/5 g/1 tsp ground coriander
2 tbsp/30 ml/2 tbsp lime or lemon juice
2 medium onions, chopped

1 large potato, peeled and cubed
1 lb/450 g/1 lb mixed prepared vegetables, such as: cauliflower florets (flowerets); green beans, stringed and sliced; shelled peas; washed spinach, tough stems removed; etc.
2 ripe tomatoes, peeled and chopped
approx. 8 fl oz/225 ml/1 cup water
salt, pepper and sugar to taste

1 Fry the chillies (chilis) and garlic in the ghee or oil with the spices, and lime or lemon juice for 5 minutes.

2 Add the onion, and stir over a high heat until it begins to brown.

3 Add the vegetables, water and seasoning and simmer, un-covered and stirring occasionally, until the potato is cooked and most of the liquid evaporated – about 20 minutes. Serve hot.

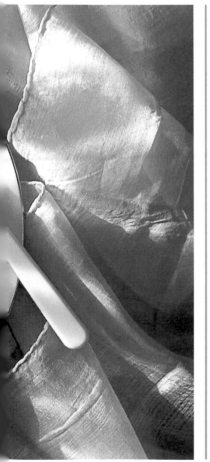

Above, left: Dry potato and cauliflower.

Left: Vegetable curry.

Right: Sweet and sour cucumber salad.

Sweet and Sour Cucumber Salad

1 cucumber	1 tsp/5 g/1 tsp sesame seed oil
2 tsp/10 g/2 tsp finely chopped fresh ginger root	2 tbsp/30 g/2 tbsp sugar
	2 tbsp/30 ml/2 tbsp vinegar

1 Select a dark green and slender cucumber; the fat pale green ones contain too much water and have far less flavour. Cut it in half lengthwise, then cut each piece into slices. Marinate with the ginger and sesame seed oil for about 10–15 minutes.

2 Make the dressing with the sugar and vinegar in a bowl, stirring well to dissolve the sugar.

3 Place the cucumber slices on a plate. Just before serving, pour the sugar and vinegar dressing evenly over them and toss well.

Hot and Sour Cucumber – Sichuan Style

1 cucumber	2 tbsp/30 ml/2 tbsp vinegar
1 tsp/5 g/1 tsp salt	1 tbsp/15 ml/1 tbsp chilli (chili) oil
2 tbsp/30 g/2 tbsp sugar	

1 Split the cucumber in two lengthwise and then cut each piece into strips rather like potato chips (French fries). Sprinkle with the salt and leave for about 10 minutes to extract the bitter juices.

2 Remove each cucumber strip. Place it on a firm surface and soften it by gently tapping it with the blade of a cleaver or knife.

3 Place the cucumber strips on a plate. Sprinkle the sugar evenly over them and then add the vinegar and chilli (chili) oil just before serving.

Above: Hot and sour cucumber – Sichuan style.

Right: Spicy cabbage – Sichuan style.

Top right: Celery salad.

Spicy Cabbage – Sichuan Style

1 lb/450 g/1 lb white cabbage	2 tbsp/30 ml/2 tbsp sesame seed oil
2 tsp/10 g/2 tsp salt	
3–4 dried hot chilli (chili) peppers, soaked and finely chopped	2 tbsp/30 g/2 tbsp sugar
3 spring onions (scallions), finely chopped	2 fl oz/50 ml/¼ cup water
2 tsp/10 g/2 tsp fresh ginger root, finely chopped	2 tbsp/30 ml/2 tbsp vinegar

1 Discard the outer tough leaves of the cabbage and cut the tender heart into thin slices. Sprinkle with salt and let stand for 3–4 hours. Pour off the excess water and dry the cabbage thoroughly. Place it in a bowl or a deep dish.

2 Heat the sesame seed oil in a pan until very hot. Add the finely chopped chillies (chilis), spring onions (scallions) and ginger root. Stir for a few seconds and then add the sugar and water.

Continue stirring to dissolve the sugar. Add the vinegar and bring the mixture to the boil. Remove the pan from the heat and allow the sauce to cool, then pour it over the cabbage. Cover the bowl or plate and leave to stand for 3–4 hours before serving.

Celery Salad

1 celery	1 tbsp/15 ml/1 tbsp vinegar
1 tsp/5 g/1 tsp salt	1 tbsp/15 ml/1 tbsp sesame seed
3 pt/1.7 l/7½ cups water	oil
2 tbsp/30 ml/2 tbsp light soy	2 slices fresh ginger root, finely
sauce	shredded

1 Remove the leaves and outer tough stalks of the celery. Thinly slice the tender parts diagonally. Blanch them in a pan of boiling, salted water. Then pour them into a colander and rinse in cold water until cool. Drain.
2 Mix together the soy sauce, vinegar and sesame seed oil. Add to the celery and toss well.
3 Garnish the salad with finely shredded ginger root and serve.

Chinese Cabbage Salad

1 small Chinese cabbage	1 tsp/5 g/1 tsp salt
2 tbsp/30 ml/2 tbsp light soy sauce	1 tsp/5 g/1 tsp sugar
	1 tbsp/15 ml/1 tbsp sesame seed oil

1 Wash the cabbage thoroughly, cut into thick slices and place in a bowl.

2 Add the soy sauce, salt, sugar and sesame seed oil to the cabbage. Toss well and serve.

Note Green or red peppers (or both) can be added to the cabbage.

Five-Spice Bean Curd

4 cakes bean curd (tofu)	1 tsp/5 g/1 tsp salt
3 tbsp/45 ml/4 tbsp light soy sauce	3 tbsp/45 ml/4 tbsp rice wine or dry sherry
2 tbsp/30 ml/2 tbsp dark soy sauce	2–3 spring onions (scallions)
	2–3 slices ginger root
1 tbsp/15 g/1 tbsp white or brown sugar	2 tsp/10 g/2 tsp five-spice powder

1 Place the bean curd in a saucepan and cover with cold water. Bring to the boil, cover and cook over a high heat for 10 minutes. By then the bean curd will resemble a beehive in texture.

2 Reduce the heat and add the soy sauces, salt, sugar, wine, spring onions (scallions), ginger root and five-spice powder. Bring to the boil gently under a cover and simmer for 30 minutes. Turn off the heat and leave to cool.

3 Remove the bean curd and cut it into small slices. Serve them either on their own or as part of a mixed hors d'oeuvre.

Left: Chinese cabbage salad.

Above: Five-spice bean curd.

Right: Pickled vegetables.

Pickled Vegetables

USE FOUR TO SIX OF THE FOLLOWING VEGETABLES OR MORE:

cucumber	green beans
carrot	garlic
radish or turnip	8 pt/4.5 l/9 pt cold boiled water
cauliflower	6 oz/175 g/¾ cup salt
broccoli	2 oz/50 g/2 oz chilli (chili) peppers
green cabbage	½ oz/15 g/3 tsp Sichuan
white cabbage	peppercorns
celery	2 fl oz/50 ml/¼ cup Chinese
onion	distilled spirit (or white rum, gin
fresh ginger root	or vodka)
leek	4 oz/100 g/4 oz ginger root
spring onion (scallion)	4 oz/100 g/½ cup brown sugar
red pepper	
green pepper	

1 Put the cold boiled water into a large, clean earthenware or glass jar. Add the salt, chillies (chilis), peppercorns, spirit, ginger and sugar.

2 Wash and trim the vegetables, peel if necessary and drain well. Put them into the jar and seal it making sure it is airtight. Place the jar in a cool place and leave the vegetables to pickle for at least five days before serving.

3 Use a pair of clean chopsticks or tongs to pick the vegetables out of the jar. Do not allow any grease to enter the jar. You can replenish the vegetables, adding a little salt each time. If any white scum appears on the surface of the brine, add a little sugar and spirit. The longer the pickling lasts, the better.

Aubergine (Eggplant) with Sichuan 'Fish Sauce'

1 lb/450 g/1 lb aubergines (eggplants)
4–5 dried red chilli (chili) peppers
oil for deep frying
3–4 spring onions (scallions), finely chopped
1 slice ginger root, peeled and finely chopped
1 clove garlic, finely chopped

1 tsp/5 g/1 tsp sugar
1 tbsp/15 ml/1 tbsp soy sauce
1 tbsp/15 ml/1 tbsp vinegar
1 tbsp/15 ml/1 tbsp chilli (chili) bean paste
2 tsp/10 g/2 tsp cornflour (cornstarch),, mixed with 2 tbsp/ 30 ml/2 tbsp water
1 tsp/5 ml/1 tsp sesame seed oil

1 Soak the dried red chillies (chilis) for 5–10 minutes, cut them into small pieces and discard the stalks.
2 Peel the aubergines (eggplants), discard the stalks and cut them into diamond-shaped chunks.
3 Heat the oil in a wok and deep-fry the aubergines (eggplants) for 3½–4 minutes or until soft. Remove with a slotted spoon and drain.
4 Pour off the oil and return the aubergine (eggplant) to the wok with the red chillies (chilis), spring onions (scallions), ginger root and garlic. Stir a few times and add the sugar, soy sauce, vinegar and chilli (chili) bean paste. Continue stirring for about 1 minute. Finally add the cornflour (cornstarch) and water mixture, blend well and garnish with the sesame seed oil. Serve either hot or cold.

French (Green) Beans a la Sichuan

1 lb/0.5 kg/1 lb beans
½ oz/15 g/½ oz dried shrimps, soaked
2 tbsp/30 g/2 tbsp Sichuan preserved vegetables
1 spring onion (scallion), chopped
1 slice ginger root, peeled and finely chopped

½ tbsp/7.5 g/½ tbsp salt
½ tbsp/7.5 g/½ tbsp sugar
1 tsp/5 ml/1 tsp sesame seed oil
1 tbsp/15 ml/1 tbsp vinegar
oil for deep-frying

1 Wash and cut the ends off the beans; snap them in half if they are too long. Finely chop the soaked shrimps and Sichuan preserved vegetables.
2 Heat up the oil, deep-fry the beans for 1–2 minutes or until soft, scoop out and drain. Pour off the excess oil leaving about 1 tbsp/15 ml/1 tbsp in the wok; stir-fry the finely chopped ginger root, dried shrimps and Sichuan preserved vegetables; add the beans with salt, sugar and 2 tbsp/30 ml/2 tbsp water or stock. After 1–2 minutes add onions, vinegar and sesame seed oil; blend well; serve either hot or cold.

Below: Aubergine (eggplant) with Sichuan 'fish sauce'.

Right: French (green) beans à la Sichuan.

Vegetarian 'Lion's Head' Casserole

4 cakes fresh bean curd
4 oz/100 g/4 oz fried gluten
2 oz/50 g/½ cup cooked carrots
4–5 dried Chinese mushrooms,
soaked
2 oz/50 g/⅓ cup bamboo shoots
6 cabbage or lettuce hearts
5 large cabbage leaves
1 tsp/5 g/1 tsp fresh root ginger,
finely chopped
2 tbsp/30 ml/2 tbsp rice wine or
dry sherry

1 tbsp/15 g/1 tbsp salt
1 tsp/5 g/1 tsp sugar
1 tsp/5 g/1 tsp white pepper
(ground)
2 tsp/10 ml/2 tsp sesame seed oil
1 tbsp/15 g/1 tbsp cornflour
(cornstarch)
1 oz/25 g/2 tbsp ground rice or
breadcrumbs
oil for deep-frying
flour for dusting

1 Squeeze as much liquid as possible from the bean curd using muslin (cheesecloth) and then mash.

2 Finely chop the gluten, carrots, mushrooms and bamboo shoots. Place them with the mashed bean curd in a large mixing bowl. Add 1 tsp/5 g/1 tsp salt, the finely chopped root ginger, ground rice, cornflour (cornstarch) and sesame seed oil and blend everything together until smooth.

3 Make 10 'meatballs' from this mixture and place them on a plate lightly dusted with flour. Trim off any hard or tough roots from the cabbage or lettuce hearts.

4 Heat the oil in a wok or deep-fryer. When hot, deep-fry the 'meatballs' for about 3 minutes, stirring very gently to make sure that they are not stuck together. Scoop out with a slotted spoon or strainer and drain.

5 Pour off the excess oil leaving about 2 tbsp/30 ml/2 tbsp in the wok. Stir-fry the cabbage hearts with a little salt and sugar. Add about 1 pt/600 ml/2½ cups water and bring to the boil. Reduce the heat and let the mixture simmer.

6 Meanwhile, line the bottom of a casserole with the cabbage leaves and place the 'meatballs' on top. Pour the cabbage hearts with the soup into the casserole and add the remaining salt, ground pepper and wine or sherry. Cover, bring to the boil, reduce the heat and simmer for 10 minutes.

To serve, take off the lid and re-arrange the cabbage hearts so that they appear between the 'meatballs' in a star-shaped pattern.

Right: Vegetarian 'lion's head' casserole.

Right: 'Pock-marked woman' bean-curd.

'Pock-Marked Woman' Bean-Curd

3 cakes of bean-curd
4 oz/100 g/½ cup minced (ground) beef (or pork)
¼ tsp/1 g/¼ tsp salt
1 tsp/5 g/1 tsp salted black beans
1 tbsp/15 ml/1 tbsp chilli (chili) paste

3 tbsp/45 ml/4 tbsp stock
1 leek or 3 spring onions (scallions)
½ tbsp/7.5 ml/½ tbsp soy sauce
1 tbsp/15 g/1 tbsp cornflour (cornstarch)
Sichuan pepper, freshly ground

1 Cut the bean-curd into ½-in/1-cm square cubes; blanch for 2–3 minutes to get rid of its plaster odour; remove and drain. Cut the leek or onions into short lengths.

2 Heat up the oil until smoking; stir-fry the beef or pork until it turns dark in colour; add salt, stir a few times, then add salted black beans. Crush them with the cooking ladle to blend well with the meat, then add chilli (chili) paste; continue stirring.

3 When you can smell the chilli (chili), add stock followed by the bean curd and leek or spring onion (scallion). Reduce heat; cook gently for 3–4 minutes; add soy sauce and the cornflour (cornstarch) mixed in a little water; stir gently to blend well and serve with freshly ground Sichuan pepper as a garnish.

Top right: White salad.

White Salad

3 dried mushrooms, reconstituted
2 tsp/10 ml/2 tsp soy sauce
1 tsp/5 ml/1 tsp mirin
4 oz/100 g/¼ lb daikon radish
1 small carrot

salt
½ cake konnyaku (arum root)
(optional)
2 oz/50 g/½ cup French (green)
beans

DRESSING

7 oz/200 g/scant 1 cup bean curd
1 tbsp/15 g/1 tbsp white sesame
seeds
2½ tbsp/40 ml/2½ tbsp white

miso
1 tbsp/15 ml/1 tbsp mirin
1 tsp/5 g/1 tsp sugar

GARNISH

1 sheet nori seaweed

1 Remove the stems of the mushrooms and slice thinly. Place in a small saucepan and add the soy sauce and mirin; simmer over very low heat for 10–15 minutes. Leave the mushrooms in any remaining stock to cool.

2 Cut the daikon radish and carrot into threads. Salt and set aside for 10 minutes, then knead until the vegetables become soft. Rinse, squeeze out excess moisture and pat dry.

3 Rub the konnyaku with salt, then rinse and pound with a rolling pin or a wooden pestle. Cut into julienne strips. Saute in a dry frying pan for a few minutes, then set aside to cool. Top and tail the beans and parboil.

4 Wrap the bean curd in clean dry towels, weight with a chopping board and set aside for 20–30 minutes to drain. Press the bean curd through a sieve.

5 Toast the seame seeds with a little salt in a dry frying pan. When they give off a nutty aroma, transfer to a suribachi or heavy frying pan and grind until oily. Blend in the bean curd and the remaining dressing ingredients.

6 Make sure the vegetables are all perfectly dry, and stir into the dressing. Mound the salad in small deep individual bowls. Lightly toast the nori seaweed and cut with scissors into threads. Set a small mound of nori on each serving to garnish.

Left: Deep-fried bean curd in broth.

Right: Red and white salad.

Deep-Fried Bean Curd in Broth

11 oz/300 g/scant 1½ cups bean curd	2 tbsp/30 g/2 tbsp kuzu, potato flour or cornflour (cornstarch)

DIPPING SAUCE

⅓ pt/200 ml/2 cups dashi	3 tbsp/45 ml/4 tbsp mirin
1 tbsp/15 ml/1 tbsp light soy sauce	

GARNISHES

⅔ oz/20 g/⅔ oz daikon radish	1 spring onion (scallion) or young leek
1 tbsp/15 g/1 tbsp fresh root ginger	1 tbsp/15 g/1 tbsp dried bonito flakes

1 First drain the bean curd; set a weight such as a chopping board or dinner plate on the bean curd. Set aside for at least 30 minutes to drain.
2 Grind the kuzu or flour finely in a suribachi or mortar and pestle; or simply crush with a rolling pin to make a fine powder.
3 Cut the drained bean curd into 4 pieces and roll in the kuzu flour. Set aside.
4 Make the dipping sauces by combining the ingredients in a small saucepan, bring just to a simmer and keep warm.
5 Peel and grate the ginger. Set aside. Peel and grate the daikon radish and set aside. Slice the spring onion (scallion) or leek into very fine slices. Place the bonito flakes in a small bowl.
6 Fill a small saucepan or deep-fryer with vegetable oil to a depth of 3-in/7-cm and heat to 350°F/180°C. Deep-fry each piece of bean curd separately for 6–8 minutes, until golden.

Drain the bean curd briefly on absorbent kitchen paper. Arrange each piece of bean curd on a serving dish, and top with the garnishes. Either pour the warm dipping sauce over or serve separately.

Red and White Salad

4 in/10 cm daikon radish	½ tsp/2.5 g/½ tp salt
1 medium carrot	

DRESSING

3 tbsp/45 ml/4 tbsp rice vinegar	1 piece 1½-in sq/4-cm kombu seuweed
3 tbsp/45 ml/4 tbsp mirin	
1 tbsp/15 ml/1 tbsp dashi	shredded orange or lemon rind to garnish
pinch salt	

1 Scrape the daikon radish and carrot. Cut into 'needles'.
2 Salt the vegetables and set aside for 10 minutes. Knead thoroughly until the daikon radish becomes soft and translucent, then squeeze to press out as much water as possible.
3 Combine the dressing ingredients in a small saucepan and bring to the boil. Remove from heat and chill. Add 2 tbsp/30 ml/2 tbsp of the chilled dressing to the vegetables. Mix and knead; squeeze to press out the dressing. Discard the excess dressing.
4 Put the kombu in a clean bowl and put the vegetables on top. Pour the remaining dressing over them. Cover the bowl and refrigerate for at least 30 minutes – the salad will have a better flavour if it is left overnight. Refrigerated in a tightly sealed container, it will keep for up to 2 weeks.
5 Serve cold or at room temperature in small portions, garnished with a few shreds of orange or lemon peel.

Right: Cucumber and wakame salad.

Cucumber and Wakame Salad

1 cucumber or 2 small Japanese cucumbers	½ oz/15 g/½ oz dried wakame seaweed, reconstituted
½ tsp/2.5 g/½ tsp salt	

DRESSING

3 tbsp/45 ml/4 tbsp rice vinegar	1 tbsp/15 ml/1 tbsp sugar
2 tbsp/30 ml/2 tbsp dashi	¼ tsp/1 g/¼ tsp salt
2 tbsp/30 ml/2 tbsp soy sauce	2 tbsp/30 ml/2 tbsp mirin

GARNISH

½ oz/15 g/½ oz ginger, chopped
into fine needles

1 Slice the cucumber in half lengthwise. Scrape out the seeds. Cut into paper-thin slices.
2 Dissolve ½ tsp/2.5 g/½ tsp salt in 3½ fl oz/100 ml/½ cup cold water, add the cucumber, and leave to soak for 20 minutes. Put the cucumber into muslin (cheesecloth) to drain.
3 Squeeze the cucumber gently to remove excess moisture.
4 Combine the dressing ingredients in a small saucepan, and heat to dissolve the sugar. Remove from heat and chill. Trim the wakame seaweed and chop coarsely. Combine the wakame and cucumber in a bowl and spoon the chilled dressing over them. Toss gently.
5 Arrange neat mounds of salad in individual bowls. Garnish with a little chopped ginger.

Right: Ensalada de col.

Cabbage Salad

½ (head) cabbage, shredded	1 small handful walnuts or almonds
1 or more avocados, diced	
1 or more tomatoes, sliced	1 medium carrot, shredded
1 red onion, thinly sliced	1 cooked beetroot (beet), sliced
2 sticks celery, chopped	1 handful coriander leaves, chopped
1 small jicama, diced or sliced	
1 small handful raisins	4 oz/100 g/1 cup cheese, diced

1 Mix the cabbage with any or all of the above. Make a vinaigrette-type dressing, but use lime juice (or half-and-half lime juice and wine vinegar) with the olive oil, instead of just vinegar. Use two parts of olive oil to one part lime juice, and add a pinch of dry mustard to help the dressing emulsify when you shake it.

Above: *Guacamole.*

Basic Guacamole

½ *dried red chilli (chili),* 2 *large or 4 small avocados, very*
preferably arbol *ripe*
1 clove garlic

1 Seed and shred the chilli (chili) pepper; pound in a mortar with the garlic and 1–2 tbsp/15–30 ml/1–2 tbsp water. Leave for 5–10 minutes. Mash the avocado with an old-fashioned wooden potato masher. Mix in the chilli (chili) garlic paste, strained through a tea-strainer. This is good for a dip; for a garnish, you can double the amounts of garlic and pepper.

Fancy Guacamole

basic ingredients, as above *1 tbsp/15 g/1 tbsp chopped*
1 medium tomato *coriander*
½ small white onion *salt*

1 Peel, seed, and finely chop the tomato. Chop the onion finely in a food processor. Add these ingredients to the guacamole. Salt to taste – the basic recipe really does not need salt.
2 For further variations, omit the red pepper or the garlic or both, and add one finely chopped serrano. You may also wish to add chopped coriander. None of this will necessarily make a better guacamole than the other, just different.

Right: Tomato salad.

Stuffed Peppers

5 medium crisp green or red peppers	4 fl oz/100 ml/½ cup water
1 fresh green chilli (chili), seeded and chopped	1 tbsp/15 g/1 tbsp tomato purée (paste)
1 small onion, finely chopped	½ tsp/2.5 g/½ tsp dried oregano
2 tbsp/30 ml/2 tbsp olive oil	2 fl oz/50 ml/¼ cup lime juice
	salt, pepper and sugar to taste

FILLING

2 fresh green chillies (chilis), or canned Jalapeño peppers (these are hot)	1 large onion, thinly sliced
	8 oz/225 g/1 cup cream cheese
	4 tbsp/60 g/5 tbsp pomegranate
1 tbsp/15 ml/1 tbsp olive oil	seeds (optional)

1 Prepare the peppers a day in advance. Char 4 of them evenly over a gas flame or under the grill (broiler) until the skin blisters. Wrap in a tea (dish) towel and leave to cool, then rub off the skins under running water.

2 Fry the chillies (chilis) in the oil with the onion until softened, then add the water, tomato purée (paste), oregano, lime juice and seasoning. Simmer for 5 minutes, add the prepared peppers and cook for 10 minutes, turning once, until just tender.

3 Remove the peppers to a serving dish. Boil up the marinade vigorously until it reduces to a few tablespoonfuls, pour over the peppers, cover and refrigerate overnight.

4 To make the filling, char, seed and chop the remaining pepper, and seed and slice the chillies (chilis) finely lengthways.

5 Heat the oil and soften the onion, chillies (chilis) and pepper for about 10 minutes. Cool.

6 Stir in the cream cheese and two-thirds of the pomegranate seeds, if used, and season to taste.

7 Stuff the peppers and serve chilled, sprinkled with the remaining pomegranate seeds if used.

Tomato Salad

1–2 fresh red chillies (chilis)	1 tbsp/15 ml/1 tbsp olive oil
3 large tomatoes	½ tbsp/7.5 ml/½ tbsp lime juice
3–4 spring onions (scallions), finely chopped	salt to taste
handful fresh coriander, finely chopped	

1 Split and seed the chillies (chilis) and soak them in cold salted water for an hour. Rinse them and slice finely.

2 Peel the tomatoes. Loosen the skins by first pouring boiling water over them, letting them stand for 1 minute, then refreshing in cold. Halve the peeled tomatoes and scoop out the seeds. Either slice the flesh or cut into chunks.

3 Lightly stir in the rest of the ingredients, season and chill for half an hour before serving.

VARIATION Add 6–8 oz/150–225 g/1½–2 cups cubed or sliced mozzarella or feta cheese for a refreshing starter or a light lunch.

Mexican Omelette

Above: Mexican omelette.

Right: Som tam thai.

knob of butter
4 eggs, lightly beaten with a little seasoning
1 tbsp/15 g/1 tbsp chopped spring onion (scallion)
1 fresh green chilli (chili), seeded and thinly sliced

2 tbsp/30 g/2 tbsp cooked sweetcorn
3 oz/75 g/¾ cup Cheddar cheese, grated
½ ripe avocado, peeled and sliced

1 Melt the butter in an omelette pan and pour in the eggs.
2 Sprinkle on the spring onion (scallion), fresh chilli (chili), sweetcorn and cheese.
3 As soon as the cheese melts, arrange the avocado slices on one half of the omelette, fold over and serve immediately.

Som Tam Thai

6 cloves garlic
11 oz/300 g/11 oz green papaya, julienned
7 pieces small green chilli (chili)
¼ cup unsalted peanuts, roasted
¼ cup dry shrimp

½ cup French (green) beans, cut in 1-in/2.5-cm pieces
6 cherry tomatoes, quartered
¼ cup lemon juice
1 tbsp/15 g/1 tbsp palm sugar
1 tbsp/15 ml/1 tbsp fish sauce

1 Take the garlic and a little papaya and the chilli (chili) and pound lightly. Add the peanuts, shrimp, beans, tomatoes and rest of the papaya. Mix well.
2 Add the lemon juice, sugar and fish sauce. Mix and place on a plate. Eat with raw vegetables and morning glory, sticky rice, French (green) beans and roast chicken.

Issaan Shredded Bamboo Shoot

2 cups fresh bamboo shoots, julienned
2 tbsp/30 g/2 tbsp pounded roasted rice
¼ cup spring onions (scallions), sliced

10 mint leaves
2 tbsp/30 ml/2 tbsp lemon juice
½ tbsp/7.5 ml/½ tbsp fish sauce
2 tbsp/30 g/2 tbsp sliced red onion
½ tbsp/7.5 g/½ tbsp dry pounded red chilli (chili)

1 Boil the bamboo shoots in water until tender, but not soft. Throw away water and rinse the shoots, and then add all the rest of the ingredients. Mix well. Serve with roast chicken and raw vegetables.

Ajaad salad.

Roast aubergine (eggplant) salad.

Ajaad Salad

2 cups white vinegar
⅓ cup sugar
1 tsp/5 g/1 tsp salt
½ cup cucumber, quartered and sliced
¼ cup shallots, sliced
2 pieces fresh red chilli (chili), sliced in to thin rounds

1 To make the satay, mix together the white vinegar, sugar and salt. Bring to the boil and reduce to a quantity equalling 1 cup.
2 When ready to serve, mix all the other ingredients together and pour the satay over the top.

Roast Aubergine (Eggplant) Salad

3 pieces long green aubergines (eggplants), weighing approx 11 oz/300 g/11 oz in total
1 oz/25 g/⅛ cup minced (ground) pork
2 oz/50 g/¼ cup shrimp, dry
2 oz/50 g/½ cup shallots
5 pieces fresh small green chilli (chili)
2 tbsp/30 ml/2 tbsp lime juice
1 tsp/5 ml/1 tsp fish sauce
¼ tsp/1 g/¼ tsp sugar

1 Place aubergine (eggplant) in a moderately hot oven and roast until soft. Remove skin, slice into 1-in/2.5-cm pieces. Sauté pork until done, rinse dry shrimp in hot water, dry and then mix all the ingredients together and place on plates. Eat with rice.

Mixed Fried Vegetables

¼ cup oil

2 oz/50 g/½ cup mange-tout (snow) peas

2 oz/50 g/½ cup kale, sliced

2 oz/50 g/½ cup cabbage, sliced

2 oz/50 g/½ cup brocoli, flower and stem

2 oz/50 g/½ cup cauliflower florets (floweretes)

2 oz/50 g/½ cup asparagus, cut into 2-in/5-cm pieces

2 oz/50 g/½ cup chinese cabbage, sliced

2 oz/50 g/½ cup mushrooms, halved

2 oz/50 g/½ cup fresh baby corn, halved

½ cup chicken stock

½ tsp/2.5 ml/½ tsp ground white pepper

3 tbsp/45 g/4 tbsp garlic, finely chopped

4 tbsp/60 ml/5 tbsp oyster sauce

¼ tsp/1 ml/¼ tsp black soya sauce

1 tbsp/15 ml/1 tbsp white soy sauce

1 Heat wok very hot and add oil. Place all vegetables in a bowl, add the stock and white pepper. Place the garlic in the wok, stir well and add the vegetables all at once (watch for flames).

2 Stir fry until almost cooked although the vegetables should still be slightly crisp. Add the oyster sauce and two soya sauces. Mix well and serve. Eat with rice or with any other food.

Mixed fried vegetables.

NOODLE & RICE DISHES

From India
MUSHROOM PILLAU 248
PLAIN RICE 248
FRIED RICE 249
RICE WITH LENTILS 251

From Japan
PORK ESCALOPE (CUTLET) ON RICE 255
THIN SUSHI ROLLS 256
FOX NOODLES 256
MOON VIEWING NOODLES 257
CHICKEN AND EGG ON RICE 257
BUCKWHEAT NOODLES IN HOT BROTH 258
CHILLED BUCKWHEAT NOODLES 258

From China
FRIED RICE CHIU CHOW STYLE 251
SHANGHAI VEGETABLE RICE 252
BEGGARS' NOODLES 252
TEN VARIETY FRIED RICE 254
FRIED RICE-NOODLES 254
CHINESE CABBAGE, MUNG BEAN NOODLES, DRIED SHRIMPS AND
SHREDDED PORK 255

From Thailand
SWEET RICE NOODLES 259
FRIED NOODLES WITH CHICKEN, VEGETABLES AND GRAVY 260
SHRIMPS (PRAWNS) WITH RICE NOODLES 260
FRIED RICE WITH SPICY SAUCE 261
NOODLE SOUP 262
SHRIMP- (PRAWN-) FRIED RICE 263
CURRIED NOODLES 263

Mushroom Pillau

2 tbsp/30 ml/2 tbsp oil
2 bay leaves
2 in/5 cm cinnamon stick
4 cardamoms
1 large onion, finely chopped

6 oz/175 g/1½ cups mushrooms, sliced
12 oz/325 g/1⅔ cups basmati rice, washed and drained
1 tsp/5 g/1 tsp salt
30 fl oz/825 ml/3¾ cups water

1 Heat oil in a large saucepan over medium high heat. Add the bay leaves, cinnamon and cardamoms and let them sizzle for a few seconds.
2 Add the onion and fry until soft. Add the mushrooms and fry for about 5 minutes until all the moisture has been absorbed.
3 Add the rice and salt and stir fry for 2–3 minutes. Add the water and bring to the boil.
4 Cover tightly, lower heat to very low and cook for about 20 minutes until all the water has been absorbed. Fluff the pillau with a fork and serve hot.

Plain Rice

12 oz/325 g/1⅔ cups basmati rice

30 fl oz/825 ml/3¾ cups cold water

1 Rinse the rice three or four times in cold water. Drain.
2 Place the drained rice in a large saucepan and pour in the measured amount of water. Bring it to the boil rapidly over a high heat. Stir.
3 Lower heat to very low, cover and cook for about 20 minutes until all the water has evaporated.
4 Fluff the rice with a fork and serve hot.

Above: Mushroom pillau.

Right: Fried rice.

Fried Rice

12 oz/325 g/1⅔ cups basmati
rice, cooked and cooled
3 tbsp/45 ml/4 tbsp ghee
2 bay leaves
2 in/5 cm cinnamon stick
4 cardamoms
3 large onions, finely sliced

3 green chillies (chilis), cut
lengthwise
1 tsp/5 g/1 tsp salt
½ tsp/2.5 g/½ tsp sugar
2 tbsp/30 g/2 tbsp raisins
(optional)

1 Heat the ghee in a large frying pan over medium high heat.
Add the bay leaves, cinnamon, cardamoms and let sizzle for a
few seconds.
2 Add the onions and chillies (chilis) and fry until the onions
are golden brown.
3 Add the rice, salt, sugar and raisins and continue frying until
the rice is thoroughly heated up.

Shanghai Vegetable Rice

14 oz/400 g/2 cups long grain rice	about 8 oz/225 g/½ lb Chinese sausages
1 lb/450 g/1 lb green cabbage or spring greens	2 tbsp/30 ml/2 tbsp vegetable oil
1½ tbsp/22.5 g/1½ tbsp dried shrimps	¾ oz/20 g/1½ tbsp lard
	1½ tsp/7.5 g/1½ tsp salt

1 Wash and measure the rice. Simmer in the same volume of water for 6 minutes. Remove from the heat and leave to stand, covered, for 7–8 minutes. Wash and dry the cabbage. Chop into 1½×3-in/4×7.5-cm pieces, removing the tougher stalks.
2 Soak the dried shrimps in hot water to cover for 7–8 minutes, then drain. Cut the sausages slantwise into 1-in/2.5-cm sections.
3 Heat the oil and lard in a deep saucepan. When hot, stir-fry the shrimps for 30 seconds. Add the cabbage and toss and turn for 1½ minutes until well coated with oil. Sprinkle the cabbage with the salt. Pack in the rice. Add 4–5 tbsp/60–75 ml/5–6 tbsp water down the side of the pan. Cover and simmer very gently for about 15 minutes. Transfer to a heated serving dish.

Beggars' Noodles

3 spring onions (scallions)	1 lb/450 g/1 lb wheat flour
3 tbsp/45 ml/4 tbsp soy sauce	noodles, flat or Ho Fen noodles, or
3 tbsp/45 ml/4 tbsp wine vinegar	spaghetti

SAUCE

3 tbsp/45 ml/4 tbsp peanut butter	3 tbsp/45 ml/4 tbsp sesame seed
2 tbsp/30 ml/2 tbsp sesame paste	oil

1 Coarsely chop or shred the onions. Mix the soy sauce and vinegar together. Mix the peanut butter, sesame paste and sesame seed oil together.
2 Place the noodles in a saucepan of boiling water and simmer for 10 minutes, or spaghetti for about 10–12 minutes. Drain.
3 Divide the hot noodles into 4–6 heated large rice bowls. Sprinkle evenly with the spring onion (scallion). Add a large spoonful of the peanut butter and sesame mixture to each bowl of noodles. Pour 1 tbsp/15 ml/1 tbsp soy sauce and vinegar mixture over contents of each bowl.

Above: Shanghai vegetable rice.   *Right:* Beggars' noodles.

Ten Variety Fried Rice

Above: Ten variety fried rice (left) and fried rice-noodles (right).

Opposite, left: Chinese cabbage, mung bean noodles, dried shrimps and shredded pork.

8 oz/225 g/generous 1 cup rice	2 spring onions (scallions)
4 oz/100 g/½ cup shrimps	3 eggs
4 oz/100 g/½ cup shrimps	salt
4 oz/100 g/½ cup cooked ham or pork	4 oz/100 g/⅔ cup peas
	2 tbsp/30 ml/2 tbsp soy sauce

1 Wash the rice in cold water just once, then cover it with more cold water so that there is about 1 in/2.5 cm of water above the surface of the rice in the saucepan. Bring it to the boil; stir to prevent it sticking to the bottom of the pan when cooked. Replace the lid tightly and reduce the heat so that it is as low as possible. Cook for about 15–20 minutes.

2 Peel the shrimps, dice the ham or pork into small cubes the size of the peas. Finely chop the onions. Beat the eggs with a little salt; heat up about 1 tbsp/15 ml/1 tbsp oil and make an omelette; set aside to cool.

3 Heat up the remaining oil, stir-fry the finely chopped onions, followed by the shrimps, ham or pork, and peas; stir, adding a little salt, then add the cooked rice and soy sauce. Add the omelette, breaking it into little bits. When everything is well blended it is ready to serve.

Fried Rice-Noodles

1 lb/450 g/1 lb rice-noodles	2 oz/50 g/½ cup celery
1 oz/25 g/1 oz dried shrimps	1 oz/25 g/¼ cup leeks
2 oz/50 g/¼ cup pork	1 tsp/5 g/1 tsp salt
2 oz/50 g/⅓ cup bamboo shoots	2 tbsp/30 ml/2 tbsp soy sauce
3–4 small dried Chinese mushrooms	4 tbsp/60 ml/5 tbsp stock
	4 tbsp/60 ml/5 tbsp oil

1 Soak the rice-noodles in warm water until soft; soak the dried shrimps and mushrooms. Cut the pork, bamboo shoots and leeks into matchstick-sized shreds.

2 Stir-fry the pork, bamboo shoots, shrimp, celery and leeks in a little hot oil, add salt and stock; cook for about 2 minutes, remove.

3 Heat up the remaining oil; stir-fry the rice-noodles for about 2–3 minutes; add the other cooked ingredients and soy sauce; stir for a further 2 minutes until there is no juice at all left; serve hot.

Chinese Cabbage, Mung Bean Noodles, Dried Shrimps and Shredded Pork

1¼ lb/550 g/1¼ lb Chinese cabbage

4 oz/100 g/¼ lb mung bean noodles

SEASONING

1 tsp/5 g/1 tsp salt

2 tsp/10 g/2 tsp cornflour (cornstarch)

½ tsp/2.5 ml/½ tsp sesame seed oil

½ tsp/2.5 g/½ tsp sugar

3–4 tbsp/45–60 ml/4–5 tbsp peanut oil

2 oz/50 g/¼ cup dried shrimps

2 oz/50 g/¼ cup fillet (tenderloin) of pork

3–4 slices fresh root ginger

1½ pt/900 ml/3¾ cups chicken stock

1 tsp/5 g/1 tsp salt

2 tsp/10 ml/2 tsp Chinese yellow wine

1 Cut the Chinese cabbage into ½×2-in/1×5-cm pieces. Soak the mung bean noodles and the dried shrimps in water for about 15 minutes until they are softened. Shred the pork and mix the meat with the ingredients.

2 Heat 3–4 tbsp/45–60 ml/4–5 tbsp oil in a karai or wok and add the ginger slices and shredded pork, stirring to separate. Then add the dried shrimps.

3 Add the Chinese cabbage, stir and mix well. Pour in the chicken stock and bring the contents to the boil. Reduce the heat and simmer for 15 minutes. Add the mung bean noodles and simmer for a further 2–3 minutes. Finally add salt and Chinese yellow wine and serve.

Pork Escalope (Cutlet) on Rice

14 oz/400 g/2 cups short grain white rice

¾ pt/450 ml/2 cups water

4 breaded pork escalopes (cutlets)

1 small onion

1 pt/600 ml/2½ cups dashi

3½ fl oz/100 ml/½ cup mirin

3 fl oz/75 ml/5 tbsp soy sauce

6 eggs

1 Cook the rice in the water. While the rice is cooking and resting, prepare the topping. Prepare and deep-fry the pork; drain on absorbent kitchen paper and slice diagonally into 1-in/3-cm strips. Set aside and keep warm.

2 Peel and slice the onion. Combine the dashi, mirin and soy sauce in a saucepan and bring to the boil. Add the onion and simmer until soft.

3 Lightly mix the eggs with chopsticks and slowly pour over the onion. Stir once when the egg is nearly set.

4 Half fill 4 large bowls with hot rice and neatly arrange a sliced breaded pork escalope (cutlet) on each bowl. Before the egg is completely set, ladle a quarter of the egg mixture over each bowl, distributing all the liquid, and taking care that the egg mixture does not completely cover the escalopes (cutlets).

Above: Pork escalope (cutlet) on rice.

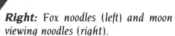

Right: *Fox noodles (left) and moon viewing noodles (right).*

Left: *Thin sushi rolls.*

Far right: *Chicken and egg on rice.*

Thin Sushi Rolls

vinegared rice made from 7 oz/
200 g/1 cup uncooked rice
2 oz/50 g/¼ cup takuan pickle
½ cucumber, 6-in/15-cm long
2 sheets nori seaweed

1 tsp/5 ml/1 tsp rice vinegar,
mixed with 3 tbsp/45 ml/4 tbsp
water
freshly made wasabi horseradish

1 Prepare the vinegared rice. Shred the takuan pickle. Slice the cucumber into narrow strips. Toast the nori by moving it over a flame for a few seconds until it changes colour and becomes fragrant, and halve each sheet of nori.

2 To make the takuan pickle rolls, lay one half sheet of nori on a bamboo rolling meat. Moisten your hands with the vinegar, place one-fourth of the vinegared rice on the nori and spread to cover the edges, leaving the top 1 in/2.5 cm uncovered. Lay half the takuan pickle in a line along the centre of the rice.

3 Holding the takuan in place with your fingers, roll up the bamboo mat to form a firm roll. Press the mat around the roll to shape it, remove the mat and with a sharp knife cut the roll into 6 slices, cutting either diagonally or straight downward. Repeat with the takuan.

4 To make cucumber rolls, lay a sheet of nori on the bamboo mat and spread over a quarter of the rice. Smear a thin line of wasabi horseradish along the centre of the rice, and lay 1 or 2 strips of cucumber on the wasabi. Roll up and cut as before.

Fox Noodles

14 oz/400 g/14 oz udon noodles

NOODLE BROTH

2 pt/1 l/5 cups dashi	1 tbsp/15 g/1 tbsp sugar
2 tbsp/30 ml/2 tbsp light soy sauce	2 tsp/10 ml/2 tsp sake
	2 spring onions (scallions)
2 tsp/1 g/2 tsp salt	4 cakes thin deep-fried bean curd

SIMMERING STOCK

⅓ pt/200 ml/2 cups dashi	1 tbsp/15 g/1 tbsp sugar
2 tbsp/30 ml/2 tbsp soy sauce	

1 Cook the noodles. Combine the noodle broth ingredients and bring to the boil; keep warm. Shred and rinse the spring onions (scallions).

2 Pour boiling water over the deep-fried bean curd to remove oil. Drain and combine with the simmering ingredients in a small saucepan and bring to the boil. Cover with a drop lid and simmer for 10 minutes.

3 Warm 4 deep bowls. Put the noodles in a sieve and immerse in boiling water for a few seconds to reheat; divide among the 4 bowls.

4 Arrange one folded cake of deep-fried bean curd and a quarter of the spring onion (scallion) in each bowl, ladle the hot broth over them and serve.

Moon Viewing Noodles

14oz/400 g/14 oz dried udon
noodles

NOODLE BROTH

2 pt/1 l/5 cups dashi	2 tsp/10 ml/2 tsp sake
2 tbsp/30 ml/2 tbsp light soy sauce	4 spring onions (scallions)
2 tsp/10 g/2 tsp salt	½ sheet nori
1 tbsp/15 g/1 tbsp sugar	4 eggs

1 Cook the noodles in plenty of rapidly boiling salted water for 10 minutes, until just cooked. Drain and immerse in cold water, stirring gently to separate the strands. Drain and set aside.
2 Combine the noodle broth ingredients and bring to the boil; keep warm. Slice the green part of the onions on the diagonal into 2-in/5-cm slices. Toast the nori and cut with scissors into rectangles 1 × 2 in/2 × 5 cm.
3 Warm 4 deep bowls. Put the noodles in a sieve and immerse in boiling water for a few seconds to reheat; divide among the 4 bowls and top with slices of spring onion (scallion).
4 Gently break an egg onto each bowl of noodles, taking care not to break the yolk. Immediately ladle the hot broth over the noodles; the hot broth will slightly cook the egg. Garnish each bowl with nori and serve immediately.

Chicken and Egg on Rice

14 oz/400 g/2 cups short grain white rice	4 dried mushrooms, reconstituted
¾ pt/450 ml/2 cups water	1 pt/600 ml/2½ cups dashi
4 oz/100 g/½ cup boned chicken breast or thigh	5 fl oz/150 ml/⅔ cup soy sauce
	3 tbsp/45 ml/4 tbsp mirin
	1 tbsp/15 ml/1 tbsp sugar
4 leeks or spring onions (scallions)	4 eggs

1 Cook the rice in the water. Prepare the topping while the rice is cooking and resting. Cut the chicken into bite-sized pieces; cut the leeks or spring onions (scallions) diagonally into 2-in/5-cm lengths. Drain the mushrooms, cut off the stems and finely slice the caps.
2 Prepare each portion separately. Measure out a quarter of the dashi into a small frying pan, and add a quarter of the chicken and mushrooms. Bring to the boil and simmer for 5 minutes.
3 Add a quarter of the leeks or spring onions (scallions) and simmer for 1 more minute. Season with a quarter of the soy sauce, mirin and sugar.
4 Lightly mix the eggs with chopsticks and slowly pour a quarter of the egg mixture over the chicken and vegetables. Wait until tthe egg is half set, then stir only once.
5 Half fill a large bowl with hot rice and pour the egg mixture over the rice before the egg is fully set; the heat of the rice will continue to cook the egg. Make 3 more portions in the same way with the remaining ingredients.

Buckwheat Noodles in Hot Broth

14 oz/400 g/14 oz dried
buckwheat noodles

NOODLE BROTH

1½ pt/900 ml/3¾ cups dashi
3 tbsp/45 ml/4 tbsp dark soy
sauce
2 tbsp/30 g/2 tbsp sugar

2 tbsp/30 ml/2 tbsp mirin
2 tsp/10 g/2 tsp salt
2 young leeks or spring onions
(scallions)

1 Cook the noodles. Combine the noodle broth ingredients and bring to the boil; keep warm. Shred and rinse the leeks or spring onions (scallions). Warm 4 deep bowls.
2 Immerse the noodles in a sieve in boiling water for a few seconds to reheat. Divide among the 4 bowls.
3 Ladle the hot broth over the noodles and top with a mound of shredded leek or spring onion (scallion).

Chilled Buckwheat Noodles

14 oz/400 g/14 oz dried
buckwheat noodles

DIPPING SAUCE

1 pt/600 ml/2½ cups dashi
3½ fl oz/100 ml/½ cup dark soy
sauce
4 tbsp/60 ml/5 tbsp mirin
1 tsp/5 g/1 tsp sugar

2 young leeks or spring onions
(scallions)
1 tsp/5 g/1 tsp freshly made
wasabi horseradish
½ sheet nori seaweed

1 Cook the noodles. Combine the dipping sauce ingredients and bring to the boil; chill. Shred and rinse the leeks or spring onions (scallions). Prepare the wasabi horseradish. Toast the nori seaweed and cut with scissors into thin strips.
2 Divide the chilled dipping sauce among 4 small bowls. Mound portions of leeks and wasabi in 4 small containers. Put the drained cold noodles in 4 containers or plates and scatter strips of nori seaweed over each portion.

Above: *Buckwheat noodles in hot broth (top) and chilled buckwheat noodles (bottom).*

Sweet Rice Noodles

7 oz/200 g/1 cup medium prawns
(shrimp), peeled and cut into 3
pieces
5 oz/150 g/⅔ cup pork meat,
diced to the same size as the
prawns (shrimp)
½ cup firm bean-curd, cut into
small rectangles
5 oz/150 g/5 oz fine rice vermicelli,
uncooked
6 cups oil
½ tbsp/7.5 g/½ tbsp garlic,
chopped
½ tbsp/7.5 g/½ tbsp onion,
chopped
1 tbsp/15 g/1 tbsp marinated soy
beans
1 tbsp/15 ml/1 tbsp fish sauce
2 tbsp/30 ml/2 tbsp vinegar
5 tbsp/75 g/6 tbsp sugar
5 oz/150 g/2½ cups bean sprouts
½ cup spring onion (scallion)
sliced intro 1½-in/4-cm pieces
2 pieces fresh red chilli (chili),
julienned lengthwise
2 tbsp/30 g/2 tbsp pickled garlic,
sliced

1 Fry the prawns (shrimp) and pork in a wok until brown and very cooked then fry bean curd the same way.
2 Soak the noodles in water for 1 minute. Drain well.
3 Place the oil in a wok, heat well and add noodles. Cook until lightly brown. Remove noodles and drain well. Remove all oil from pan except for 2 tbsp/30 ml/2 tbsp. Add garlic and onion, fry lightly and add pork, prawns (shrimp) and bean curd, add marinated soy beans, fish sauce, vinegar and sugar. Fry until thick and sticky.
4 Reduce heat and add the noodles. Mix well, then place on a large plate in a mound. Decorate with bean sprouts, spring onion (scallion), chilli (chili) and pickled garlic. Serve as hors d'oeuvre.

Fried Noodles with Chicken, Vegetables and Gravy

4 fl oz/120 ml/½ cup oil	2 tbsp/30 g/2 tbsp sugar
11 oz/300 g/11 oz flat rice noodles (Kwetio)	1 tsp/5 g/1 tsp ground white pepper
1 tsp/5 ml/1 tsp black soya sauce	6 cups chicken stock
2 tbsp/30 g/2 tbsp garlic	14 oz/400 g/14 oz kale, cut into
6 oz/200 g/1 cup chicken breast, boneless, sliced	11×2-in/4-cm pieces (or broccoli)
2 tbsp/30 ml/2 tbsp white soya sauce	2 tbsp/30 g/2 tbsp cornflour (cornstarch), mixed with a little water

1 Heat oil in a wok, add noodles and fry lightly. Add black soya sauce, fry lightly and remove.
2 Place rest of oil in the pan, add the garlic and chicken, fry lightly. Add white soya sauce, sugar, white pepper and chicken stock. Boil well, add vegetables. Boil, then add cornflour (cornstarch). Boil for one minute and pour over noodles on plate. Serve with sliced fresh red chilli (chili) in vinegar, fish sauce, sugar and ground chilli (chili).

Prawns (Shrimp) with Rice Noodles

1 oz/25 g/1 oz bacon	1 oz/25 g/1 oz garlic, chopped
¼ cup coriander, leaf and stem roughly chopped	5 cups glass noodles, soaked in cold water for 10 minutes
1 oz/5 g/1 oz ginger, pounded	1 tsp/5 g/1 tsp butter
1 tbsp/15 g/1 tbsp white peppercorns, crushed	3 tbsp/45 ml/3 tbsp black soy sauce
6 large prawns (shrimp)	2 pieces coriander root

SOUP STOCK

1¼ pt/50 ml/3 cups chicken stock	½ tbsp/7.5 ml/½ tbsp sesame seed oil
2 tbsp/30 ml/2 tbsp oyster sauce	½ tsp/2.5 g/½ tsp sugar
2 tbsp/30 ml/2 tbsp black soy sauce	1 tsp/5 ml/1 tsp brandy or whisky

1 Place stock ingredients in pot and boil for 5 minutes and cool.
2 Take fire proof casserole, place bacon in the bottom, add the coriander root, ginger, pepper, prawns (shrimp) and garlic. Then place noodles on too. Add the butter, soy sauce and stock.
3 Place on fire cover, bring to a boil for 5 minutes. Mix with tongs. Add chopped coriander root, cover, cook until prawns (shrimp) are cooked. Remove excess stock and serve. May be done with prawn (shrimp) or lobster tail also.

Fried Rice with Spicy Sauce

2 tbsp/30 ml/2 tbsp peanut or corn oil	1¾ lb/750 g/4 cups cooked rice
	3 tbsp phrik nam plaa sauce

1 Heat the oil in a wok or pan, add the rice and mix well, stir-frying for 1 minute. Add the sauce, mix well and cook for 1 more minute. Remove from the heat.

2 Serve accompanied by preserved salted eggs, cucumber slices, fried eggs and raw vegetables.

Left: Fried noodles with chicken, vegetables and gravy.

Fried rice with spicy sauce.

Noodle Soup

7 oz/200 g/1¾ cups pork loin, cut into thin slices
15 oz/400 g/4 cups thin rice vermicelli noodles (sen lek or sen mii)
5 oz/150 g/1¼ cups bean sprouts
4 oz/100 g/1 cup pork liver, boiled and sliced thinly
1 tsp/2.5 g/1 tsp chopped preserved cabbage
64 fl oz/1.8 l/8 cups chicken stock

12 fish balls
3 oz/75 g/½ cup minced (ground) pork
1 spring onion (scallion), cut into ½ in/1 cm pieces
2 tbsp coriander leaves and stems, cut into ½ in/1 cm pieces
2 tbsp/30 g/2 tbsp chopped garlic, fried in oil until golden
½ tsp/2.5 g/½ tsp ground white pepper

1 Boil the pork loin for about 15 minutes, cool slightly and cut into ½ in/1 cm thick strips. Set aside.

2 Cook the noodles and bean sprouts together lightly in boiling water for 3 minutes – don't cook until very soft. Drain and place in deep soup bowls, with the bean sprouts underneath. Place the sliced pork, liver and preserved cabbage on top of the noodles.

3 Boil the chicken stock in a pan, add the fish balls and boil for 3 minutes. Remove with a slotted spoon and add to the bowls.

4 Put the minced (ground) pork in a small pan with 12 fl oz/325 ml/1½ cups of the chicken stock and heat gently, mixing well until the pork is cooked, about 4–5 minutes. Add the spring onion (scallion), coriander, garlic and pepper, and then pour into the bowls. Top with more chicken stock as needed to fill each bowl.

5 Serve accompanied by fish sauce, chilli powder, sugar and phrik dong (sliced fresh red chillies in vinegar), all in separate bowls. Add these according to individual taste.

Noodle soup.

Prawn (Shrimp) Fried Rice

½ cup oil
6 oz/200 g/1 cup small prawns (shrimp), peeled
1 tbsp/15 g/1 tbsp garlic, chopped
3 eggs, mixed
1 tomato, cut into 6 pieces
⅓ cup sliced onion
4 cups cooked rice

1 tsp/5 g/1 tsp salt
1 tsp/5 g/1 tsp sugar
1 tsp/5 g/1 tsp ground white pepper
⅛ cup spring onion (scallion)
½ cup cucumber, peeled and sliced

1 Place a wok on fire, add oil. When hot, add the garlic and mix, then add the prawns (shrimps) and fry for one minute. Add eggs, tomato and onion. Then add rice, salt, sugar, white pepper and spring onion (scallion). Mix well over hot fire for 5 minutes.
2 Place on plates, with cucumber slices. Eat with whole spring onions (scallions) and ran sliced cucumber.

Curried Noodles

48 fl oz/1.35 l/6 cups thin coconut milk
11 oz/300 g/¾ lb boneless skinned chicken breasts, cut lengthwise into ½ in/1 cm thick slices
1 tbsp/30 ml/1 tbsp white soya sauce

1 tbsp/30 ml/1 tbsp black soya sauce
2 tsp salt
15 oz/400 g/4 cups dried or 7 oz/200 g/2 cups fresh egg noodles (ba mii)
peanut or corn oil for frying

CHILLI PASTE
4 dried red chillies, chopped roughly
1 tbsp/15 g/2 tbsp chopped shallot

2 tsp/10 g/2 tsp sliced ginger
1 tsp/5 g/2 tsp coriander seeds
1 tsp/5 g/2 tsp turmeric

1 Dry-roast the chilli paste ingredients in a 350°F/180°C/gas 4 oven until fragrant, about 8–10 minutes, then pound until fine with a mortar and pestle or in a blender.
2 Heat 8 fl oz/225 ml/2 cups of the coconut milk in a pan or wok, add the chilli paste and fry for 2 minutes, then add the chicken and soya sauces. Stir-fry for 3 minutes, then add the rest of the coconut milk and bring to a boil for 3 minutes. Add the salt and remove from the heat.
3 Fry 4 oz/100 g/1 cup of the noodles in hot oil until crisp. Remove and drain well. Boil the rest of the noodles in water until firm but tender, about 6–8 minutes, and drain.
4 Place the boiled noodles in serving bowls, and pour the chicken mixture on top. Garnish with the fried noodles.
5 Serve accompanied by bowls of diced shallots, pickled cabbage and chilli powder.

Curried noodles.

ACCOMPANIMENTS

From India

From Mexico

From Japan

From Thailand

Yogurt with Boondi

3 oz/75 g/1½ cups boondi
12 fl oz/325 g/1½ cups unsweetened yogurt
½ tsp/2.5 g/½ tsp salt
½ tsp/2.5 g/½ tsp chilli (chili) powder
pinch of paprika
pinch of garam masala

1 Soak the boondi in a little cold water for 10–15 minutes.
2 Beat the yogurt in a bowl until smooth. Add the salt and chilli (chili) powder and stir.
3 Gently squeeze the boondi to remove the water and add to the spiced yogurt. Mix well and chill. Before serving sprinkle with paprika and garam masala.

Above: Yogurt with boondi.

Left: Yogurt with cucumber.

Yogurt with Cucumber

12 fl oz/325 ml/1½ cups unsweetened yogurt
1–2 green chillies (chilis), chopped
2 tbsp/30 g/2 tbsp coriander leaves, chopped
½ cucumber, finely sliced
½ tsp/2.5 g/½ tsp chilli (chili) powder
½ tsp/2.5 g/½ tsp ground roasted cumin
½ tsp/2.5 g/½ tsp salt

1 In a bowl whisk the yogurt until smooth.
2 Add all the other ingredients and stir in well. Chill.

Yogurt with Potatoes

16 fl oz /450 ml/2 cups unsweetened yogurt
10 oz/275 g/2½ cups potatoes, boiled and diced into ¼-in/0.5-cm cubes
1 small onion, finely chopped
½ tsp/2.5 g/½ tsp salt
¼ tsp/1 g/¼ tsp ground black pepper
½ tsp/2.5 g/½ tsp ground roasted cumin
1 green chilli (chili), chopped
1 tbsp/15 g/1 tbsp coriander leaves

1 Beat the yogurt in a bowl until smooth.
2 Add the potatoes, onions, salt, pepper and cumin and gently mix. Chill.
3 Serve sprinkled with the chilli (chili) and coriander leaves.

Yogurt with Aubergine (Eggplant)

6–8 tbsp/90–120 ml/about ½ cup oil
1 small aubergine (eggplant), cut into small pieces
12 fl oz/325 ml/1½ cups unsweetened yogurt

½ tsp/2.5 g/½ tsp salt
½ tsp/2.5 g/½ tsp ground roasted cumin
½ tsp/2.5 g/½ tsp chilli (chili) powder

1 Heat the oil in a karai and fry the aubergine (eggplant) pieces until brown. Drain.
2 In the bowl whisk the yogurt until smooth. Add the salt, cumin and chilli (chili) and mix thoroughly.
3 Place the fried aubergine (eggplant) pieces in a bowl and pour over the spiced yogurt. Chill.

Above: Yogurt with aubergine (eggplant).

Mint Chutney

2 oz/50 g/2 oz mint leaves, washed
2 oz/50 g/¼ cup tamarind juice
2 tbsp/30 g/2 tbsp onions, chopped
2 cloves garlic

¾ in/2 cm root ginger
2–3 green chillies (chilis)
½ tsp/2.5 g/½ tsp salt
½ tsp/2.5 g/½ tsp sugar

1 Blend all the ingredients together until you have a smooth paste. Serve with any fried foods. (Can be stored in an airtight jar in the refrigerator for one week.)

Above: Yogurt with potatoes.

Right: Mint chutney.

Tomato Chutney

1 tbsp/15 ml/1 tbsp oil
½ tsp/2.5 g/½ tsp panch phoron
1 lb/450 g/2 cups tomatoes
½ tbsp/7.5 g/½ tbsp salt

1 tbsp/15 g/1 tbsp sugar
1 tsp/5 g/1 tsp cornflour
(cornstarch), mixed with a little
milk

1 Heat the oil in a small saucepan over medium heat. Add the panch phoron and let them sizzle for a few seconds.
2 Add the tomatoes, cover and cook until the tomatoes are soft. Add the salt and sugar and cook a further 10 minutes.
3 Thicken with the cornflour (cornstarch) mixture and remove from the heat. Chill.

Coriander Chutney

3 oz/75 g/3 oz coriander leaves
4 cloves garlic
3 tbsp/45 g/4 tbsp desiccated
(shredded) coconut
2 green chillies (chilis)

2–3 tbsp/30–45 ml/2–3 tbsp
lemon juice
½ tsp/2.5 g/½ tsp salt
¼ tsp/1 g/¼ tsp sugar

1 Chop the sprigs of coriander and throw away the roots and lower stalk.
2 Blend the coriander with all the other ingredients until you have a smooth paste. Serve with any fried foods. (Can be stored in an airtight jar in the refrigerator for one week.)

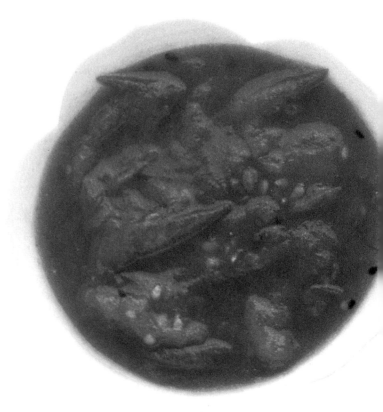

Tamarind Chutney

4 oz/100 g/4 oz tamarind
12 fl oz/325 ml/1½ cups hot
water
¼ tsp/1 g/¼ tsp chilli (chili)
powder

1 tbsp/15 ml/1 tbsp lemon juice
2 tbsp/30 g/2 tbsp brown sugar
¼ tsp/1 g/¼ tsp salt

1 Soak the tamarind in the water for about 30 minutes. Squeeze the tamarind and strain.
2 Combine the tamarind juice with the other ingredients and chill.

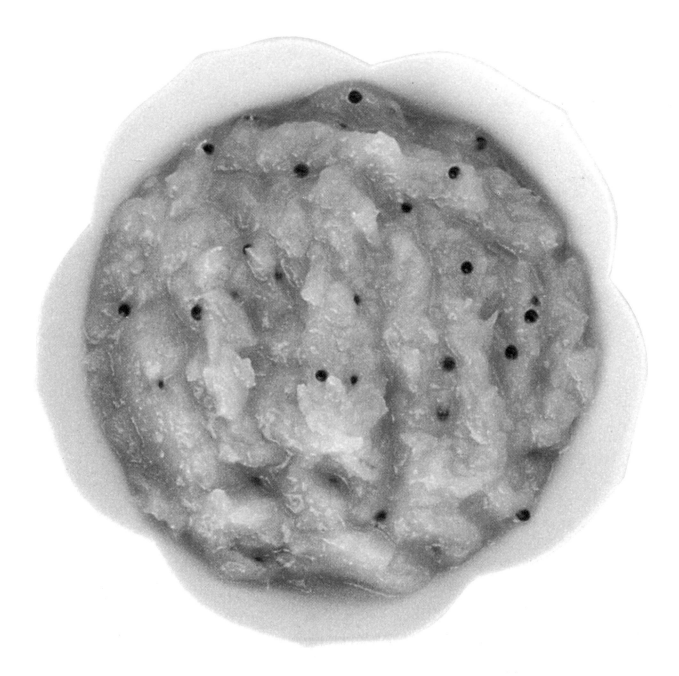

Top left: *Coriander chutney.*

Centre left: *Tomato chutney.*

Bottom left: *Tamarind chutney.*

Above: *Pineapple chutney.*

Pineapple Chutney

½ tbsp/7.5 ml/½ tbsp oil
½ tsp/2.5 g/½ tsp whole mustard seeds
8 oz/237 g/1 cup canned pineapple, crushed and drained

big pinch of salt
1 tsp/5 g/1 tsp cornflour (cornstarch) mixed with a little milk

1 Heat the oil in a small pan over medium heat. Add the mustard seeds and let them sizzle for a few seconds.
2 Add the drained pineapple and salt and, stirring occasionally, cook for about 10 minutes.
3 Thicken with the cornflour (cornstarch) mixture and remove from the heat. Chill.

Above: Tomato, cucumber and onion relish.

Tomato, Cucumber and Onion Relish

8 oz/225 g/1 cup tomatoes, chopped into ¼-in/0.5-cm pieces
8 oz/225 g/2 cups cucumber, cut into ¼-in/0.5-cm pieces
4 oz/100 g/1 cup onions, chopped
2–3 green chillies (chilis)

½ tsp/2.5 g/½ tsp salt
¼ tsp/1 g/¼ tsp sugar
3 tbsp/45 ml/3 tbsp lemon juice
2 tbsp/30 g/2 tbsp coriander leaves, chopped

1 Mix all the ingredients together in a small bowl. Cover and set aside to chill. Serve with any Indian meal.

Mixed Vegetables Pickled in Sake

4 leaves Chinese cabbage
4 leaves red cabbage
1 small turnip
½ cucumber
1 medium carrot
1 oz/25 g/3 tbsp raisins
salt
3½ fl oz/100 ml/scant ½ cup sake

1 Wash and trim the vegetables. Cut the Chinese cabbage and red cabbage into small 1 × 1 in/3 × 3 cm pieces. Halve the turnip and slice into half moons. Cut the cucumber into small chunks and cut the carrot into sticks. Chop the raisins coarsely. Carefully pat the chopped vegetables dry with paper towels.
2 Place the vegetables in a glass or ceramic bowl and sprinkle with salt, stirring to ensure that all the vegetables are salted. Set aside for 10 minutes.
3 Knead the vegetables and squeeze to press out as much water as possible.
4 Place the vegetables in a clean ceramic bowl and mix in the raisins. Sprinkle over the sake. Set a drop lid or plate on the vegetables and top with a weight. Set aside for about 20 minutes. Drain and rinse the vegetables and serve small quantities on individual dishes.

Right: Mixed vegetables pickled in sake.

Sweet Pickled Ginger

4 oz/115 g/4 oz fresh root ginger
2–3 tsp/10–15 g/2–3 tsp salt
3½ fl oz/100 ml/scant ½ cup rice vinegar
3 tbsp/45 ml/4 tbsp water
1 tbsp/15 ml/1 tbsp sugar
a little pickled plum juice or red food colouring (optional)

1 Wash the ginger roots thoroughly, peeling away any discoloured skin. Sprinkle lightly with salt, put into a bowl or jar, cover and set aside for 1–2 days.
2 Drain the ginger and put in a clean glass or ceramic bowl or jar. Combine the vinegar, water and sugar (and red colouring if required) in a small saucepan, bring to the boil and pour over the ginger. Cover the bowl or jar and set aside for at least 7 days. To serve, cut paper thin slices of ginger along the grain and serve a little on individual plates. Sweet pickled ginger will keep for several months in the refrigerator.

Salt Pickled Vegetables

1 Chinese cabbage or 2 cucumbers or 2 daikon radishes
1 oz/25 g/2 tbsp salt

1 Wash and trim the vegetables. Chinese cabbage: cut off the base of the cabbage and cut the cabbage lengthwise into six or eight pieces. Cut each piece into 2 in/5 cm chunks. Cucumber: peel and seed the cucumbers and cut into ½ in/1 cm slices. Daikon radish: Peel, quarter and cut into 2 in/5 cm lengths. Lightly pat the vegetables with paper towels to dry.
2 Layer the chopped vegetables with salt in a large glass or ceramic bowl, beginning and ending with a layer of salt. Cover with a drop lid or plate slightly smaller than the top of the bowl, and top with a weight such as a jar of water.
3 Leave the bowl in a cool dark place for 3–4 days. The brine will quickly rise above the level of the vegetables.
4 To serve, remove the required quantity of pickled vegetable from the bowl; rinse, squeeze and cut into small pieces. Serve in small quantities or pickled in individual dishes. The pickles may be flavoured with a drop of soy sauce to taste. The remaining pickles will keep for 2–3 months in the brine.

Left: Chili con queso.

Below: Fresh salsa.

Chili Con Queso

Fresh Salsa

1 *medium onion, finely chopped*
1 *oz/30 g/2 tbsp butter*
8 *oz/250 g/1 cup canned tomatoes, chopped*
1–3 *serrano chillies (chilis)*

12 *oz/350 g/3 cups grated cheddar (or Jack) cheese*
4 *fl oz/120 ml/½ cup sour cream (optional)*

1 Fry the onion gently in the butter until it is translucent. Add the tomatoes and chilli (chili) peppers; simmer, stirring frequently, until thickened. Add the cheese, stirring as you do. Cook, stirring constantly, until the cheese melts. For a thinner dip, add the cream.

small handful of coriander leaves
1 *large onion, red or white*
one 24-oz/650-g/24-oz can tomatoes

1–4 *cloves garlic*
2 *serrano chillies (chilis), or 1 jalapeno*

1 Wash the coriander and remove the coarser stems and roots. A gringo might use as little as a teaspoon of chopped coriander; a Mexican would probably use half a bunch – about a handful, before chopping.

2 Chop the onion and tomatoes finely, the garlic, chilli (chili) pepper and coriander very finely. Put them all in a large bowl. Squish them together with your hand, squeezing and rubbing to blend and increase flavour.

3 You can also use a food processor. Chop the garlic and pepper first; then add the onion, and chop some more; then add the rest. The traditional way to make it is to grind the ingredients together in a pestle and mortar.

SALSA VARIATIONS: Roast one or two Poblano or Anaheim chillies (chilis) over an open flame; when they are charred all over, remove the skin. Remove the seeds and veins; chop; add to the salsa.

Use fresh tomatoes instead of canned: either peel them (dip in boiling water for 10–30 seconds) or leave the skins on. Remove the tomato seeds, or not, as you feel inclined.

For a thicker salsa, use a can of crushed tomatoes with added tomato purée (paste).

If you like, add any of the following: a pinch of oregano; and/ or 1 tbsp/15 ml/1 tbsp wine vinegar or lime juice; and/or 1 tbsp/15 ml/1 tbsp olive oil.

Fresh coriander seeds are a wonderful addition to salsa – a strong argument for growing your own.

In the absence of fresh serrano chillies (chilis), shred a red chilli (chili) and grind it in a little water with the garlic; leave to soak for a while; and add this paste to the tomato, onion and coriander.

For a rock-bottom-basic dipping salsa, add the same chilli (chili)/garlic paste to half a can of commercial tomato sauce.

Green Salsa

one 10-oz/300-g/10-oz can	*2–4 cloves garlic*
tomatillos	*1 tbsp/15 g/1 tbsp chopped fresh*
1 small white onion	*coriander*
2–4 serrano chillies (chilis)	

1 Smash the lot together in a food processor – this is a fine-grained sauce. Alternatively, chop finely; mash together; and grind in a pestle and mortar.

2 If you are using fresh tomatillos, remove the dry outer husk, but don't be tempted to skin or seed them – there will be nothing left. You can increase the coriander as much as you like. A really basic salsa verde consists only of tomatillos, chilli (chili) peppers and coriander.

Corn Tortillas

1 lb/450 g/4 cups masa harina	*1 tsp/5 g/1 tsp water*
½ pt/300 ml/1¼ cups water	

1 Work all the ingredients together in a large bowl. If the masa is sticky, it is too wet: add some more masa harina, and work it in. If it breaks up, it is too dry: add some more water slowly. You will not harm the dough by handling it repeatedly – indeed, it seems to improve it – and obviously there is no rising or proving time. Ground dried chillies (chilis) and even grated hard cheese (similar to Parmesan) may be added to the dough to make flavoured tortillas.

2 The traditional way to shape tortillas, by slapping a ball of masa from hand to hand until it grows into a flat sheet, is extremely difficult to learn as well as being somewhat time-consuming. A tortilla press is a much easier method – use two plastic bags to stop the tortilla sticking to the press – but if you can't get a tortilla press, just roll out a ball of dough between two plastic bags, using a regular-sized rolling pin. Plastic bags are much less likely to stick then the waxed paper recommended in some books. Corn tortillas can be anything from 1–2 in/3–5 cm in diameter – these are used for appetizers – to about 6 in/15 cm.

3 Cook the tortillas on a comal, a round cast-iron or earthenware baking sheet used directly over the fire; a griddle or heavy frying pan will do equally well. Each tortilla is cooked for a couple of minutes on each side; they are done when the edges begin to lift, and they are slightly browned. Given that half a dozen people can easily dispose of a couple of dozen tortillas in one meal, you can see why most people buy their tortillas ready made: a dozen tortillas can be an hour's work, but can be bought quite reasonably at the grocer's store or tortilleria.

4 The best way to re-heat tortillas is over a direct flame; pat them with damp hands if they are uncomfortably dry. Alternatively, use a microwave; or a comal; or an oven set at about 150–200°F/70–90°C (Mark ¼), with the tortillas wrapped in paper towels and a damp cloth and foil around the lot.

5 To fry tortillas, use ½–1 in/1.2–2.5 cm of very hot oil (corn oil or peanut oil – or lard, for traditionalists), and fry to taste. After 30–60 seconds, the tortillas will be limp and flexible; after two or three minutes, they will be hard and crisp, and are known as tostadas. For home-made cornchips or tostaditas, cut 4 in/10 cm tortillas into quarters, and fry them in plenty of oil until they are brown and crisp.

Flour Tortillas

1 lb/450 g/4 cups plain (all-	*1 tsp/5 g/1 tsp baking powder*
purpose) flour	*1 tbsp/15 ml/1 tbsp lard*
1 tsp/5 g/1 tsp salt	*6 fl oz/180 ml/¾ cup cold water*

1 Mix all the dry ingredients; cut in the lard; add enough water to make a stiff dough. Roll on a lightly floured board, or use plastic bags as for corn tortillas.

Right: Making tortillas in Toluca market.

Green Chilli (Chili) Dip

10 fresh green chillies (chilis), cut into 2-in/5-cm strips
10 garlic cloves
6 peeled shallots
3 cherry tomatoes

1 tbsp/15 g/1 tbsp dry salted mackerel or anchovy – fried thoroughly
1 tbsp/15 g/1 tbsp spring onion (scallion)
1 tbsp/15 g/1 tbsp fresh coriander leaves

1 Pan roast the chillies (chilis), garlic, shallots and cherry tomatoes until fragrant.
2 Roast lightly with the fish. Add 2 tbsp/30 ml/2 tbsp hot water, the spring onion (scallion) and coriander. Mix well. The result should be of a saucy consistency and a touch salty. If not, add more water or fish sauce as required. Serve with fresh cabbage, sliced cucumbers, French (green) beans and/or fried or roasted fish.

North-eastern Spicy Dip

6 garlic cloves
1 tbsp/15 g/1 tbsp sliced shallot
1 tsp chopped galangal (ka)
2 tbsp/30 g/2 tbsp finely chopped anchovies
1 tbsp/15 ml/1 tbsp lemon juice

1 dried red chilli, pounded finely
1 kaffir lime leaf, torn into small pieces
½ stalk of lemon grass, sliced finely

1 Dry-fry the garlic, shallot and galangal for 3 minutes over medium heat, then chop finely. Pound with the rest of the ingredients with a mortar and pestle or in a blender.
2 Serve accompanied by cabbage, green (string) beans, fresh basil and sticky rice.

Above: Green chilli (chili) dip.   *Right:* North-eastern spicy dip.

Spicy Meat and Tomato Dip

6 dried red chillies, chopped
3 tbsp/45 g/3 tbsp chopped
shallots
1 tbsp/15 g/1 tbsp sliced lemon
grass
1 tbsp/15 g/2 tbsp chopped garlic
2 tsp/30 ml/2 tsp shrimp paste
2 tsp/30 ml/2 tsp salt
2 tbsp/30 ml/2 tbsp peanut or
corn oil

3 oz/75 g/½ cup raw chopped
pork
8 cherry tomatoes, diced
4 fl oz/100 ml/½ cup water
lemon juice, to taste
fish sauce, to taste
sugar, to taste
1 oz/25 g/1½ tbsp coriander
leaves

1 Pound the chillies, onion, lemon grass, garlic, shrimp paste and salt together with a mortar and pestle or in a blender until fine.

2 Heat the oil in a wok or pan and add the chilli mixture and the pork and tomatoes. Cook until thick, about 15 minutes, then add the water and cook again for 10 minutes until thick.

3 Adjust the seasoning to taste with lemon juice, fish sauce and/or sugar. Garnish with the coriander leaves.

4 Serve accompanied by raw or slightly cooked vegetables, sticky rice, and if you can buy it, crispy pork rind (often sold under the Spanish name 'chicharrones').

Phrik Nam Plaa

2 fl oz/50 ml/¼ cup fish sauce
10 fresh small green chillies, sliced
into small circles

1 tsp/5 g/1 tsp sliced shallot
¼ tsp/a pinch of palm sugar
1 tbsp/10 ml/1 tbsp lime or lemon
juice

1 Mix all the ingredients together well. This is good for accompanying almost all Thai food, especially rice. Just sprinkle a little on your food to liven it up.

Below: *Spicy meat and tomato dip.*　　**Right:** *Fermented dip for vegetables and rice.*

Fermented dip for vegetables and rice

20 fl oz/550 ml/2½ cups thin coconut milk
3 oz/75 g/¾ cup dried salted mackerel (the smellier the better) or anchovies
1½ oz/40 g/⅓ cup galangal (ka), sliced
1½ oz/40 g/⅓ cup lemon grass, sliced

1 tbsp/10 g/1 tbsp finely sliced kaffir lime leaves
1½ oz/40 g/⅓ cup krachai, cut into lengthwise matchsticks
4 oz/100 g/1 cup green (string) beans, cut into 1 in/2.5 cm pieces
2 oz/50 g/½ cup shallots, halved
2 oz/50 g/½ cup bamboo shoots, cut into ¼ in/5 mm cubes

5 oz/150 g/1¼ cups catfish fillets, skinned and cut into pieces
6 fresh small whole red chillies

4 baby white aubergines (eggplants), the size of large grapes
fish sauce, to taste (optional)

1 Heat the coconut milk in a pan, add the salted fish, boil for 1 minute, add the galangal and lemon grass, boil again, then add the catfish, chillies and lime leaf and cook for another minute. Add the krachai – don't stir it in – and bring back to a boil. Simmer for 3 minutes, add the rest of the ingredients and cook for another 2 minutes. Taste for saltiness and add fish sauce as necessary. Serve hot or cold – this dish can be refrigerated for 2–3 days to enhance the flavours.
2 Serve accompanied by raw vegetables and rice.

Left: Green mango salad.

Green Mango Salad

12 oz/350 g/3 cups green unripe mango flesh, cut into long matchsticks
1 oz/25 g/¼ cup unsweetened grated coconut, dry-fried until light brown
1 oz/25 g/¼ cup dried shrimps

3 tbsp/45 g/3 tbsp sliced shallots
5 fresh small green chillies, chopped
1 tbsp/5 g/1 tbsp palm sugar, or to taste
fish sauce, to taste (optional)
lime juice, to taste (optional)

1 Mix all the ingredients together. If not salty enough add a little fish sauce; if not sour enough, add lime juice.

Satay Sauce

4 oz/100 g/⅔ cup shelled raw peanuts
3 oz/75 g/¾ cup finely chopped onion
2 tbsp/30 ml/2 tbsp oil
1 in/2.5 cm root ginger, peeled and grated
1 tsp/5 g/1 tsp chilli (chili) powder

2 tbsp/30 g/2 tbsp soft dark brown sugar
2 tbsp/30 ml/2 tbsp soy sauce
2 tbsp/30 ml/2 tbsp lemon juice
½ tsp/2.5 g/½ tsp spice powder
6 fl oz/175 ml/¾ cup water
salt to taste

1 Roast the peanuts in a preheated oven, shaking the pan occasionally, until lightly browned. Rub off the skins in a tea (dish) towel and return to the oven until a good deep tan. Cool and store in a plastic bag until needed.
2 Just before you make the sauce, grind the peanuts coarsely in a food processor or wrap them loosely in a tough plastic bag and crush them with a steak hammer or a heavy saucepan.
3 Brown the onion in the oil over a high heat. Add the ginger, chilli (chili) powder and peanuts and fry for a minute more, stirring.
4 Turn down the heat, add the remaining ingredients and simmer for 5 minutes. Correct the seasoning and serve hot or warm with grilled (broiled) or roasted meat, pork and chicken in particular.

VARIATIONS: For a smoother sauce, or one suitable for marinating and basting grilled (broiled) or barbecued meats, especially kebabs, blend or process the cooked sauce. It should not be too smooth.

Index

Number in *italics* refer to photographs, in addition most recipes are featured as photographs.

Picture Credits

r = right; l = left; c = centre; b = bottom; t = top.

Steve Alley and Amber Wisdom: *pp 33b; 34; 35; 36; 65; 66; 67; 68; 69; 70; 108; 109; 110; 111; 112; 113; 114; 115; 117; 151; 153; 239; 240; 272; 273.* Michael Freeman: *pp 13; 14; 38; 39; 40; 41; 42; 43; 46; 47; 48/49; 50; 51; 52; 53; 71; 72; 73; 74; 75; 118; 119; 120/121; 122; 123; 154/155; 156; 157; 198; 199; 207; 208; 209; 210; 211; 212; 213; 214; 215; 216; 217; 218; 219; 220; 221; 222; 223; 224; 225; 226/227c; 248; 249; 250; 266tr; 267; 268; 269; 270.* John Heseltine: *pp 59; 60; 61; 62; 63; 64; 106; 107; 148; 149; 150; 188; 189; 190; 192; 194; 195; 226b; 235; 236; 237; 238; 271.* House Food Industrial Company (Japan): *pp 6; 7; 8; 9; 10; 11.* Ian Howes: *pp 55; 56; 57r; 227; 228; 229; 230; 231; 232; 266l.* Jane Taylor, Sonia Halliday Agency: *p 179l.* Liba Taylor *pp 32; 33t; 37; 152; 275.* Trevor Wood and Michael Bull: *pp 2/3; 54; 78; 79; 80; 81; 82; 83; 84; 85; 104l; 116; 128; 129; 130; 131; 132; 133; 134l; 164; 165; 166; 167; 168; 169; 170; 197br; 271.*